BEYOND CONFLICT AND CONTAINMENT

*trans*action/**Society** Book Series

BEYOND CONFLICT AND CONTAINMENT
Critical Studies of Military and Foreign Policy

Edited by

MILTON J. ROSENBERG

Transaction Books
New Brunswick, New Jersey
Distributed by E.P. Dutton & Co., Inc.

Unless otherwise indicated, the essays in this book originally appeared in *trans*action/ **Society** magazine.

Transaction Books
Rutgers University
New Brunswick, New Jersey 08903

Library of Congress Catalog Card Number: 79-189565
ISBN: 0-87855-038-0 (cloth); 0-87855-534-X (paper)

Printed in the United States of America

Contents

Preface

For the past decade, *trans*action, now **Society**, has dedicated itself to the task of reporting the strains and conflicts within the American system. But the magazine has done more than this. It has pioneered in social programs for changing the social order, offered the kind of analysis that has permanently restructured the terms of the "dialogue" between peoples and publics, and offered the sort of prognosis that makes for real alterations in economic and political policies directly affecting our lives.

The work done in the magazine has crossed disciplinary boundaries. This represents much more than simple cross-disciplinary "team efforts." It embodies rather a recognition that the social world cannot be easily carved into neat academic disciplines; that, indeed, the study of the experience of blacks in American ghettos, or the manifold uses and abuses of agencies of law enforcement, or the sorts of overseas policies that lead to the celebration of some dictatorships and the condemnation of others, can best be examined from many viewpoints and from the vantage points of many disciplines.

The editors of **Society** magazine are now making available in permanent form the most important work done in the magazine, supplemented in some cases by additional materials edited to reflect the tone and style developed over the years by *trans*action. Like the magazine, this series of books demonstrates the superiority of starting with real world problems and searching out practical solutions, over the zealous guardianship of professional boundaries. Indeed, it is precisely this approach that has elicited enthusiastic support from leading American social scientists, many of whom are represented among the editors of these volumes.

The subject matter of these books concerns social changes and social policies that have aroused the long-standing needs and present-day anxieties of us all. These changes are in organizational life styles, concepts of human ability and intelligence, changing patterns of norms and morals, the relationship of social conditions to physical and biological environments, and in the status of social science with respect to national policy making. The editors feel that many of these articles have withstood the test of time and match in durable interest the best of available social science literature. This collection of essays, then, attempts to address itself to immediate issues without violating the basic insights derived from the classical literature in the various fields of social science.

As the political crises of the sixties have given way to the economic crunch of the seventies, the social scientists involved as editors and authors of this series have gone beyond observation of critical areas and have entered into the vital and difficult tasks of explanation and interpretation. They have defined issues in a way that makes solutions possible. They have provided answers as well as asked the right questions. These books, based as they are upon the best materials from *trans*action/**Society** magazine, are dedicated to highlighting social problems, and beyond that, to establishing guidelines for social solutions based on the social sciences.

The remarkable success of the book series to date is indicative of the need for such "fastbacks" in college course work and, no less, in the everyday needs of busy people who have not surrendered the need to know or the lively sense required to satisfy such knowledge needs. It is also plain that what superficially appeared as a random selection of articles on the basis of subject alone, in fact, represented a careful concern for materials that are addressed to issues at the shank and marrow of society. It is the distillation of the best of these, systematically arranged, that appears in these volumes.

THE EDITORS
*trans*action/**Society**

Beyond the Cold War:

The Pragmatic and Prophetic Modes in Policy Science

MILTON J. ROSENBERG

The foreign and military policies of the United States have never been more vigorously nor more acrimoniously debated than during the last five or six years. It was during these years that attentive sectors of the American public, growing increasingly dismayed by the Vietnam war, began to look beyond that war to the context of policies in which it was set.

While this shift in public mood was underway a parallel shift was occurring in those social sciences which presume to address basic issues of international and arms policy. In increasing number, though never anything near a majority, American policy scientists undertook a critical analysis of the main perspectives and purposes of this nation's international and arms policies and of the fruits of those policies.

The resulting scholarly work has exerted some detectable influence upon the policy-making process itself, not so much by altering the basic convictions of those who sit in the highest councils of power as by energizing the informed criticism to which they must inevitably respond. As that informed criticism grows more politically potent, through its representation in Congress and through its partial acceptance within the major and minority political parties, some alteration in foreign and arms policy becomes increasingly likely. Indeed, as this volume goes to press, some major props of our classic Cold War stance seem to be dissolving: the Senate is in revolt against the kind of foreign aid that has been practiced since the Marshall Plan; a confusing but portentous Sino-American thaw is occurring; American participation in the land war in Indochina is being ended (though, in the view of many critics, the American aspect of that war is being shifted to the air and our geopolitical passion for dominance over Southeast Asia has *not* yet been put aside); the research, development and deployment aspirations of the military are now receiving unrelenting critical scrutiny in Congress.

In short, a struggle over basic arms and foreign policy is underway and, with every election year, it becomes more apparent that the struggle is being waged through the American political process itself. The outcome of the struggle cannot be readily predicted and neither hard-liners nor "conciliationists" have any claim to sanguine assurance. But the flowering of post-Cold War critical scholarship in policy issues makes it likely that, when the Vietnam conflict has finally been ended, we will not again relapse into unquestioned reliance upon the certitudes of "protracted conflict" and "containment."

From its beginning in 1963, *trans*action (now **Society**) has been a major vehicle through which policy scholars outside the policy establishment have addressed the general public. Some outstanding contributions are gathered together in this volume.

Some of the essays included examine the U.S. foreign aid program and delineate the disappointing realities that have all too often been obscured by altruistic rhetoric. The aspiration to use economic and military aid to construct a stable international environment serving American security and national interest is closely analyzed. Similarly, a number of the authors have analyzed available data to show just how the AID program has worked to enrich American corporations and the small commercial and political elites of developing nations, while failing, in fact, to assist the economic development of those nations or to improve the opportunities of most of their citizens.

Another section of the volume contains some crucial articles on American military policy. The extremely high (and, in the long run, possibly unbearable) costs of present military policy are examined closely. The costs scrutinized are economic—but not only economic. Also examined is the likelihood that modern nuclear weapons and the strategic theories by which they are deployed to preserve the "delicate balance of terror" are far from fail safe. The conditions under which the great powers may inadvertently slide toward Armageddon are examined along with some major prospects for fending off that possibility through arms reduction alternatives and through basic revision of arms postures and the strategic uses to which they are put.

In another section the *moral* costs of interventionism, as exemplified by Vietnam atrocities, are reckoned and discussed with illuminating, if disquieting, candor.

The volume closes by addressing the possibilities for

change in elite leadership styles and in the roles played by social scientists as they examine and research the policy works of those elites.

The essays reprinted here do not require further specific introduction. They speak for themselves, at least as regards the particular issues that each addresses. Taken together they provide a useful sample of the new critical scholarship on foreign and military policy.

What does require further discussion—particularly so as to outline the shape of the forest in which the succeeding articles stand as trees—are the two trends of change that I have already alluded to. The first is the discernible shift toward a new temper in policy studies, a shift that might be characterized as moving from a *pragmatic* to a *prophetic* style; from working within the Cold War dynamic to a deeply critical stance toward that dynamic. The second is the trend (or at least the temptation) within the policy establishment toward revision of the perceptions and purposes which have sustained the Cold War foreign policy of the Western alliance. These two main trends are, of course, so closely related as to be almost obverse sides of the same dynamic: the academic critics of containment and protracted conflict receive cues from and exert significant influence upon disaffected persons and groups who stand closer—whether as legislators or bureaucrats—to the settings in which policy decisions are made.

But the influences that have prompted and reinforced scholarly dissent derive from a number of other sources as well. A few of these are immediately evident to anyone who has spent the last ten years in the disarrayed academic culture of the United States. One of these influences has been the political dismay voiced by the most ethically responsive of the college students during the decade of the sixties. Beginning with the first "teach-ins" in 1965, these students came increasingly to question the motives and methods of the American policy elite and of persons and institutions functionally bound up with it.

Though initially organized around the issue of the Vietnam war, student protest went far beyond that issue. Not only Left activists but more conventional liberals began to question the pattern of policy in which the Vietnam war was set. The outcome was an assault upon the mythwork of two decades of Cold War. Particularly susceptible to contemptuous rejection was the representation of the Communist world as undifferentiated, as conspiring for world domination, and as ready to use immolative nuclear surprise toward that end.

A second and related theme originated on the far left of the emerging student movement but diffused rapidly over the moderate left and toward the middle of the political spectrum. This was a renewal of critical hostility toward American corporate, governmental and military institutions. It took its force from a deep suspicion that these institutions were either inadvertently or conspiratorially influential in the emergence of a new American imperialism—a *Pax Americana* which could be maintained only by blighting the legitimate aspirations of emerging nations, by ready recourse to conventional war and by willingness to risk nuclear war to defend or extend American power.

To be sure, during the second half of the decade of the sixties the student movement waxed and waned in its immediate political significance as it shifted toward and away from ideological extremity. But it conveyed enough anguish and enough approximation of relevantly pointed analysis to affect a significant number within the contiguous professoriat. Social science academics were particularly sensitive to another embittered complaint voiced by their students in those years: that the social disciplines had been complicit in the drift or, as the ideological simplicists saw it, the forced march toward an American empire.

There can be no doubt that this accusation exposed and activated long-smoldering sensitivities. Few, if any, of the academics who responded to this assault believed that their disciplines had been guilty of anything more than sloth and smugness, of living the unexamined professional life. But this laxity began to appear sinful enough. By adhering to the received doctrine of "value-free" inquiry, by obsessive investment in perfected methodology and by faith in "incrementalism" (things are improved slowly, in piecemeal progression from the unbearable present to a slightly less unbearable future) the policy sciences had taken on a completely pragmatic cast. But this was a pragmatism of style rather than consequence, an incrementalism of aspiration rather than achievement. According to some who felt the problem most deeply, what had really happened in the Cold War era was that the social sciences had, at last, been largely incorporated into the network of ruling and managing institutions. Most academic men of intellect and of scientific aspiration had come to accept role definitions which limited them to assisting in the implementation of major policies and put far beyond their reach any wholehearted indulgence in skepticism about those policies, any direct examination of their moral import, or any open advocacy of radically different alternatives.

Partly in response to the *j'accuse* voiced by their students, which achieved its effect through reactivating inner doubts of older provenance, some policy scholars came to believe that they and their colleagues had been trapped in the dynamic of the Cold War. They came to see that the *Realpolitik* of protracted East-West conflict—a guiding view which they or their professions had helped to formulate and popularize—had generated many profoundly dysfunctional consequences. One of these was that it hampered accurate analysis of the political life of the Communist states and, particularly, of their relations with one another.

Even more injurious to scholarship and to the prospect for developing humane and truly wise policy was the influence of the Cold War rationale upon our understanding of smaller nations emerging into, or aspiring toward, autonomy and modernity. The prevailing policy style required suspicion, manipulation and, sometimes, suppression of any "new nation" moving toward a socialist organization of its institutions; especially when that nation's elite found inspiration, or even an applicable rhetoric, in Marxist concepts. The official, most readily supported scholarship served to augment this approach, usually by focusing upon "revolution" or "internal war" as a process that could be undermined or deflected if its dynamic were properly understood and if the details of any local instance were adequately described.

But in this area other modes of scholarly response— less tied to official policy and thus less interventionist and manipulative in purpose—could also be discerned. Especially noteworthy in the sixties was the considerable investment of research resources and intellect in "area studies"; that is, in the description of regional cultural and institutional systems and in the analysis of how they were likely, in the near future, to process the urge toward modernization.

Some such work, particularly that done in Southeast Asia, was coordinated to the American government's aspiration for continuing influence over the emerging or developing states. However, area research in other locales—especially when conducted by anthropologists, sociologists and geographers—often deviated considerably from the assumptions and purposes set by Cold War *Realpolitik*. In general it stressed that political and institutional development were bound to violate the narrow criteria treasured by a policy elite over-preoccupied with geopolitical definitions of American security and national interest. By so doing it called into question the realism of those criteria and the wisdom of the policies designed to actualize them.

The existence and persistence of this brand of area studies during the last decade is instructive. It highlights that there were only limited accuracy and justice in the arraignment of the policy sciences by those students and younger scholars who insisted that the academy had been taken into captivity by the policy establishment. It also suggests that the amount of scholarly deviance from the main, governmentally sanctioned trend will be a function of a number of other background factors. In the case of area studies and their analysis of development and modernization it is clear that deviance and independence were facilitated by a number of special factors. Among these were the existence of a stable scholarly tradition, of a style of intellectual craft and a set of organizing categories that predated the Cold War; the availability of considerable professional support and some financial support from agencies outside the government; and perhaps the recruitment of researchers from disciplines that have usually been considered marginal by the empowered elite. This last point, put simply, is the suggestion that sociologists, anthropologists, social psychologists and geographers may, when compared to typical political scientists and economists, be sufficiently distant from direct power and influence so as to be more capable of useful deviance from received policy doctrine.

Whatever its complex sources, no such deviance from the main trend is observed when we examine the history, over the last two decades, of another major body of work developed by American policy scientists. I speak here of the rise and prosperous influence of the strategic intellectuals, of deterrence theory and the new "rationality" in the processing of arms-policy decisions.

In no other domain of Cold War policy studies have scholars had greater influence upon basic policy making; and in no other domain have they operated with more sanguine, even enthusiastic, acceptance of the model of international reality offered to them by their clients and sponsors.

This is not the place to rehearse the fascinating history of the rise of the new strategic intellectuals. It must suffice to note what they have wrought—and then it will be easy to understand why deterrence theory and its many applications have recently come under rather scornful and angry criticism; why, for at least some students and legislators and for many academics, it has become the perfect symbol of the misuse of policy science in the Cold War era.

In general the most remarkable achievement of the strategic intellectuals was that they were able to update

Clausewitz and to persuade themselves and their governmental clients that even nuclear war can be correctly
viewed as the "continuation of policy by other means."
At any rate, they contended, prudence requires us to
live with the fact that the Communist powers will be
disposed to play the Clausewitzian game with post-
Clausewitzian weapons.

Thus it was argued that national security, at the least,
and probably effective pursuit of our geopolitical
interests as well, required that the United States build a
potent nuclear assault force. For the only sure way to
prevent our nuclear destruction by the Soviet Union was
to achieve and display a "credible" second strike
capability. The ready and full display of our power of
retributive destruction would inhibit the Soviet Union's
elite from being tempted to attack us in their search for
world domination. This in turn meant that our nuclear
force had to be considerably larger than theirs, and that
we had to keep it "hardened"—defended as much as
possible from preemptive assault—and technologically
superior.

It was on the basis of this general perspective, as
developed at the RAND Corporation and elsewhere by
such men as Brodie, Enthoven, Kahn, Kissinger, Schelling, Snyder and Wohlstetter, that the first phase of the
nuclear arms race was energized and managed. The
outcome was that by the early 1960s we had achieved a
vast superiority in strategic weapons, a superiority that,
according to the original vision of the deterrence
theorists, should have given us a renewed sense of
security in an insecure international environment.

It might have, but for two further developments: The
USSR would not hold still; and strategic theory,
committed always to the search for guaranteed security,

evolved toward the conscious choice of a higher form of paranoid logic.

This latter characterization is not intended as a loosely applied pejorative. The basic processing rule of paranoid ideation is that whatever threat can be *conceived* is to be *believed*. The basic decision-processing rule that the strategic theorists fell back upon with increasing uniformity was one that they sometimes called the "conservative assumption" or the "prudential standard." In essence it asserted that the maintenance of a credible second strike capability required that the antagonist's capability for successful preemptive assault be overestimated rather than underestimated. Why not *correctly* estimated? Because that was made impossible, or at least unconfirmable, by the ambiguities that bedevil any attempt to assess technological developments and weapons deployments requiring "lead times" of about five years.

Therefore, the working rule guiding American arms policy became, in effect, to project the worst (from the point of view of American security) missile deployments and aggressive intentions upon the Soviets as they might be five or ten years hence; and then to press on with the weapons development and deployment plans deemed necessary to meet that possible threat. Minimally this meant that, in the realm of offensive and defensive missiles and delivery systems, the nation must do everything reasonably necessary to guarantee an invulnerable second strike capability against an antagonist far more effectively armed than at present. On just this sort of systematic basis the deterrence theorists established the necessity for believing in whatever potential threat one could more-or-less realistically conceive.

But two parties, at least, are engaged in such deadly

games; and because of this the "delicate balance of terror" cannot be long stabilized. Instead, with each side falling back upon "prudential" analysis each is always running scared and thereby scaring its potential opponent. The "action-reaction cycle," as George Rathjens calls it, spirals on, spinning off more and more dysfunctional consequences with every revolution.

Most obvious of all these injurious consequences is the gigantic cost of new strategic weapons and "defensive" systems, a cost which inevitably depletes national wealth and fosters inattention to other basic domestic needs. Even more disturbing to scholars and investigative journalists who have peered closely at the modern military is their occasionally visible restiveness over the restricted utility of nuclear weapons. So vast an investment in a special and highly potent technology of destruction must, inevitably, breed the temptation to get some international political return from it. Thus on each side of the Cold War, particularly when it has turned warm, the threat of nuclear assault has been used at least once (by the USSR during the Suez crisis and by the United States during the Cuban missile crisis) to force a major concession from the antagonist. What some observers deeply fear is that continued escalation in the sophistication and potency of nuclear weapons will foster a greater proclivity for trying to score geopolitical points by going to the nuclear brink.

Even more unnerving is the possibility that the nuclear arms race may yet produce the sort of technological breakthrough that would create the conviction that an effective preemptive assault—one that would disable much of the opponent's second-strike capability—has at last become feasible. Furthermore under such new conditions the application of the logic of "prudentialism" might stimulate pre-preemption.

One can imagine—even if one cannot fully credit it as possible—the crucial moment in such a scenario: "Our intelligence reports indicate that with their new SS-15, MIRVed, 17-headed missiles now almost fully deployed they are beginning to think that they may be able to pull off a full counterforce assault against us and then ride out the remainder of our second strike under their field-force, ABM shield. They might elect that option the next time we are standing eyeball to eyeball— probably during the coming Iraqi crisis. Our only effective defense is to deny them the opportunity of preemption by pre-preempting them now."

I have dwelt upon these matters, and risked disrupting the organization of this essay, partly because of a longstanding and troubled concern with deterrence theory and its influence upon the policy process. Beyond that confessional and indirectly apologetic note, the simple standard of judiciousness requires, as well, that I label the foregoing as extremely speculative. Indeed, I have employed a variant of the "conservative assumption" in analyzing the consequences of a theory which proceeds through its radical application.

Yet it should be clear that however bizarre and excessive such speculations may seem, they are not uniquely conceived here. Rather, they have for some time been agitating apparently competent observers, including a few former members of the defense establishment itself. And the prevalence of such concerns highlights a question of more immediate pertinence to our present inquiry: taking deterrence theory as an instance in which intellectual work has had very significant (and possibly dangerous) consequences, what can we learn from it for the future management and application of policy-science endeavors?

Several tentative answers (or perhaps they are merely

cautionary considerations) come to mind. And though they bear particularly upon strategic science and deterrence theory they also reflect a broader type of critical sensibility that can probably be applied across the general range of policy science endeavors.

I might add that, in general, the cautionary considerations shortly to be proferred seem also to have occurred to most of the authors represented in this volume. Or so one might gather from the tenor of their contributions, from the orbit of their apparent intellectual intentions. It appears, then, that the new style in policy scholarship, as represented by the essays in this book, is guided by awareness of a special set of deficiencies characteristic of the older style; and though these deficiencies are most readily discovered in the work of the deterrence theorists, they are sometimes also visible in other sectors of Cold War policy science.

Perhaps the most obvious failing—and one that is particularly evident in the work of the deterrence theorists—is that the nonproximate effects of policy recommendations are rarely examined. To recommend the pursuit of strategic security through "hard-point" ABM defense of ICBM sites and not to consider what the deployment would probably suggest to "prudent" Soviet strategists is, to say the least, shortsighted. Similarly, to recommend "pacification" of South Vietnam without reckoning the likely consequences of the removal of perhaps two million peasants from their villages is equally hasty. Or, for that matter, to wage a long-term Cold War (and to warm it up occasionally) without any projective analysis of how this will affect American political life and how it might disrupt the delicate balance of pluralism, speaks of a similar failure of *intellectual* responsibility.

In general, at its worst the policy scholarship of the Cold War period seemed to ignore a stricture familiar to any thoughtful social scientist. And that is: when initiatives are inserted into a functionally integrated national or international system they are likely to make waves, to produce systemic consequences other than those immediately intended. Thus, a good portion of the challenge facing a policy scholar is to organize his interpretations and put forward his recommendations with an acute sense of second order, tertiary and, for that matter, nth effects.

If he does this with the certainty of a seer he has lapsed into *hubris* or a special variant of ideational madness. But if he avoids the challenge with a shrug over "incalculable contingencies" his performance must be faulted as verging on intellectual irresponsibility. Though this seems to have been a deficiency in much of the policy scholarship of the last 25 years, it is, within sizeable limits, a correctable one. The essays in this volume do, I think, reflect the aspiration to think through, beyond tomorrow, and also to think across— that is, from the political, military or economic sector in which a policy initiative is contemplated to contiguous sectors in which it might produce untoward or unmanageable effects.

A second failing seems evident in the work of most leading deterrence theorists and in the efforts of some political-area experts, particularly those who have specialized in studying the Communist nations and in developing worried assessments of the international aspirations of those nations. Too often, these scholars seem unaware of the perspective afforded them by the modern sociology of knowledge. They seem not to understand that their work usually tends to strengthen some groups engaged in the struggle for political power (in this case the power to control major foreign and military policies) while weakening others. Nor do they usually seem aware of, or interested in, the related proposition that a body of intellectual work may take on the social function of providing "guiding myths." In this instance this means providing overviews or "philosophies" of international relations which, by their diffusion *as* overviews, affect the very substance of international relations, actually closing out some channels down which the stream of major events might otherwise flow.

Putting this more concretely, a good deal of the deterrence-oriented analysis of strategic problems and a fair amount of the containment-oriented work in area studies and in comparative political systems have served the more apocalyptic military as well as various other elite, hard-line enthusiasts. By summoning expert opinion, and by displaying data gathered or estimates projected by experts, those who helped to foster and maintain the Cold War (whether located on the Western or Communist side) were able to defend and extend their case. And thus they were able to exert significant and continuing control over policy.

It is a matter of instructive paradox that, at the same time, those at the elite level who so disported themselves were further impassioned and motivated by their experts' readings of international and strategic reality. A situation of mutual reinforcement between the experts and their most powerful clients, between the proposers and the disposers, helped to keep the Cold War dynamic going—perhaps even after it had reached its own intrinsic culmination.

All of this is elaboration upon the simple theme that

establishment policy intellectuals operate within an institutional matrix that maximizes the likelihood that their interpretations and projections will become self-fulfilling prophecies. What, then, is the necessary corrective? It is *not* to abandon the search for organizing overviews; nor to put aside the building of ambitious integrative theories from which a broad range of particular judgments can be derived. Intellectual endeavor in any scientific or quasi-scientific realm must reach toward system. The ambition for system is inevitably generated by intellectual activity itself. But it should be possible to extend one's inquiry to the question of how the inquiry itself alters the issues or opportunities being studied.

In practical and historically anchored terms this suggests, for example, that the deterrence theorists might have studied and reported upon the ways in which deterrence-guided decisions might prevent either of the great protagonist nations from finding a way out of the action-reaction cycle in arms acquisition. Or they might have asked how correctives could be built into their own analytic procedures so as to limit overestimation of the potential enemy's future missile force or of his temptations to expend that force. Or they might quite simply have stressed to their clients that the underlying assumptions in their studies and recommendations were not the only assumptions possible.

One practical value of the sociology of knowledge as a mode of intellectual sensibility is that it alerts the scholar to the sociopolitical forces that have influenced his scholarship and to the sociopolitical consequences his scholarship may foster. Thus sensitized, the policy scholar is likely to produce a better product—at least in

the sense that it helps policy makers to better understand the limits of the conceptual systems that have
been constructed or confirmed for them by the scholars
they have commissioned. And possessing this special
kind of sophistication, policy makers, as well as their
political opponents and critics, can be at least partially
freed from the tyranny of polarized or routinized
perception. It is just this sort of freedom which enables
escape from the present historical moment, which
stimulates the aspiration toward mastery and transformation of present structures rather than allowing
entrapment in those structures.

Most of the essays reprinted here seem to reflect an
awareness of this problem. Though they are critical of
one or another aspect of American foreign or military
policy, they are not given to undifferentiated rejection
of American policy. They do not propose simple
overviews of the internation dynamic; particularly, they
avoid reducing that dynamic to the polar opposite of
the Cold War protracted conflict model. Perhaps some
useful self-doubt has been acquired and will ultimately
have its effect, not only upon the achievements of the
policy-oriented disciplines but also upon the ways in
which those achievements will be put to use in the
future.

A last critical point concerning yet another deficiency
of policy studies during the Cold War era ought to be
registered, though it is far more applicable to the field
of strategic studies than to any of the other realms of
policy science. It involves a complaint that must be
directed not at those who did the work but at those
who did not.

The overwhelming and unnerving problem that the
great nations faced within a few years after the shaping

up of the Cold War was how to handle the nuclear weapons that they and their potential antagonists now possessed. How, if at all, were these weapons to be used? Or rather, how could it be guaranteed that they would not be used when the East and West blocs were launched upon a long and dangerous contest of wills? Many subsidiary problems needed close analysis. Much relevant data needed to be gathered and sifted. Inventiveness in the design of alternative plans for negotiation and arms control was urgently required.

The established social sciences such as sociology, anthropology, political science and social psychology might have proved pertinent to these tasks if not fully adequate to them. But in the main, members of those disciplines remained diffident. Except for a sizable contingent of political scientists, they did not rush in to confront the challenge illumined in the dawn of a new nuclear arms technology. Undoubtedly this was partly because, except for the political scientists, they had not been invited. The intellectual vacuum was filled by new claimants—by physicists, by scholars trained in analytic philosophy, by occasional mathematicians and economists and by men-of-all-work, generalists attached to the military or somehow resonant to its temper.

It might well be argued that with a fuller representation of all of the relevant disciplines, strategic studies and, thus, the ultimate shape of strategic policies might have taken a different turn. The blame certainly lies partly with those in political or institutional power who failed to issue the invitation. But it lies also with those too timorous to presume where they had not been invited.

The lesson that may have been learned by now is that social scientists have a responsibility to address important policy issues whenever those issues involve variables and processes encompassed by their disciplines. The essays brought together in this volume seem in the main to reflect that sense of responsibility. And they reflect it not only in relation to arms policy and deterrence but rather as it bears upon the whole range of policy issues that must be clarified if internation stability and distributive justice are to be served through scholarly effort.

Having come thus far, I am aware of a number of deficiencies in the exposition I have attempted. They are due to the need to cover large and complex matters briefly and to the resultant reduction of subtle color tones to black, white and a small number of intermediate shades of gray. Thus, a few clarifications and elaborations may not be amiss at this point.

Though I have argued that the dynamic of the Cold War drew a large portion of policy scholarship toward distortive error, I do not mean to suggest that it lacks all merit. To the contrary, significant contributions were made in many areas of policy study. And, overall, social scholarship has profited considerably from the effort to comprehend the institutions and processes through which great modern states wage protracted, yet limited, competition with one another.

Though I have suggested that much of the policy scholarship of the last 25 years contributed to the maintenance of the Cold War and to some aspects of its style, I do not mean to suggest that the policy sciences played any major causal role in its initiation. Rather, I would cast my lot with the school of history that assumes the flow of ideas to be far more influenced by the uses of power than are the uses of power directed by the flow of ideas. Regarding the origins of the Cold War,

with sectors of the elite committed to the main-
maintenance of protracted conflict;
participation in policy studies by relevant disciplines that have, so far, been grossly under-
represented.

t something more is needed, something that comes
r to rectifying an underlying malaise or weakness of
t in conventional policy science approaches. Just
t that malaise is and how it might be put aside are, I
k, illuminated by the essays in this book when they
compared to more conventional policy scholarship.
The present authors seem to have recovered some
se of the "prophetic style" that I alluded to earlier.
this I mean the aspiration to use social inquiry so as
directly advance human welfare, to redress the gross
crepancy between guiding values and present realities.
e other basic component of the prophetic style is—to
voke the Quaker injunction sometimes quoted by
vocates of the new approach in policy studies—that
e must "speak truth to power." At its minimum level
is means that values and moral concern cannot be put
side as one takes on the scientific stance; that social
tellectuals are obliged to evaluate policies and pro-
rams in terms of their probable humane and inhumane
ffects.

At another level this injunction suggests that the
scholar's basic obligation to the society he serves, and, if
this does not sound too misty, his obligation to
mankind and its hope for peace and polity, is to
maintain a position of critical independence. For the
social scholar the temptation to confirm his intellectual
identity by gaining access to, and influence upon, the
policy process is well-nigh universal. However, the
related danger is also well known and often experienced.

I have perhaps been more influenced by the conventional historians than by their revisionist critics.
Thus, it seems to me that the Cold War had about it
something of the ineffable quality of historical inevita-
bility, though to be sure, the background conditions
which made it inevitable were, perhaps, products of still
earlier policy choices which need not have been elected.

But even if the postwar turn toward protracted
conflict between East and West was inevitable, it clearly
does not follow that it need be eternal. Indeed, it seems
a certainty that it cannot be, for nothing in the relations
between states is particularly stable—and certainly not
conflict which, by its nature, plays itself out toward
some reorganization of the internation system.

A last elaboration of what has gone before should be
noted: though the American and Soviet elites, together
with the elites of their respective major allies, joined in
mutual prosecution of their protracted conflict, neither
was bound within an absolutely uniform consensus.
Western observers cannot penetrate completely the haze
that envelops the recent policy history of the Soviet
Union. But from the evidence picked up when the
"circulation of elites" is occurring, and from the
reflections of intraelite policy debate that glance off the
pages of *Pravda* and *Izvestia,* this much seems clear:
both hard-line and conciliationist positions have been
heard in the highest decision-making councils of the
Soviet Union. Vacillations between tough and mild
postures in Soviet initiatives toward the Western powers
cannot be taken, as some Sovietologists have done, as
merely a kind of trickery intended to keep the West
confused, and thus to maximize the gain that will accrue
whenever the stance shifts from cooperativeness to
belicosity.

As regards the West, the picture is quite clear. At many important junctures in the Cold War, the elites of our allies have opposed and limited some aspects of American policy. And within the American policy elite, including not only the President and his immediate advisors, but the higher bureaucrats of the State and Defense Departments, the Senate as a total body and various committees of the House, debate and dis-agreement grew broader and deeper with each passing year of the sixties.

Undoubtedly the Vietnam war speeded the reexamination of basic policy commitments, but that reexamination had already begun toward the end of the Eisenhower administration. This is not the place, nor is it necessary, to examine the many issues now being contested. Whether they concern our policies toward Southeast Asia, strategic weapons programs, the extent and purpose of foreign aid, military withdrawal from Europe, the future of our alliances, our relations with China or a dozen other salient problems, all such issues relate to a more basic question. That question is whether we should continue in protracted conflict with the Communist world or seek a deep stabilization. Concerning such stabilization of the international order there is a subsidiary but still crucial issue: whether it is to be sought through conventional balance-of-power settlement or through a diminished American involve-ment in the world and acceptance of various trends of change in the international system. Among these are trends toward polycentrism, toward regional groupings and toward the growth of "functional," intergovern-mental institutions through which separate sovereignties may gradually be pooled, thus reducing the importance

of nations in the processing o problems.

The task of this essay, as I discuss trends of change in p relate them to trends of cha establishment. I have given far to the former than to the latter. my characterization of the inaccurate, it then becomes nece question. It is one toward which the hope that the long frustra deferral of hope that gave the C especially painful quality may ye question is: how can the social scie their policy-study aspects, contribu bearable, a more promising and prod of the relations between states?

There will be no great surprise presume to offer. They follow rather critique of the older style of policy s endorsement of the newer style as e succeeding essays.

Obviously, the first part of the an been given: policy scholarship will be m the formulation of wise policy the more scholarship. And increased adequacy, gested, will require, among other things t

1. attention to the nonproximate eff innovations;
2. awareness of the special social role scientist, of his myth-providing functi
3. awareness of the ever-present danger will be too narrowly defined throug

One may be gradually and inadvertently drawn into a kind of scholarly functioning in which the ambition to "tell it like it is" is subverted by anxiety over whether anyone in a position to act upon the message will listen and, if he does listen, whether he will be motivated by what he hears.

The proper response to this dilemma is not found in the facile insistence that scientific accuracy and ultimate social good cannot be served from within government or through governmental sponsorship. If power corrupts, it does not follow that access to the wielders of power need do so. If it is not debased by a yielding to grandiosity, by confusion of one's partial truth with eternal and total verity, the prophetic stance can sometimes be achieved within establishment circles and institutions. Irving Horowitz's essay in this volume can be read as an examination of the opportunities for, and the limits upon, the exercise of the prophetic style when one is located within, or has direct access to, the institutions responsible for making and executing governmental policy.

Yet government is not the only or the ultimate source of policy. However muddled and sluggish the institutions of modern political democracy may be, they do continue to make influence over policy available, both to competing subelites and to broad social interest groups as they engage in advocacy and competition, as they use the political process itself.

This leads me to my last point—and it is the one that I feel most urgently and would want to urge upon those engaged in policy studies. The prophetic style now surfacing in the new, post-Cold War approach to policy studies has yet another outlet, another exciting opportunity. It can and should address the general public. In our country attentive publics do exist but the *general* public remains distressingly inattentive to problems of foreign and military policy. Any increase in its sophistication, and any elevation of the motive to achieve sophistication, is bound to improve the quality of policy design—if only by forcing policy makers toward greater differentiation and also toward greater responsiveness to the humane aspirations of ordinary citizens.

Public education on the complexities of issues of military and foreign policy is, then, a task that policy scholars themselves can advance. And public journals like the one from which the essays reprinted here have been drawn comprise a main vehicle for that effort. But ours is a differentiated public, a truly plural society, not only as regards economic interests and the divergence of ethnic traditions, but also as regards claims and influences upon the making of basic policy decisions. If the policy scholar has come to the point where he feels strongly and clearly that policy ought to be moved in one rather than another direction he has the opportunity, if not the obligation, to assist that movement. He can do this by putting his knowledge and his skills directly to work in the building of attentive publics that will enter into political struggle to advance the process of policy alteration.

In the present era that has been the turn taken by many policy scholars who have lent their analytic abilities and their specialized knowledge to the "peace movement." With some limited success that movement has been working to build a large, attentive public that might, through political action and organization, strengthen the influence over foreign policy of the sizable group of American legislators who are now attempting to bring the Cold War to its full termination. The last article in this book—and the only one that did not originally appear in *trans*action—affords an illustration of one way in which, as I see it, policy scholars can contribute to the public political process.

Though it might go without saying I shall risk the obvious to make one last cautionary point: there is in this sort of role just as much danger that one will inadvertently be drawn away from his primary obligation to "tell it like it is" as in the role of the policy scientist employed or favored by governmental agencies. But truth, partial or otherwise, is there for the grasping if one relies upon those methods and past achievements of policy science that are already in hand. If one guards against the failure of nerve, and against its defensive false face—the presumption of ultimate, grandiose certainty—one can, within the realm of policy studies, serve both scholarship and profoundly humane purpose.

FOREIGN AID

Corruption and Commerce
in
Southeast Asia

LUCIEN M. HANKS

Anarchy is merely the lack of institutional authority. There will always be government in terms of voluntary social organizations formed to do specific things—putting out fires, protection against thieves, different kinds of schools. If you want the service, you support it and participate; if you don't want the service, nobody can make you use it or pay for it. Karl Hess, as quoted by James Boyd in "From Far Right to Far Left and Farther with Karl Hess," *New York Times Magazine,* December 6, 1970.

Though scholars attuned to the niceties of labeling may wish to alter Karl Hess' definition of anarchy, it covers about what I mean when I use the word. Here I shall claim that something approaching these voluntary relations between government and people exists in Southeast Asia and appears to have existed for some time. Clearly this usage of "anarchy" has nothing to do with civil disorder, armed insurrection, rapidly changing heads of state or ineffective rulers. Though Southeast

Asia has suffered and continues to suffer from most of these afflictions during the present century, this is anarchy only in a vulgar sense.

Most observers have confined themselves to describing the extensive and often ruthless powers of the rulers. Out of our concern with uncurbed power, we have affixed the label "oriental despotism," considering it a kind of disease for which we from the free enterprise democracies prescribe cures by constitutional governments, while our socialist neighbors recommend nationalization of commerce. Not least known among the diagnosticians of societal disorder was President Lyndon B. Johnson who declared his "Five Points for Peace" during an interview over three television networks on December 19, 1967. During the course of his statement, he told his listeners that "The overwhelming majority of the people of Vietnam want a one man-one vote constitutional government."

Such a statement was bound to please all who take pride in American exports, yet few in the audience knew that no constitution, no parliamentary government in Southeast Asia has lasted more than a decade. As for liberty through nationalization of the economy, the experiences of Indonesia and Burma have done little more than to start their economies along the road to a tail-spinning decline.

We may expect heads of government to indulge in rhetorical excesses, but experts too write variations on these same political remedies. An old Burma hand, Frank N. Trager, wrote as follows about General Ne Win's 1960 resignation after two years of military rule:

> [By their resignation] They [General Ne Win and his corps of officers] provided a demonstration lesson in non-bureaucratic efficiency and puritanical incorruptibility; they also provided a sufficiently different, if

not unique, example of military and civilian support for national ideals and a commitment to democratic processes and goals.

Aside from misplaced praise, here we find success on the part of a head of government attributed to respect for democratic forms. In fact, three years later, in 1968, General Ne Win again seized the government of Burma, dissolved the parliament and threw opposition leaders into prison, where some were quietly assassinated.

The foregoing exemplifies a widely held misconception of the nature of government and its relations to the people of Southeast Asia. Like fifteenth century Flemish painters who portrayed Jesus in the costume of a local peasant, our statesmen and expert journalists all ascribe western social rules to a scene which in fact works quite differently.

To understand Southeast Asia we must strip away our own political ascriptions. We tend to assume, for example, that government stands or should stand above the populace like a parent providing functional services intended to maintain law and order. According to this view, if a government is weak, the social order will dissolve into an Hobbesian state of raw and brutish nature. Even experts believe that government should rule all the people within a given territory and that the significant difference between governments arises from whether they are organized as monarchies, oligarchies or democracies, and that despotism comes, if not from dictatorship, from the absence of a rule of law under a constitution. Alas, good King Wenceslaus and bad President Harding! Forgetting our own American revolution, many of us continue to divide governments of the world into legitimate powers that have appeared because of due process and the usurpers who come to power by force of arms.

From these beginnings we regard the world's land mass as a mosaic of nation states, each with its well-defined frontier. Within these bounded areas dwell people whose societal order is shaped like a pyramid, with a ruler at the top, the populace at the bottom. From our particular North American position on the surface of the earth, Southeast Asian governments appear to be arbitrarily depriving the people under their jurisdictions of their human rights. In what follows I shall describe an alternative interpretation of societal order, hoping that it will stand nearer to what we once called reality.

The world knows Sukarno as the battler against the colonial Dutch, founder of the Indonesian Republic, and a man who served both as prime minister and president. What I want to call attention to is that despite his eclipse in 1966, a monument to him still stands in the center of Jakarta, a monument too big to move or to demolish without special attention by a government now more concerned with off-shore oil leases.

There it stands in the center of an enormous square perhaps half a mile in breadth, without a tree or bush to interrupt one's gaze. The Sukarno monument is a gigantic pillar, perhaps 200 to 300 feet in height (if memory serves), surmounted by flame-like figures, while statues and fountains adorn the base in quasi-baroque fashion. At first glance, an American would recognize in it a national monument to the founder of a country, something a little more flamboyant than the Washington Monument but with the same intent. Looking more closely, however, one notices that there are no pilgrim tourists at the base, and if the column has one, the elevator to the top has long since broken down. Never did I see more than a few pedicab drivers napping around its base, though people said the enormous weedy space around the monument was sometimes used for fairs and military parades. As one enquires further, differences begin to mount. The plan provides for boulevards radiating from the monument in eight directions, somewhat like the Arc de Triomphe at the Place de l'Etoile in Paris, and as in Paris, drivers make their way along the shaded avenues at the circumference. The radial boulevards, however, go no farther than the limits of the park, failing to continue into the crowded city or to alter the traffic flow of the city itself. Then, suddenly one remembers that Sukarno is still living and that the monument was not built posthumously by admirers wishing to perpetuate his memory. Rather Sukarno built it himself for his own glory.

Spending public funds for such self-glorification affronts our sense of propriety. But if the money were private funds from some corporate operation, we might even applaud the effort, for more costly buildings and monuments than this have been erected in our country to sell chewing gum or automobiles. Yet it is in this sense that the Sukarno monument should be understood for as we shall see, Southeast Asian governments are like corporate enterprises, and like all corporate enterprises they must advertise. This monument is a hard-sell appeal to the Indonesian people; it conjures up a dream world where every passerby perceives in this giant column the magnetic strength of President Sukarno. And he too was in its spell, seeing himself there at the center of the great park surrounded by millions of people, overflowing into the streets beyond. He could dream of delivering at the foot of the column an address carried by loudspeaker to every corner of the park and by radio to every island of Indonesia. The last word said, he stands to receive the ovation. Such was the dream, for in fact he ruled precariously amid revolts and factions ever scheming his overthrow, from West Irian to the outlying islands off Sumatra. Sukarno yearned for that center of power over the widely scattered realm, but he never attained it for more than a moment or two. So today, after his overthrow, a few school boys are about the only ones to climb around on the statues and dry fountains.

So much for the dream. The actual relationship between government and people in this part of the world is loosely contractual, based on a verbal or unspoken agreement between a leader of an armed force and one or more autonomous villages. If a Southeast Asian government does stand at the center with all the autonomous villages under its control, we must remember that it has fought its way there in competition with other armed groups. No ready-made seat awaits a governor, for each one must build and occupy his own.

Historically, capitals were frankly surrounded by fortifications, with armed men standing at the gates to keep the populace out. The old Thai capital at Ayuthia stood well protected on an island in the Chao Phraya river, the common people living across the river. Go to Ava in Burma or Hue in Vietnam, and again the centers of government were fortifications. In Angkhor Vat and Angkhor Thom we are less sure of the disposition of the armed forces, but we know that each of these walled-off edifices enclosed the special rites required for governing the Khmer Empire. These rites seem to have taken place at spots selected by Brahmins and geomancers which would enable each new monarch to control his fluctuating realm, and Fa Hsien, the 12th-century Chinese visitor to Angkhor Thom, had to secure special permission before being allowed to pass the gates. And those who entered were like prisoners; they had to obtain permission to depart.

Beyond the fortifications lay the villages. Any cluster of newly arrived settlers, having enquired of existing higher authority. In time, with new settlers, population grew to 20,000 or more people, each locality living under the rule of an elected headman with his council of elders, more self-sufficient than a New England town. In the vast majority of places, the headman, with his elders, still takes care of maintaining the roads and bridges, looks after the indigent, settles disputes among the inhabitants, appoints committees to manage local festivals, sometimes maintains a school, always drawing on village labor or produce for their purposes. If one seeks ready-made pyramids of authority, they exist in the local organization of villages, each following the plan prescribed by its own particular ethnic heritage.

Government beyond the village level often grows out of one of these villages. To become a controlling ruler of more than one village requires the successful completion of four steps: An aspirant first gathers a modest group of fighters, equipping them with available weapons. With their help he establishes a monopoly, perhaps simply by setting up toll gates on some highway. By threatening to confiscate the wares of itinerants, the would-be leader hopes to gather enough produce and money to maintain his fighters or to enlarge their numbers. With tolls carefully set to get the most return without diverting traffic to alternate routes, and having successfully defeated possible competitors for the business, a man is then ready to extend his enterprise to a new level by offering "protection" to nearby villages. Any spot troubled with brigands may be willing to acquire protection for the safety of its inhabitants, and should the normal supply of brigands have been villages where free land was available, planted itself where it wished without need for an authorizing grant of land or a certificate of incorporation from some depleted, convincing substitutes can be mustered among the aspiring ruler's armed men. Thus additional revenue flows into the coffers, so that the fighting force can be increased and bring new villages under the protective umbrella. Finally, having built a going enterprise with profits substantially exceeding the costs of the army, an old general in his declining years seeks to pass the business intact to a favorite kinsman. If in the process the organization does not dissolve into quarreling factions, the old man becomes the founder of a dynasty lasting at least two generations.

The language of business operation has more than superficial relevance. Not only do these purveyors of protective services arise out of individual initiative (a point that will be amplified in the following section) but most important for our immediate concern, they operate on a voluntary arrangement between supplier and customer villages. In Vietnam an old maxim underscores this assumed independence and may be paraphrased: The authority of the emperor stops at the village gates. That this statement has content is attested by Nghiem Dang in his *Vietnam: Politics and Public Administration* in describing administrative arrangements before the advent of the French colonial system:

All decisions of whatever importance were made at the commune (village) level by the headman, who was highly respected by the people, and the carrying out of these decisions was assured of their own free will by villagers; this was the principle of communal autonomy.

Communal autonomy is also presumed in Burma, if we may generalize from the description by Manning Nash of a single village near Mandalay: "Officials of the Agricultural Redevelopment Agency, the Agricultural

Loan Service, and the health services always get audiences with U Sein Ko, if they want to make a speech or do something in Nondwin." These governmental officials stopped at the house of U Sein Ko as a sign of respect, to gain his permission for carrying out their programs, and by his assent they gained the ear of the inhabitants. Had these government officials plunged into the village on their own, no one would have cooperated.

Many a village appears to have existed beyond the protection of any agency. Bang Chan, a village never more than a day's travel from Bangkok, existed for thirty-five years before the appointment of an administrative officer in the near vicinity. Michael Moerman reports that Ban Ping was formerly under the governor of Nan, whose authority lapsed about 1850, but "did not come under the direct authority of the national government until after the administrative reforms consequent upon the Shan rebellion of 1901-02."

Evidence of village autonomy can be found in a distinction made in some areas between an office which we may call the village chief and another one responsible for contacts with an agency of protection. In the Burmese village that Manning Nash studied, U Sein Ko was the chief to whom officials addressed their requests to enter the village, while a man of much less stature served as liaison to the protecting agency by collecting taxes and attending meetings on call. This division of labor between a manifest and actual authority occurs frequently enough not to provoke special notice, yet in northern Thailand's tribal villages the distinction between the two offices is explicit. The village chief with ritual authority from the ancestral spirit conducts village rites, settles disputes, relocates the village and so forth, while the liaison man receives a title from the protective agency, a Shan name, for in that area protection lay in the hands of Shan princes, but the village chief could only be referred to in the local language. Many of the smaller or remoter villages said they had no liaison man, since none was ever appointed.

Of course, a village chief cannot always decide freely with whom he will contract for protection; facing tommy guns, he can only give the rice and pigs demanded, if he is to save the village from destruction. Subsequently he may weigh the question of moving to some more peaceful spot. Yet with a free offer of protection before him, a village chief may well decide, after sizing up the strength of the would-be protector, to form his own defenses within the village. Happier is the village chief when a strong general has conquered his enemies, allowing the village to live in peace with payments of modest tribute. After all, a village can only continue under that minimally dependable order sufficient to reap the crop which has been planted.

Besides living without a protector, a village may in theory even deal with several protectors, but for documentation we must turn to the protective agencies which at times themselves had to make deals with other protective agencies in order to survive. The kings of Pnom Penh in Cambodia during much of the nineteenth century paid tribute both to Bangkok and Hue for their protection, uneasily pitting one against the other. A less well-known case is the little city of Cheli in Chinese Yunnan, occupied by the Thai-speaking population known as *lyy* that still lives in the region. As the Dynastic Chronicles of Bangkok tell the story, Cheli sought the protection of Bangkok, but:

> The city of *lyy* at that time (circa 1854) was a vassal city to both Burma and the Chinese Haw (governors

of Yunnan province). Therefore, even if Siam agreed to accept *Iyy* as its tributary, in case Burma or China attacked the latter, it would be most inconvenient to send out an army from Siam to protect it, for it was very remote and the route fraught with difficulties. Despite these misgivings, Bangkok persuaded the governor of Nan Province in northern Thailand to send an expeditionary force which successfully captured Cheli. On its part Bangkok was unable to defend its newly acquired vassal against the armies of Burma, so that after two years of fruitless campaigns, the Thai withdrew. So Cheli returned to forwarding tribute both to Mandalay and the governors in Chungming.

We are scarcely surprised to learn that here people declare that government, like drought, floods and famine, is a major evil in this world. Rare is the Southeast Asian village that has received a government official without expecting him to extort money and that does not pay him some fraction of his demand in order to speed him on his way. Angry officials have been known to return to the village with soldiers and massacre the inhabitants. So during edgy days whole villages may be abandoned when some unidentified stranger approaches. Even when an official comes bearing gifts, all anticipate a time when favors will have to be reciprocated. In short, East Asian villagers act like urban Americans who wish to assert their independence of the utility companies by running wires past electric meters or inserting slugs in pay telephones: they underreport their population for the head tax and the size of their fields for the land tax.

Too often the services offered are unavailing. When a buffalo or ox is stolen, one calls the police only if some near neighbor has a brother or perhaps a son in a position to activate the police for his particular benefit. Lacking this, a plaintiff must pay a fee to obtain police cooperation, and only then is he likely to obtain satisfaction, but without justice. The police may find a victim for punishment in some neighboring village and rob a distant farmer to replace a missing animal. As most villages lack the necessary connections to the police and are too poor to pay the activating fee, they are as apt to become a victim as to gain from these contacts.

Most villages have developed means of maintaining order. Each household guards its own possessions, perhaps with ferocious watch dogs, always leaving someone behind when the others leave. If, despite ordinary precautions, a cart is missing when the dawn breaks, the owner sets out on his own to track it down, following the clues that neighboring witnesses provide. Having reached the village of the suspected thief, the owner backtracks in search of a go-between who will offer a price for the return of the cart. The go-between then returns to the village with this offer, and perhaps after several trips back and forth from the thief to the aggrieved, agreement on a price is reached for the return of the property.

Villages have other procedures for keeping the peace. Before a wedding, for example, the bride price is contracted with a man of local prestige jointly named to arbitrate any differences that might arise before final payment is made. Custom prescribes division of property in case of divorce and at death, so that a wise elder can be summoned to settle disputes. Roads, trails and canals running between villages are maintained in sections agreed upon in meetings of the elders. In these ways villages hold themselves aloof from the need of an outside authority.

Protective agencies in Southeast Asia act very much like commercial operations in the occident. Both market services to consumers and seek to form monopolies of these services. In principle any customer is free to accept or reject them, though a given agency may perform almost exclusive services in certain geographical areas. At the fringes of these areas several suppliers may compete.

The analogy breaks down, though, in that commercial firms in the occident now operate under the constraints of a sovereign state. But in the days when western business firms like the Dutch or British East India Companies stood on their own, they too worked in fortified enclosures, moved their goods under armed supervision and sent out spies to determine what their competitors were doing. Today we see their counterparts disarmed, though they still surround their establishments with protective fences and admit the public only for business purposes.

Both also advertise the superior quality of their services. Southeast Asian governments underscore the invincibility of their leaders, formerly with such titles as Lord of Life, Ruler of the Plane of the Earth, and Incarnation of Siva or some other powerful deity. In taking office, the head of state was invested with the Sword of Victory, the Cloak of Invulnerability or the Toothed Discus that overpowers enemies. The rites of an audience with the head of government, where petitioners waited the epiphany of the celestial one on their knees and elbows, further dramatized the awesome character of the enterprise.

While most of these practices have yielded to less dramatic western forms, the new head of government is as much of an individual as the new president of a firm. He picks his own staff and opens liaisons with new suppliers of men and weapons. As a new corporation president locates his office in a new spot and decorates his room in a new mode, so heads of state in Southeast Asia may relocate the capital and build new palaces. Each new king of Cambodia, during the period of the Khmer Empire, erected a new temple for his reign at a place determined by geomantic experts to be most effective for controlling the realm. Subsequent kings in other countries erected temples and pagodas in their fortified cities with similar intent. Marketing consultants, research staffs and economic advisers perform comparable services for commercial executives of today.

As God helps only those who help themselves, a danger lurks in relying too heavily on promotion. Slogans and guarantees cannot long sustain an inferior product, nor can the ceremonial weapon of invincibility replace the keen-edged battle sword. The Hoa Hau and Cao Dai sects of twentieth century Vietnam exemplify a nice balance between temple cults and armed followers, but when a governor becomes too smitten with his deific power, the effectiveness of his rule is near an end. Taksin, king of Thonburi in Thailand (1767-82) was said to have considered himself a living Buddha not many months before he was deposed. Certain Burmese kings also suffered from this delusion with comparable results. More often the less soldierly and more sacred successors to power owed the continuation of their position to active ministers who kept the enterprise vital, much as the Shoguns in Japan managed the rule of an emperor too ritually occupied to leave the palace. These days the mode prescribes active heads of government, though many continue to build temples and pagodas.

Let us not confine our gaze, however, to the more or less successful governments in the capitals, but observe an even more striking parallel between them and commercial enterprises. Governmental enterprises are continually arising, particularly in the provinces, as if they were family stores or home industries which may disappear a few months after opening or persist as small operations for a decade or more, but sometimes rise to impressive proportions. In central Thailand an old man of 60 told me about having been a gang leader about the year 1910:

> There was a gang at Khlaung Kred (a neighboring village) as well as Bang Chan. In Minburi (a larger market center) were several gangs. When people from Minburi came to the temple fair at Bang Chan, the Bang Chan and Khlaung Kred gangs worked together. When the people at Khlaung Kred wanted to go anywhere, the young, armed with swords, went with them.
>
> All members of the gang went around with a sword. Anyone without a sword was someone who did not want to fight. When the two groups met, their champions would challenge each other. A good leader must have the power of invulnerability and if blood runs when they fight, that man must have lost his power.

One thinks of juvenile gangs in American cities where one challenges the other in a game of prestige. In Southeast Asia, however, the gangs did not always disappear when young men married and settled down. From other sources I learned that at Khlaung Kred the leader, no longer a youth, was an expert with the sword, trained young men in its use and provided such services as night watch in the village.

An energetic and relatively rich young man draws to himself a coterie of young men whom he feeds and entertains with trips to the cock fights and drinks at the tea house. As long as his wealth and the novelty of their ventures can hold, the gang continues as a self-indulgent group or, with the assent of the elders, as protectors of the village, but let the crop fail and the leaders fall into debt, the followers disappear.

A less affluent but more ambitious young man may set out with his followers to rob not-too-distant villages, and as long as they do not embarrass the home village, everyone looks the other way. Only when robberies become too frequent and reprisals begin, with village pitted against village, is the locally established protective agency likely to step in. In Burma after World War II, when governments were weak, villages found it necessary to enclose themselves with fortifications, which were defended by the local gang when it was not making forays to rob some neighbor.

The usual villager is not sufficiently fearless or braggadocian to enter affairs of this sort. To be sure, a variety of amulets and tattooed signs bolster everyone's courage to meet danger from the harsh words, unwanted lovers and snake bites. However, gang leaders seek out the rare and more powerful devices that help prevent bullets or knives from penetrating the flesh. Some also claim the protection of familiar spirits who warn of approaching danger or have learned from a hermit some spoken formula to render an opponent harmless. Equipped in this manner, gang leaders pit themselves to fight other gang leaders and prove their relative strength by seeing whose blood is drawn first.

Properly approached and suitably lured with food and weapons, these semidisciplined gangs are ready to join with others. Thus many a leader of some small gang, having demonstrated his prowess, has risen to controlling position over considerable groups. Indeed, the history of Southeast Asia is filled with passing reference to leaders with their gangs who appear suddenly on the scene from nowhere. The following account by D. G. E. Hall deals with a man named Daing Farani, an adventurer whose Bugi speech suggests his coming from the Celebes to the region of the Malacca straits:

Raja Kechil ruled the Johore dominions from Riau [off-shore islands near the present site of Singapore]. In 1718 the deposed Sultan [of Johore, named Abdul Jalil] intrigued with Daing Farani, a Bugis chief who served Raja Kechil in Sumatra, and was disappointed in his expectations of receiving the office of Yam-tuan Muda in Johore. The plot failed, and the fugitive Abdul Jalil was put to death while attempting to flee to Pahang. In 1722, however, Daing Farani and his Bugis followers drove out Raja Kechil and placed a son of Abdul Jalil on the throne. The new sultan was forced to appoint Daing Farani's eldest brother Yam-tuan Muda, or Under-King, of Riau, and reign as the puppet of the Bugis. From then onwards the Bugis were the real rulers of Johore.

A man named Le Quang Ba, an organizer of resistance during the French period in Vietnam, wrote the following:

In 1939, the Japanese fascists, preparing for intervention in Indochina, were giving support to many gangs which operated in frontier areas, well-armed ruffians, half smugglers, half pirates, against whom the Chiang Kai Shek and French authorities could do nothing. With Japanese support these gangs freely plundered the population. After a misdeed, they would have only to cross the frontier to escape punishment.

Le Quang Ba used the occasion to organize the villages of his area, and by dint of his success, he became an important figure to meet for all persons wishing to enter the mountains of Cao Bang province.

These fragments indicate the continuity between village leaders of gangs and heads of government. In this free enterprise many gangs may lodge in a countryside, but few survive to become a force capable of protecting a small monopoly. Of them, few increase to a size that can merit the term war lord. In the shade of a large and powerful government, the little ones tend to die away. But out among less powerful neighbors are space and fluidity enough that some may survive; a kind of Darwinian struggle takes place in such areas. Still, as larger gangs may cooperate with smaller ones against a third, survival is not entirely a matter of swords and fire power.

Undoubtedly a tendency exists for heads of large governmental enterprises to succeed each other on the basis of kinship, a tendency that has lead many to posit a controlling aristocratic class. Certainly these heads of governmental enterprises, having grown rich in office, have a more luxurious style of life than the villagers and are elevated by cults of the region to superhuman station. However, the fact remains that many a queen has been a daughter of commoners, and sons of these marriages have succeeded to headship. More important, the moment of succession is a period of intense competition not only between sons of the deceased but between his brothers, nephews and cousins, when assassination was a frequent arbiter. Most dynastic lines are broken by usurpers like Phra Phetarat of Thailand who in 1688 dethroned the old king and established a new dynastic line. This man moved from general in charge of the royal elephants directly to the throne.

The step from gang leader in the rice fields to head of a large governmental enterprise is a long one, more easily spanned in two than one generation. Buddhist doctrine, however, affirms that any man may have merit enough to rise from commoner to king, while in Islam, Allah's favor may fall upon the humble as well as the mighty, and the Mandate of Heaven in Vietnam can fall upon any shoulders. Hierarchies, like the mountains of Southeast Asia, are usually low, frequent and easy to climb though with occasional steep pitches. Indeed, some of the most famous, such as the Shwe Dagon in Rangoon and its equivalent Golden Mountains of other cities, have been entirely made by men.

If Southeast Asian villages contract freely with protective agencies, and if protective agencies come and go like firms in a free-enterprise economy, how does anarchy show itself today? We have been long accustomed to look respectfully (or at least feeling we should be able to look more respectfully) on uniformed generals and business-suited officials with their dispatch cases. When we visit the capitals of this region, the offices, Houses of Parliament and diplomatic receptions assure us that we are standing in a familiar scene.

These governments have adjusted adroitly to western expectations. Execution of enemies is carried out in seclusion rather than at the center of some festive occasion. Architects and engineers have been hired to build boulevards and parks in formerly fetid areas. Colonial governments in the nineteenth century helped set the pattern: power was centralized at the capital; post offices, railways, schools and hospitals were founded under government patronage. Laws regulating the conduct of people at large were introduced along with police, courts and jails.

Thailand missed these occidental governors, but with the help of advisers, the Thai learned to manage the same operations. W. A. Graham, an Englishman who participated in this transformation, told (in 1913) of organizing the police:

> With the time-honoured custom of collusion between officials and professional criminals strong in the land, from which many of the old chiefs (Chao Muang) derived considerable profit, it was scarcely to be expected that any genuine effort to suppress crime entirely would be made by the country justices of the old regime, even at the urgent command of the king. But by creating a monopoly of this form of industry, the chiefs no doubt exercised a sort of check ... for it was very noticeable that with the reorganization of rural officialdom and the removal of the chiefs or the curtailment of their powers and authority, violent crime of every description increased to an alarming extent and very soon passed altogether beyond the control of authorities. To meet this difficulty the Minister for the Interior devised a scheme for the maintenance of a force of gendarmerie . . . .

Such resistance to change surprised us less than the speed of accepting the new; no civil wars broke out; no one sealed himself off in some unapproachable pocket of resistance. The crime wave proved to be a short-lived period of readjustment. A new generation of governing people quickly realized that one could do as well or better with post offices or highway building as with old-fashioned protection. Westerners were introducing a wide variety of luscious new monopolies, while orientals were drinking them in. So the gamut of new monuments has grown from electric generators to housing developments with a western chorus rejoicing at "civilization," "modernization" and "development." Let any one of them return a few weeks later and look through the windows of, say, the custom house, built in a style appropriate to the turn of the century, and observe not only the (to us) extortionate prices of export and import licenses but the confiscation of merchandise for resale to the advantage of officials. This is the new way to keep the gang together.

Occidentals have also enlarged the range of weapons that the government monopolies may use in attack. From reliance solely on force, all, be they police department or education department, have learned to vary prices in order to secure a friend, to seize a source of supply in order to embarrass a rival and to obstruct rivals with suits and injunctions from the courts. They have learned the power of using radio and newspapers as weapons, of appealing to popular opinion, and the value of an election in the gaining of certain friends abroad.

Less serviceable trappings of the west have been constitutions, parliaments and political parties. Ten constitutions have been proclaimed and revoked in Thailand during a period of less than 40 years. The act of parliament in London setting out the government of Burma did not survive a decade before the take-over of a military dictatorship. Malaysia, begun in 1957, could not contain Singapore more than eight years and today stands in mortal danger from further communal rifts. The new Vietnamese constitution seems to be sufficiently loose in fit not to obstruct the serious work of running a monopoly. Nor have the instruments of socialism fared better than the democratic ones, judging by the report from Burma in the *New York Times* of September 3, 1970:

> With the rebirth of commerce, nationalized People's Stores have become the principal distribution centers for almost everything sold legally. The managers have become the principal government representatives with whom the average Burmese deals—he hates them. The manager allots the small quantities of goods he receives to customers registered with him . . . . Shortages are compounded by a distribution system in which soldiers heading a lumbering bureaucracy have replaced Indian, Chinese and European traders who at a profit to themselves used to handle goods.

So the soldiers of a military government have learned to operate a black market.

Perhaps most revealing of these assemblages of varied monopolies that form the governments is their inability to introduce the western model of central control of finances. Everywhere ministries of finance tend to remain rudimentary, unable to gain monopolies on collection of revenues and have them flow through a central treasury into the various agencies in accord with approved budgets. Instead, each agency collects and dispenses its own funds from its own particular monopolies, and in considerable measure the strength of the clique in power depends upon its ability to hand out and withdraw monopolies in return for cooperation by some local leader.

So the head of government may vary in his authority from day to day, as these self-seeking bureaus and departments manoeuvre for strength. In Burma the Antifascist People's Freedom League, the political party which furnished most of the muscle for gaining independence, turned during the 1950s from being a merely self-sufficient extension of government to the people into an adversary of government. Its collapse followed the military seizure of power by General Ne Win. In South Vietnam, generals of divisions turned against Ngo Dinh Diem, and each successive prime minister has had to tread carefully to hold or suppress his generals. In Cambodia Lon Nol waited for the moment when he could overthrow Prince Sihanouk.

These variations in power reveal themselves particularly in fluctuating territorial sovereignty, for no government, with the possible exception of Singapore, controls the geographical area within its borders. The very presence of civil wars and insurrections shows the difficulties of operation today, but even in quieter times the reins were held loosely and often indirectly from central to provincial to local government. In three instances armed forces from neighboring countries enjoyed unofficial asylum in the hills of Thailand, while Bangkok officially denied their presence. Every country has its ethnic minorities which tend to lie outside control from the capital, like the upland tribal people of South Vietnam who in the 1960s organized their own political league known as FULRO and threatened to set up their own independent state. Whole districts of Burma are now organized by Karen, Chin and Kachin minorities who forward no revenues to Rangoon.

As a result of these multiple governments, people carry on their livelihoods much like the American businessman who was quoted in the *New York Times* of October 28, 1970 in a dispatch from Cambodia:

"I pay them off," an American businessman said of the Communists, "and they leave my trucks alone." He said he operated in Cambodia the same way he found he could do business in South Vietnam. "I set up a long-term contract with the Communists," he explained.

A Cambodian government official said, "Some of the taxis and buses here pay off the Communists for the right to travel unmolested. I have been told that the Communists have a list of all the taxis and buses that have paid their fees. Those that have go through free. The others risk being shot at—or worse."

It makes little difference what the ideology of the particular governing group may be, for all seek to stay in power by the same means.

Inevitably we must ask the implications of this view of Southeast Asia for American foreign policy. If our objective is to restore order to the region, we must first abandon our view of the unrest as a stuggle between competing ideologies. Wise heads of Southeast Asian governments in search of aid from Moscow, Peking and Washington fit their ideologies to appeal to those whose support they seek. Prince Souphanouvong is no more a communist than his brother Prince Souvannaphouma is a democrat. Both came from the same aristocratic background in Laos; both competed for power, and only because one went to Washington, the other had to seek help in the other camp. The same may be said for Ho Chi Minh, Prince Sihanouk, Thanom Kittkachorn, the prime minister of Thailand, and the rest who choose their words to fit their supporters.

We must next note what the peculiar nature of governments in this area equips them to accomplish or not to accomplish. As they are agencies dependent on profit, we cannot expect them to carry out services for the general welfare any more than we can expect an American pharmaceutical firm to give away medicines to cure the sick. In a limited way they can maintain the peace in various areas by destroying small troublemakers or by incorporating them into their monopolies. With groups of approximately equal power, they can only feud or live in an armed truce. In the meanwhile what we may consider the major jobs of keeping peace and providing limited public services belong to localities with their councils of elders and local men of influence.

Washington has sought to stabilize these Southeast Asian governments with military aid as if it were dealing with institutions that can act in the public interest. Instead the aid has been used to increase new personnel and the salaries of old employees. New ventures began where profits seemed most likely, so that Asian government officials became managers of night clubs and black markets. In effect Washington acted, in the eyes of heads of Asian governments, as if it were paying a factory without placing an order for services. Saigon, for instance, failed to act like a western-styled government and build up its army to cooperate with American troops in defense of the nation, so friction rapidly developed between allies. Americans made surly remarks about being made to look like suckers, while Vietnamese were upset by the peremptory expectation of unspecified services.

Vietnamization and similar deals arranged with Thailand, Cambodia and Laos are only slightly more specific contracts. Washington is hiring troops for these entrepreneurs in order to replace American troops, but it has not specified a return service. We may well expect Saigon to continue attacking its rival the National Liberation Front and its North Vietnamese supporter, but if American troops go home in fact, Saigon may decide to continue a token war or to invade North

Vietnam as well as Cambodia and Laos. If Thailand decides to regain its lost provinces in Cambodia, Laos and Burma, Washington can only stop the flow of arms, but by then the peace will have been further broken.

Cessation of aid to Southeast Asian governments is the first step to restoration of civil order, for only by this means can governments be halted which are in the business of increasing their profits by extending their control. In most areas we may expect the aftermath of introducing arms to continue the struggle between warring factions until a balance has been restored by an equality of capability in arms. Then the black market in arms which distributes guns to whomever can pay for them will go to work in the same direction.

The villages lie beyond our reach to help through governmental channels, as they always have. The various massive programs of village redevelopment in north-eastern Thailand, designed to promote loyalty to the Bangkok government, have only bewildered the inhabitants, accustomed over centuries to self-sufficiency, and left them with facilities which they cannot manage on their own. Those villages that survive will lie outside the paths of the contenders, for stockades defended by the small arms of a village are no match for tanks and rockets. Many other areas will be as devoid of habitation as the Plain of Jars in Laos, whence inhabitants have fled to remoter valleys as well as cities. There will, however, be a diminuendo of devastation rather than a crescendo.

The old spectre of China moving into the area has been vastly overrated. The last armed invasion of any magnitude occurred in 1406, when the Ming armies occupied North Vietnam for a few years before being forced to withdraw. The North Vietnamese have learned to live with the frictions caused by a big neighbor, as have Canada and Mexico. Certainly we may expect new governments to arise along the northern borders of Laos and Burma, governments that will enjoy the backing of Peking. Yet they too may help to restore tranquility, since the Chinese are more adept than ourselves in gauging how many guns a young gang leader can have before he becomes too arrogant, corrupt or lazy. As Nghiem Dang, author of *Vietnam: Politics and Public Administration* declared:

... there exists a natural order of things called *tao* which makes men live at peace with each other." Without uttering a word, a good head of government conveys the stillness of heaven and earth to the people of his faction, while they in turn convey this stillness to the villages at large. As the villagers grow confident of being able to cope with their own problems, the stillness of heaven and earth envelopes them. Then no need remains for an active government. Chwang Tze, the Taoist sage, reports asking Confucius a rhetorical question, "Why must you ... be vehement in putting forward your Benevolence and Righteousness, as if you were beating a drum and seeking a fugitive son (only making him run away)?"

Thus local competence working without governmental constraint is seen to keep the peace.

May 1971

FURTHER READING

Laos: War and Revolution (New York: Harper & Row, 1970) edited by Nina S. Adams and Alfred W. McCoy.

The Rope of God (Berkeley, Cal.: University of California Press, 1969) by James Siegel.

The Lost Revolution (New York: Harper & Row, 1966) by Robert Shaplen.

"The Election Ritual in a Thai Village" by Herbert P. Phillips in *Journal of Social Issues,* Vol. XIV, No. 4.

Pakistan:
The Busy Bee Route
to Development

TIMOTHY NULTY and LESLIE NULTY

Along with many other causes of the 1960s, that of development aid and advice from the rich one-third of mankind to the poor two-thirds has been overtaken by considerable doubt and disillusionment. Quite apart from the vagaries of intellectual fashion, there are many sound and sometimes unpleasant reasons for the increasing discontent with the aid policies of the recent past.

In any discussion about the future direction of the development effort, and especially the rich countries' share of it, Pakistan is a particularly useful case to examine. This is true not only because Pakistan is so large (sixth in population in the world), so poor (nearly at the bottom of the international income ladder with a $50 to $60 per capita income annually) and has received such a large share of the aid cake (since 1963, between $400 million and $500 million a year). But Pakistan is also interesting because its recent history highlights so clearly many of the crucial issues disturbing students of development. These issues can be grouped under two sets of questions: First, what sort of "economic development" has taken place (in Pakistan) over the last decade and a half, how much of it has there been, and where does the economy appear to be heading? Second, what has been, and what should be the role played by foreign aid, advice and advisers?

One undoubtedly important aspect of economic development is measured by the growth of per capita national product. It is important because it is an indication of the total material resources available to the economy and, as such, it is one measure of the *potential* welfare that could be enjoyed by the country. The ultimate aim of what is generally called development is, after all, an increase in total welfare. We do know, however, that "welfare" does not always come in forms that are readily measured by the national accounts. In rich industrial countries the relationship between increasing welfare and increasing Gross National Product (GNP) has become an extremely complicated issue, largely because increasing affluence is accompanied by the diminishing marginal utility of consuming the sorts of goods and services that are measured in the Gross National Product. Such questions as whether to cut down a forest to supply a paper factory (which increases GNP considerably) or to leave it standing as a contribution to a generally healthy and enjoyable environment (which makes little measurable addition to GNP) have become critically important. In extremely poor countries, however, this sort of problem is less pressing; the need for a straightforward increase in material consumption is too obvious and too great. Thus in poor countries GNP, and especially the growth in GNP over time, is useful as an initial indicator of the economy's potential welfare.

However, using GNP data to assess Pakistan's recent economic progress poses serious difficulties. Quite apart from the inherent problems of assessing a national product of which one-half never appears on the market and much of the other can only be guessed at, anyone with an intimate knowledge of Pakistan's statistics knows perfectly well that their compilers have sometimes deliberately used arbitrary evaluations in drawing them up. For example, the fact that public expenditure on defense is included in GNP is often cited as one way in which statistical measures may give an incorrect estimate of economic growth. However, we do not think this problem is particularly important in Pakistan's recent history, partly because it affects the national accounts of many other countries in the same way and partly because in Pakistan it has been a low and stable proportion of GNP, averaging around 3.5 percent a year over the last ten years.

More serious is the extent to which statistics for Pakistan as a whole obscure (and have sometimes been intentionally used to obscure) discrepancies in the development of the two provinces—a crucial and highly sensitive political issue. In so doing, the data have led to an overstatement of overall GNP for all of Pakistan.

Nevertheless, it is difficult to deny that some growth of the sort measured by GNP data has taken place in Pakistan. The official GNP figures show an average annual growth rate of 5.4 percent since 1959-60, which is doubtless an overestimate. But the rate of growth of key commodities has so far outpaced even the highest estimated rates of population growth (3.2 percent) that

Table 1 — AVERAGE INCOME FROM AGRICULTURE PER WORKING MEMBER OF THE AGRICULTURAL POPULATION, EAST AND WEST PAKISTAN, 1951-52 TO 1967-68 (RUPEES PER HEAD IN 1959-60 CONSTANT PRICES).

	1951-52	1955-56	1959-60	1961-62	1964-65	1965-66	1966-67	1967-68
East Pakistan	714	724	688	589	652	630	585*	620*
West Pakistan	903	990	971	858	891	911	892	881

*Estimates
Source: computed by T. E. Nulty from Labor Force Survey Data and added in Gross Provincial Product Data.

Table 2 — MONEY WAGES OF PRODUCTION WORKERS IN MANUFACTURING INDUSTRY DEFLATED BY COST OF LIVING INDEX, EAST AND WEST PAKISTAN 1954 TO 1966-67 (IN RUPEES).

	1954	1955	1957	1958	1959-60	1962-63	1963-64	1964-65	1965-66	1966-67
East Pakistan	1023	903	935	957	949	986	996	n.a.	n.a.	n.a.
West Pakistan	1104	1041	1040	1066	1071	977	995	1047	1082	989

Source: computed by T. E. Nulty from Censuses of Manufacturing Industry and C. S. O. Statistical Bulletin of Cost of Living Index. N.B. After 1963-64 there is no Census of Manufacturing Industry data for East Pakistan.

it is quite clear that the per capita availability of domestically produced goods such as food grains, cotton yarn, fertilizer, electricity and manufacturing output in general is now higher than it was even ten years ago.

The potential welfare contained in this growth of the per capita national product has two aspects. The first is current welfare, represented by the level of consumption enjoyed by the entire population. Second is the welfare (consumption level) that can be expected in the future as a result of decisions made now.

Before we can decide what, if any, increase in welfare (present and future) has actually been achieved in the course of economic growth, we must know how the national product has been used. Thus, taking current welfare first, we must ask why GNP has grown and who has benefited. Later we must also analyze what is the likely pattern of future development (welfare) as a consequence of the level and distribution of present GNP.

Considerable evidence seems to show that the distribution of income, never very equal in Pakistan, has become steadily more unequal over the last 20 years. Investigations by ourselves and others suggest that the vast majority (about 75 to 80 percent) of the people of Pakistan are now no better off than they were 20 years ago. A large number, something like 15 to 20 percent, may actually be poorer in real terms, and this is in spite of the fact that real output per capita overall is supposed to have increased by 25 percent.

This increased inequality can be seen in several dimensions. East Pakistan, with 55 percent of the population of the whole nation, has become poorer in per capita terms in relation to the less populous and richer western province. In 1951-52 the average per capita income in East Pakistan was 85 percent of that in West Pakistan, but by 1967-68 the ratio had fallen to 62 percent. Within each province the rural population (roughly 90 percent of the total in the East and 75 percent in the West) has lost ground compared to the urban sector, and in both provinces and in all sectors the wealthiest classes have greatly improved their position relative to everyone else.

Table 3 — EAST AND WEST PAKISTAN: GROSS PROVINCIAL PRODUCT PER CAPITA (IN CONSTANT 1959-60 RUPEES).

	East Pakistan	West Pakistan	East % West
1950-51	291	345	84.3
1955-56	268	377	74.9
1959-60	283	377	75.1
1963-64	302	416	72.6
1966-67	290	462	62.8

Source: Unpublished provincial accounts

The trend towards increasing income inequality is shown also in the National Household Surveys of Income and Expenditure, although they cover only a short period (three years) and despite the fact that like all such sample surveys based on voluntary replies to a questionnaire, they understate the income share accruing to the richest classes.

It is also clear that the share of profits in the national economy has been growing steadily, increasing from 2.3 percent of GNP in 1954 to 5.7 percent in 1966-67. Of course this is bound to be a natural concomitant of development in any "free" market economy. But since two-thirds of the profits in large-scale manufacturing, along with the profits of 80 percent of the financial institutions in Pakistan, are directly controlled by 20 or

Table 4 – PERSONAL INCOME DISTRIBUTION, EAST AND WEST PAKISTAN, 1963-64 AND 1966-67 (ALL FIGURES ARE PERCENTAGE SHARES OF TOTAL HOUSEHOLD INCOME).

| | Income Classes | | | | | |
| | top 1% | | top 5% | | bottom 10% | |
	1963-64	1966-67	1963-64	1966-67	1963-64	1966-67
East Pakistan:						
Rural and urban	3.5	3.6	11.1	11.0	5.7	5.1
Rural	2.0	3.0	9.5	10.0	5.7	5.1
Urban	8.0	9.0	21.0	20.0	5.0	4.5
West Pakistan:						
Rural and urban	5.5	7.1	15.0	16.6	5.2	4.9
Rural	5.2	6.8	10.0	11.7	5.8	5.9
Urban	6.7	8.3	20.0	22.5	5.1	4.8
All Pakistan	4.9	6.1	13.0	14.3	5.7	4.7

Source: Pakistan Central Statistical Office Quarterly Survey of Household Income and Expenditure, July 1963-June 1964 and July 1966-June 1967.

Notes: It is important to remember that sample surveys almost always understate the share of income going to upper income groups, since these groups tend not to report their correct total household income. This is further complicated in developing countries by the difficulty of distinguishing between "personal" and "business" income, since most firms are family enterprises. Although in computing this distribution some adjustment has been made to the raw data to allow for underreporting in upper income groups, the adjustments have been made in such a way as to make it likely that the increase in inequality shown in this table would be a conservative estimate.

This table is computed in terms of average income *per capita* for each income class; often data of this sort is presented only on the basis of household income. Since household income and household size are correlated differently in different countries, international comparisons can only be made with great care.

Table 5 – ALL PAKISTAN PROFITS AND HIGH-LEVEL SALARIES IN ALL
NON-AGRICULTURAL SECTORS RELATED TO GNP AND PRIVATE DOMESTIC SAVINGS
(ALL FIGURES ARE % OF GNP AT CURRENT MARKET PRICES).

	(A)* % share of profits & high-level salaries	(B)* all income & corp. tax	(C) (A)-(B)	(D) private domestic savings as % of GNP÷(C)
1950-51	25.4	0.8	24.6	24.0
1955-56	21.0	1.1	19.9	14.1
1959-60	25.5	1.2	13.7	13.2
1963-64	31.9	1.7	30.2	25.2
1966-67	33.3	1.3	32.0	18.7

*3-year averages centered at the stated year

Sources: Pakistan C. S. O. Statistical Bulletins, Censuses of Manufacturing Industry, Labor Force Surveys, Government Budgets and other government sources.

30 families (a fact generally acknowledged, even by the government) these data give some idea of the steady concentration of resources in the hands of the wealthiest groups.

The inequalities we have been illustrating have been defended and justified as a deliberate and necessary part of development policy by Pakistani economists and by foreign advisers, on the grounds that they will lead to faster growth and greater future welfare. Dr. Mahbub ul Haq, until recently the chief economist of the Pakistan Central Planning Commission, quoted J.M. Keynes on the development of Western capitalist economies in support of his view:

In fact, it was precisely the inequality of the distribution of wealth which made possible those vast accumulations of fixed wealth and of capital improvements which distinguished that age from all others. . . . If the rich had spent their new wealth on their own enjoyments the world would long ago have found such a regime intolerable. But like bees they saved and accumulated not less to the advantage of the whole community because they themselves held narrower ends in prospect.

Mahbub ul Haq himself writes:

What is important and intellectually honest is to admit frankly that the heart of the growth problem lies in maximising the creation of this surplus. Either the capitalist sector should be allowed to perform the role, or, if this is found inefficient because of the nature of the capitalist sector in a particular country or is distasteful politically, the state should undertake it. It would be wrong to dub the consequent emergence of surplus value as "exploitation": its justification is economic growth.

The underdeveloped countries of today cannot be too fussy about . . . ownership of "surplus value." Nor with the "revolution of rising expectations" are they allowed much political time to be fastidious about the means they choose to get rapid growth.

The view of Gustav Papanek, formerly with the Harvard Development Advisory Service mission to the Pakistan Central Planning Commission, was the same:

The problem of inequality exists but its importance must be put in perspective. First of all the inequalities in income contribute to the growth of the economy which makes possible a real improvement for the lower income groups.

Haq, the Pakistani government and most Western economists and advisers have successfully advocated that public policy should aim at fostering the same process in Pakistan as that described by Keynes for nineteenth-century Britain. On the one hand this was to be done by increasing the share of national income which went to the wealthy (on the grounds that they would be able to save a large proportion of it) and on the other hand by creating powerful incentives for the rich to invest their savings by guaranteeing very high returns to invested capital. (Returns have normally been around 50 percent per annum and have frequently exceeded 100 percent).

An extreme form of this review of development was expressed in conversation by an eminent American adviser to the Pakistani government who acknowledged that one reason why state enterprises appeared to be unprofitable was corruption at the top, with managers skimming off much of the profits. He then proceeded to defend this on the grounds that, being rich, the corrupt managers had a high propensity to save and invest the stolen funds, whereas if the profits were turned over to the government a larger proportion of them would be dissipated in wages and other current expenditure. High-level corruption was thus cited as a positive contribution to economic growth.

Has the approach taken by the Pakistani government, with the wholehearted encouragement of virtually all foreign agencies, been successful even on its own terms? Have the foundations for rapid self-sustained growth, leading to increased welfare for everyone in the future, actually been laid?

Certainly the government has carried out the two parts of its program. The distribution of income, as we have described, has been deliberately, heavily and increasingly biased in favor of the wealthy minority. The greater part of Pakistan's increased income has gone to the upper 20 percent of the population and most of it to a tiny and rich clique at the very top. What evidence is there that this group has not "spent their new wealth on their own enjoyments . . . but like bees . . . saved and accumulated"?

Everything has been done to encourage the rich to invest their wealth: tax holidays for industrial investments, tariff barriers against foreign competition, a highly favorable exchange rate for imported raw materials and equipment, subsidized prices for publicly owned power and low and stable wages, not to mention the complete subjection of any serious labor or political movement that might have challenged the distribution of income aimed at by the government. (Whether the recent elections in Pakistan represent a real challenge to this state of affairs remains to be seen.) All this should have encouraged high rates of domestic savings.

How have Pakistan's capitalists responded to this

policy? Certainly the consensus in the foreign establishment is that they have admirably fulfilled their intended role. This is clearly the central thesis of Gustav Papanek's *Pakistan's Development: Social Goals and Private Incentives.* Although the book was published before the urban riots of 1968-69, one would have expected the events of that winter and spring to have raised doubts and questions in the minds of foreign observers. In many cases this did occur temporarily. However, the assessment of Pakistan's progress published in the Pearson Commission report in the fall of 1969 essentially affirms and justifies Pakistan's chosen strategy.

In the very earliest days of Pakistan's development it is possible that the emerging class of capitalists did save and reinvest a fairly high proportion of its growing income. In those early days their economic and social position was not yet secure; there was rivalry and suspicion from the older land-owning and professional civil service elite that controlled the government, and there was little foreign aid and no domestic capital market to supply them with funds to supplement their own savings. These conditions rapidly changed, however: lines of communication, common interests and cooperation with other sections of the elite classes were quickly developed and, under the Ayub regime, firmly cemented. The distinctions and barriers within the ruling classes began rapidly to disappear.

Moreover, borrowing from overseas, and especially foreign aid, increased enormously. Government agencies were set up to channel aid and domestic funds into the private sector. As the boards of directors of these agencies were composed of high civil servants and the leading industrialists, it is not surprising that almost all of the funds went to the small group of wealthy and favored entrepreneurs who had managed to get to the top and who were represented on the boards. In addition, a large banking network was built up by the same group, each major industrial family having its own bank and/or insurance company. Virtually all loans and advances by the banking system went to these families at rates of interest far below what was, or would have been a free market rate had the supply of finance not been so thoroughly monopolized. Since 1960-61, between two-thirds and three-quarters of the value of all loans made by private banks have been made to (at the most generous estimate) .0008 of the population, or less than 1,000 households in a nation of over 100 million people. In order to attract funds to cover these advances, the banks have built up an extensive network of local branches but, because of their strong monopolistic position, have collectively managed to keep interest rates paid on bank deposits very low.

Thus it has become possible for the small class of dominant capitalists to finance investment from outside sources on very advantageous terms without resorting to savings out of their own income. No statistically significant trend can be established for the share of private domestic saving in GNP; yet with more and more of the nation's income going to the rich there ought to have been a clearly observable upward trend *if* the rich had been using their income to save and accumulate like the bees they are supposed to resemble. This conclusion is reinforced when we recognize that the official data on "private savings" includes private luxury-house building (which has been considerable) and investment financed by state-run firms out of their current income (such as the railroads, power companies, and the like). Rather, as the following table shows, it is Government Savings, that is, the surplus of government revenue over current expenditure, and the Net Inflow of Foreign Resources (aid plus foreign loans) that have shown the most dramatic rise.

If we look at the data on private domestic savings, we note that in 1966-67, these accounted for 5.9 percent of GNP. In the same year, gross profits in large-scale industry amounted to 3,290 million rupees, or 5.7 percent of GNP. If the captains of industry actually saved the high proportion of their profits usually attributed to them (75 percent is frequently given), this would imply that the entire remainder of the private sector managed to save only 1.5 percent of GNP. Given that these other sectors have accounted for over 70 percent of GNP, and given what we know about investment that actually took place in sectors other than large-scale manufacturing, this proposition concerning savings out of manufacturing profits is highly suspicious.

The conclusion that appears to come out of this is that on the whole the rich have not used their own rapidly increasing incomes to finance their investments but instead have been able to rely on investment funds at low rates of interest provided by foreigners (through aid and loans) by the rest of the Pakistani population (through the monopolistic financial system), and by the Pakistani government (which in fact again means the rest of the Pakistani population, since most government revenue is provided by a highly regressive indirect tax system). What then have the rich done with their share of the pie? Although they may not have saved like the prodigious bees that were supposed to be their model, the wealthy class of Pakistan has certainly performed remarkable feats of consumption, a fact immediately

Table 6 – CONTRIBUTIONS TO SAVINGS AND INVESTMENT IN PAKISTAN
(MILLION RUPEES AT CURRENT MARKET PRICES UNLESS OTHERWISE SPECIFIED).

Years**	Investment				Saving				net inflow of foreign resources*	as % of GNP
	public	private	total	private as % of total	govt. saving	as % of GNP	private saving	as % of GNP		
1950-51	427	543	870	62%	-260[1]	-.9%	1285	5.9%	+155[2]	0.7%
1955-56	757	710	1467	48%	266	.9%	671	2.8%	-529	2.1%
1959-60	1553	1269	2922	44%	688	2.1%	1072	3.2%	-1062	3.2%
1963-64	3753	2978	6731	45%	875	2.0%	3327	7.6%	-2495	5.6%
1966-67	5166	3875	8041	48%	1491	2.5%	3578	5.9%	-2973	4.9%

*including aid; the "net inflow of foreign resources" is the balance of payments deficit.

**in order to smooth out short-term fluctuations the figures given for each year are three-year averages centered at the stated year (1955-56=average of 1954-55, 1955-56 and 1956-57). Because of rounding errors and averaging the sums of the three "savings" items do not exactly equal "total invesement."

1. i.e., budget deficit.

2. indicates net outflow from Pakistan.

Source: computed from data in C. S. O. Statistical Bulletins, Government Budgets and other government sources.

obvious to any casual visitor to that country. We have already mentioned luxury housing, which probably accounts for at least 10 percent of measured private investment. In addition, imports of automobiles were five times as great in 1964-65 as they were before Mohammed Ayub Khan came to power in 1958, and they have not stopped growing since. The same is true of Hasselblad cameras, Akai tape decks and private airplanes. In addition, a considerable proportion of the surplus that has not been consumed has been exported to foreign havens.

Although not financed by entrepreneurs out of their own income, we have seen that private investment has nevertheless grown at a steady rate (albeit not as dramatically as one might have expected, given the resources that have been directed toward the entrepreneurial class). If, then, it could be established that the investment that has taken place up to now has actually laid a firm foundation for future growth, then an argument could be made that, regardless of how it has been achieved, who has paid the cost and who received the benefits, the net effect of the last 20 years is that a positive and major step on the road to development has been taken. Such a view would be very much in line with the thinking of those who made and supported Pakistan's development strategy.

However, such a conclusion is unfortunately open to doubt. Rather, the indications are that the step that has been taken leads directly to the kind of economic cul-de-sac that has become such a depressingly familiar pattern in Latin America and elsewhere: inefficient industries producing inappropriate goods behind high protective tariffs for monopoly prices.

Some observers supporting the official position have

argued that in Pakistan this is not the case. They contend that there has been sufficient diversification into investment goods and into industries where Pakistan has a comparative advantage so that Pakistan will not fall into the usual pattern of stagnation following an initial burst of industrialization based on highly protected consumer goods industries designed to provide locally what was formerly imported. This sanguine view has been challenged by other observers and the statistical methods and empirical evidence used by the "optimists" to support their case are open to serious question. But leaving aside for the moment the question of "product mix," there is no shortage of other reasons to be wary of these hopeful predictions.

Many industries in Pakistan are run very much below plant capacity, contrary to what one would expect in an economy where capital is supposed to be one of the scarcest resources. Such a state of affairs continues to exist, however, largely because capital has intentionally been made artifically cheap by foreign aid and an overvalued exchange rate. The licensing policy for imports and other forms of market protection for many industrial products result in high rates of return being earned even on inefficiently invested capital.

One common influence contributing to an inefficient industrial structure is the practice of overinvoicing capital goods imports as a way of avoiding restrictions on the export of capital. Once a Pakistani buyer has obtained an import license for a certain consignment of goods, he comes to an agreement with the overseas supplier to inflate the invoice, with a certain share of the excess being anonymously deposited in a numbered bank account overseas by the supplier on behalf of the buyer. After the 1958 military regime came to power,

Ayub Khan declared a temporary amnesty to anyone who repatriated capital that had been illegally exported. Ninety-six million dollars were turned in. This was only the tip of the iceberg, and yet the amount represents about 7 percent of total export earnings for the five years previous to the amnesty.

Overinvoicing also runs counter to development needs by distorting the factors influencing investment decisions. A power industrialist can be reasonably certain of being able to establish a sufficient strong monopolistic position and to obtain enough protection from foreign competition to be able to produce almost anything at a profit. To take just one example, the sole spark plug factory in Pakistan is, as a result of a total ban on imports of spark plugs, able to break even when operating at only one-ninth of installed capacity.

In these circumstances the decision as to what sort of factory to build becomes partly dependent on which supplier offers the best deal on the invoicing of equipment; it is much less related to the question of which sort of factory would be most profitable, either to the individual entrepeneur in terms of local market conditions or to the nation in general.

To go back now to the question of the industrial structure established by the chosen development strategy, the policy of keeping capital cheap, along with the high level of protection and the unequal distribution of income, has led to consumer goods industries receiving a much higher share of investment resources than is desirable in an economy that is supposed to be aiming at rapid self-sustained growth. In Pakistan, intermediate and capital goods industries have been more difficult to establish profitably, because sophisticated foreign imports are available to those able to obtain licenses permitting them to import such machines (at prices lower than those warranted by market demand). In contrast, the returns to investing in the assembly of foreign components, using sophisticated imported machinery, are relatively high, especially when the final goods are aimed at the middle- and upper-class market which, as we have seen, has been getting increasing shares of the growing national economy.

We would like to give just one example of how a policy measure, which might appear at the outset as a rational attempt to relax existing constraints on growth, is seen after its implementation to be yet another means of assuring the perpetuation of the status quo. In underdeveloped economies one of the most overriding considerations of economic policy is how best to allocate extremely scarce key resources. In Pakistan, foreign exchange is one of the economy's scarcest resources, and the government is faced with the need to ration foreign exchange while at the same time desiring to assure that it is spent on imports essential for development. The strategy chosen has been to keep the price of imports down (through overvaluation of the rupee) as an inducement to domestic investment. Demand and supply for foreign exchange are equated through a licensing system by which the government can ensure that foreign exchange is spent on desirable goods. Thus before claims to foreign exchange can be obtained it is necessary for the importer to obtain a license for the particular goods he requires. Because foreign exchange is in short supply, licenses are restricted in number and inevitably are subject to black market bidding in the form of bribery and personal influence on relevant authorities. In the Pakistani context the operation of bribery and personal influence inevitably assures the success of the richest and most influential. On the one hand they can always outbid competitors because of their greater financial resources and on the other hand their political and social standing makes them less vulnerable to prosecution for their illegal acts. This creates barriers to entry for small businessmen and hinders the diversification of industry by restricting the growth of complex backward and forward linkages. In addition, since the rationing system for the issue of licenses was calculated to allot to each license holder enough imported raw materials to permit a certain given proportion of his installed capacity to be utilized, there was an inducement for entrepreneurs to choose techniques that used relatively large amounts of imported capital and raw materials and to install much more capacity than necessary, in an attempt to monopolize output of the particular commodity. The cost of the resulting unutilized capacity was easily covered by the high rate of tariff protection and the monopoly position of the producer. Although the import licensing system has now been run down to some extent, giving rather more scope to competitive bargaining, the damage is already done. The monopolistic structure of industry is now entrenched, and the original beneficiaries of government policy are now strong enough to maintain their own barriers to further competition; dismantling the original policy cannot easily reverse this situation.

However, if we could establish that the errors of the past were at least vulnerable to forces for change, the problems would not appear so intractable. But by now, the lucky few who made it to the top during the initial period of expansion have acquired a powerful vested interest in the existing economic structure from which they have benefited so handsomely, but which is neither efficient nor suited to rapid future growth. In order to protect this vested interest they are forced to extend and solidify their control of the political system, joining forces with the two other ruling groups, the landowners and the senior civil service and army. The rich are thus likely to become more powerful and considerably richer while the poor proliferate and military government follows military government in an atmosphere of economic stagnation. This vicious circle, with its many Latin American precedents, is perpetuated by the fact that although discontent may be widespread and may occasionally break out in random acts of violence, all real socioeconomic interests that might have acted as countervailing forces have been undermined from the very beginning by the development policy that has been pursued. This policy, in its effort to provide every incentive and safeguard for every interest of the entrepreneurial class upon which it placed its faith as the driving force of development, has succeeded in creating a small class of wealthy, privileged monopolists who are now in a virtually unassailable position—freed by that very policy from the pressures of business competition, organized labor movement or political opposition and with no strong interest in efficiency, change or even, necessarily, in development itself.

Some observers have argued that the recent elections in Pakistan hold the promise of fundamental change. Although some aspects of the election results caused surprise (in particular the magnitude of Zulfikar Ali Bhutto's People's Party in the West) they have been much overplayed. We seriously doubt that they portend any profound change in the social or economic structure which we have outlined.

In the first place, the Pakistan military under Yahya Khan has declared that the constituent assembly which has been elected must produce a constitution a) which is acceptable to the army and b) within 120 days. If these two conditions are not met there will be a return to military rule. For the assembly to meet these conditions and to make a serious impression on the basic structure which we have been discussing would be extremely difficult even if the assembly were sympathetic to major reform, which is, itself, dubious. The only issue on which progress is at all likely to be made is the provincial problem. Here, Sheikh Mujibur Rahman, whose party won overwhelmingly in the East, is both too deeply committed to Eastern autonomy and too strongly placed in the assembly (where he has a narrow absolute majority) for the *assembly* not to make some move in this direction. How much autonomy the *military* is prepared to accept and whether they could keep control of the East if they eventually disbanded the assembly and restored the military regime, are open questions. Our own considered view is that 1) the military would accept some autonomy for the East but not as much as Mujib has been claiming; 2) if the military did decide eventually to jettison the assembly, it could probably keep control of the East. Therefore, we will probably see some softening of Mujib's position on the subject of autonomy and a compromise among the various conflicting interests in the assembly, which would, in any configuration, fall far short of "fundamental change." Alternatively, Pakistan could easily be back at square one if the military decided that the assembly had gone too far in giving autonomy to the East.

However, the provincial question is only one aspect

of the pattern we have been discussing. The others—social and economic questions within each province—are most unlikely to be affected by the election. Mujibur Rahman is not by any stretch of the imagination a left-wing revolutionary, or even reformer. He is not even, by any normal usage of the term, a socialist. The provincial issue aside, his internal social and economic policies are scarcely distinguishable from Ayub Khan's Muslim League or, indeed, from the status quo. His appeal, his strength and his success are based entirely on Bengali nationalism. His only serious rival in the East is Maulana Bhashani, who really does advocate sweeping internal changes. Bhashani, however, boycotted the elections and thus left Mujib to stand virtually uncontested, solely on the issue of autonomy. If we may draw historical parallels, Sheikh Mujib represents Pakistan's version of bourgeois nationalism, largely content with the internal state of affairs but wanting independence from the external colonial power.

In West Pakistan a good deal has been made of Zulfikar Ali Bhutto as a radical left-wing force. His success in winning a majority of West Pakistani seats, thus coming second only to Mujib in the country as a whole, has been interpreted as a real threat to the establishment. Again we find such an analysis very doubtful.

Bhutto is the scion of a large feudal landowning family in one of West Pakistan's most conservative and traditional regions, the Sind. He is not noted for displaying an enlightened attitude towards his own peasants or estates and serious land reform has never been part of his electoral program. He was a leading Minister in the Ayub regime for many years during the time when the policies we have discussed were being pursued. There is no evidence that he was unsympathetic to the development strategy being followed. He left the Ayub government over the issue of the peace settlement with India at the Tashkent conference in 1965; and continuing the struggle to regain Kashmir from India has been an important part of his political program and the focus of his popular support. In Pakistan, challenging India's right to Kashmir, whatever the historical merits of the case (and Pakistan does have a relatively strong case for its position) simply means increased demand for armaments at the expense of social improvement, with virtually no hope of success, either military or political. Under these circumstances, the use of the Kashmir issue in Pakistan is suspiciously similar to the familiar political tactic of diverting attention from pressing internal problems by concentrating on foreign villainy.

The press, both in Pakistan and in the West has often characterized Bhutto as the leader of the revolutionary left because of his overtures to China and his support for nationalization. This is a gross misinterpretation of the situation. External relations between Pakistan and China have virtually nothing to do with internal policies. They depend on the configuration of world political forces, the desire for an ally against India, the need not to become too dependent for arms on one country, the desire to play off one country against another, and so forth. This belongs to the realm of international power politics and the strategy for playing this game often has little to do with ideology or internal policy. It is entirely plausible for a leader to be warmly "pro-Peking" in external matters and yet on internal matters to advocate precisely the opposite of everything the Chinese Revolution is supposed to stand for. To deduce from his "pro-Peking," "anti-American" speeches that Bhutto is a left-wing radical requires either a thorough misunderstanding of the facts or a desire to play upon certain Western prejudices.

Secondly, although to many in the West "nationalization" is associated with socialism, it is important to remember that in an almost totally illiterate society, with few qualified, efficient or even honest administrators, nationalization often merely means a shift of control from one section of the elite, say, private industrialists, to another such as the civil service. Given the increasingly close relationship, through marriage among other things, among the various sections of the ruling elite, this is not very much of a shift at all. In these circumstances the slogan of "nationalization" is little more than a cipher, by itself it does not necessarily imply any fundamental change in the underlying socioeconomic structure.

In any case Bhutto himself has never been very clear about his policies in this direction. Although frequently calling for "nationalization" he has made ambiguous and conflicting statements about its actual scope, direction and method of implementation. A close look at Bhutto's statements over the last few years reveals little genuine ideological content or consistency behind the electioneering slogans. Were Bhutto to become president, the most one would expect would be a relatively minor reshuffle of power within the ruling class (some families would decline, others rise, very much like a palace coup in pre-revolutionary Russia or in many Latin American countries today), there would be a few token measures such as nationalizing a few of the banks but basically nothing would change for another ten years—until the pot once again boils over.

With this general background, how are we to evaluate the role of the Western foreign aid and advisory effort? Most advisers and aid administrators see themselves as technocrats, (in many cases sincerely dedicated to the cause of economic development), whose job it is to help determine and implement that allocation of the available resources that will most effectively promote economic and social development. As such they produce a great many worthy papers arguing cogently against stepping into this or that economic pitfall. In Pakistan various aid and advisory agencies have frequently campaigned for such unexceptionable and even progressive causes as lower guaranteed prices for food grains in the face of recent surpluses, more rigorous and objective appraisal of development projects, more rational management of foreign exchange, land reform, educational reform and so forth. It is therefore understandable that they react indignantly to suggestions that they have contributed to the difficulties, inefficiencies and anomalies that in many cases they have actively worked against.

The point is that good intentions and worthy papers, even when presented to cabinet ministers, do not measure the real impact that foreign agencies, advisers and aid have made. What we must try to assess is the extent to which foreign involvement has served to support and maintain an economic structure, which, once established, generates its own self-perpetuating indigenous lines of development.

One outstanding example of this sort of problem is revealed in the balance of payments-foreign exchange situation already referred to. Most aid agencies in Pakistan have actively encouraged revision of the official exchange rate in view of the inefficiences that have resulted from maintaining the present rate and the consequent need for import licensing. However, it is clear that it has been the ready availability of foreign exchange supplied by aid to finance Pakistan's large international deficits (arising from overvaluation of the official exchange rate) that has enabled the government thus far to avoid devaluation. There is thus a built-in inconsistency in the agencies, which on the one hand press their own governments for greater donations and on the other chastise their hosts for making use of the opportunities these sums create.

A second aspect of the aid effort that contributes to the difficulty of properly measuring its true impact is the ambiguity in the role of the aid-advisory agencies. Such agencies almost inevitably acquire a vested interest in self-perpetuation; no one really wants to work himself out of a job, while promotion and/or transfer to equivalent positions requires some proof of "success" in achieving stated aims. Thus, aid agencies have an interest in showing themselves to be "useful" to the host government. It is often the case that in the view of the host government the most useful function of an aid or advisory agency is its performance as a public relations unit in the international aid "stakes." Under these circumstances it is in the best interest of the aid agency to present only the rosy side of an economy's development efforts. This interest readily reinforces the second tendency of aid agencies to prove "success" by demonstrating that their advice is seen to be taken and also seen to work. Thus there is a built-in influence in the relations between advisers and host governments that assures that the advisers will concentrate their efforts on those policy problems least in conflict with vested interests in the host country and that are most likely to evoke a positive response from the host government. Advisory groups working independent of aid-giving governments often refer to this as "pragmatism." But inevitably this relationship leads to emphasis on policies quickly and easily reflected in GNP data and relative neglect of policies with perhaps longer gestation periods or with less easily measurable impact such as education.

In Pakistan, as in many other countries, it is difficult, then, to avoid the conclusion that the foreign establishment has underwritten a socioeconomic system and a development strategy that have produced a monopolistic economic structure that is neither efficient, dynamic nor equitable. Such an economy can achieve the objective of steady growth only by continued dependence on continual injections of foreign resources to substitute for domestic savings and to subsidize inefficient investment decisions. Whether the policies of foreign agencies have been adopted in the honest belief that the model cited earlier by Haq would be the best way to achieve a rapid improvement in the lot of the entire population or whether out of a deliberate wish to create "a dependent class of puppets in preparation for neo-colonialist exploitation" is largely irrelevant. Foreign aid and advice in Pakistan have in fact encouraged and enabled a small class of wealthy monopolists to extend their control over the economy, the government and the society and also provided an intellectually respectable argument to justify this pattern to the rest of the world by setting up the model of high savings-investment through redistribution of income and government-financed incentives.

Our conclusion must be that in assessing the development experience of Pakistan, even if we accept the questionable premises upon which the chosen growth strategy has been based, the actual performance of the economy has been inefficient. It has not justified the a priori assumptions about the propensity to save of the rich, or even of the capitalists. The subsidy element of foreign aid has made possible "growth" as measured by national income accounts; it has also permitted the beneficiaries in the socioeconomic elite to raise their consumption levels to standards that foreign advisers themselves are hard put to exceed. But there is little convincing evidence that it has either encouraged or succeeded in laying a foundation for truly self-sufficient or self-sustaining development. On the contrary, the evidence shows that the pattern that has been established is one of political instability and continued dependence on external sources. Seen in this context, we might take heed of the words of the Cambridge University student warning his mates against careers as foreign advisers: "foreign aid is using the money of the poor people in rich countries to pay the rich people in poor countries for their allegiance to the rich people in the rich countries."

February 1971

FURTHER READING:

Economic Development in South Asia (London: International Economic Association; New York: Macmillan, 1970) edited by E.A.G. Robinson and Michael Kidron.

Political Economy of Development (Berkeley: University of California Press, forthcoming) edited by N. Uphoff and W. Ilchman.

"Overinvoicing, Underutilization and Distorted Industrial Growth" by Gordon Winston in *Pakistan Development Review,* Winter 1970.

"Foreign Assistance: Objective and Consequences" by Keith B. Griffin and J. L. Enos in *Economic Development and Cultural Change*, April 1970.

Passage to Pakistan

HYMAN P. MINSKY

When I was approached to join the Pakistan Institute for Development Economics for the summer of 1968, I viewed it as an adventure. I am neither an expert in the economics of development nor particularly knowledgeable about the special problems of international trade, industrial, agricultural and labor organization that might be relevant to a country such as Pakistan. My special interest is in the economics of advanced capitalist countries, what is usually called Keynesian economics. My most recent work has dealt with financial institutions and economic policy in the United States. I suppose I was to act as a gadfly, to get the staff to think about problems they weren't attacking. I don't feel I was successful.

Karachi, the headquarters of the Ford Foundation supported institute, was not a major seat of British power in India prior to independence. As a result it lacks many amenities of colonial life. At the time of independence, 1948, Karachi was a city of 350,000. Last summer the population was estimated around 3.5 million.

As the city has grown, developments of detached homes have been built. Many, including those in the area of the Ford Foundation staff flat, are built on a scale that would be considered lavish in the affluent West. By contrast, little in the way of modern workers' housing was visible. Uncounted numbers live in huts built out of straw and mud, or often in leantos placed up against garden walls of the lavish homes.

It was claimed that there weren't many street sleepers (as there are, notoriously, in Calcutta). I didn't do much wandering around Karachi at night, but when I did, I usually saw a good many people sleeping in doorways and vacant lots. In the morning and afternoon, nap-takers were always visible in the green centerstrips of the boulevards.

Pakistan is a most unnatural state. The two parts, East and West, are separated by 1,200 miles of India. The peoples of East and West are different in language, culture, way of life and appearance. The West Pakistani, tall and often handsome by European standards, identify with Persian culture; the East Pakistani, the people of Bengal, are shorter and darker. They look toward the subcontinent: one might say they are Indian rather than Persian.

To both East and West Pakistan, partition was an economic calamity. In the east, Calcutta, the principal city of Bengal, was cut off from its hitherland in East Pakistan. The jute mills and jute plantations were separated. In the west, the Punjab, potentially one of the world's richest agricultural lands, was split. The headwaters of the rivers that water the Punjab are in India, and the land of the Punjab is in Pakistan. Prior to the twentieth century, the British had built a vast barrage system which takes water from the five rivers of the Punjab to irrigate the adjacent low-lying plain. The Punjab was the largest stretch of irrigated land in the world. It could be the base of a very prosperous agriculture. But India has moved to divert these waters to its own uses. Partition made a very poor part of the world poorer.

Most of East Pakistan, moreover, is the alluvial plain of the Ganges and the Brahmaputra, two mighty tropical rivers carrying huge amounts of water, regularly flooding beyond their banks. The control of such rivers, like the Amazon and Orinoco of South America, is beyond present competence. In addition, if the rivers of East Pakistan were to be controlled, the dams and reservoirs would have to be in India and China.

The government and especially the military are dominated by the people of West Pakistan, mainly the people of the Punjab. This is a legacy of British discrimination—the Punjab was settled by Moslem and Sikh veterans of the British legions. Many in East Pakistan view independence as having substituted a Punjabi for a British colonial overlord: a change that was not an improvement. Economically, the exploitation of the East by the West takes the form of using the foreign exchange earnings of the East—mainly derived from jute production—to finance the economic development of the West.

Dramatic stories have been told by people such as Gustav Papenek of the Harvard Advisory Service about the success of the development programs in Pakistan. Like most dramas, these stories are fictitious. The numbers used to detail the growth in Gross National Product are to a large extent the result of arbitrary valuations by government and foreign statisticians. For example, as a result of the procedure used to determine these numbers in a heavily populated poor country, an increase in the number of troops shows up as a growth in national income.

Furthermore, some of the substantial increases in manufacturing output that took place in the 1960s really decreased income. American and Pakistani economists at the institute showed that much of the industrial progress in Pakistan has resulted in negative value added, if international prices are used to measure the value of commodity inputs and outputs. Let me explain. West Pakistan grows cotton. Cotton has a good international market; the dollar price of a bale is known. The government encourages the development of manufacturing of cotton goods. It sets a tariff on cotton goods; in addition it gives a bonus in the form of a favorable exchange rate to the exporter of cotton goods. But as a result of the inefficiency of manufacturing, the raw cotton would have earned more dollars on the international market than the domestically produced cotton goods.

A complicated system of multiple exchange rates and export bonuses makes it profitable for the manufacturer to engage in such uneconomic production. For example, raw cotton worth $100 in the international market is turned into cotton cloth worth $90 in the international market. However, if the effective exchange rate is four rupees to the dollar for raw cotton and eight rupees per dollar for cotton goods, $100 of raw cotton would bring 400 rupees, $90 of cotton goods would yield 720 rupees. To an exporter, given these exchange rates, if it only cost 100 rupees to manufacture the cotton goods, private profits would result from the processing of cotton even though to the national economy a $10 loss takes place. In addition to using multiple exchange rates, the government raises the domestic price of cotton goods by import licensing and tariffs so that manufacturing for the local market is profitable. The protection of West Pakistan's manufactures in East Pakistan's markets is one way in which the East Pakistanis believe they are being exploited by the West Pakistanis.

Pakistan was a major recipient of American aid. Part of this aid was military. It was a "bulwark against Communism" in the Dulles scheme of the world. Part of the American and other Western aid was used to replace the waters of the Punjab that India had diverted to irrigation in India. This need to offset the impact of partition sent a billion or more dollars of aid down the drain in terms of effecting a substantial increase in productive capacity.

American aid is viewed by many Pakistanis as a racket. This is so because AID (Agency for International Development) fosters an industrial structure inconsistent with capabilities of the economy; it stands in the way of the development of indigenous industry and it is often blatantly corrupt.

One of the standard operating procedures in Pakistan is the systematic overinvoicing of aid consignments. Aid takes the form of an official authorization of a Pakistan enterprise to spend money on American machinery. What price is charged for, let us say, the textile machinery to be purchased? Evidence indicates that one price is quoted by American manufacturers when the funds are free to be spend on Japanese, German, Swiss, etc., textile machinery. Another, higher price is quoted when funds must be used to purchase American machinery. These prices are typically higher than what the same equipment sells for in the States. Thus there is a difference between what the American manufacturer would charge if he were selling under world market conditions and what he charges in the protected AID market. As for the Pakistani manufacturer, it is not his own money, and so he is not especially concerned about getting the minimum price. This is especially true once it is recognized that funds in New York, London or Switzerland are worth much more to a rich Pakistani than the official exchange rate indicates.

What happens to the difference between the price at which the firm would be willing to sell and the price at which it does sell? A remarkable fact in this corrupt situation seems to be that the AID officers who initial such projects (and pass over the overinvoicing) don't seem to get any of the funds that are floating around credited to their own bank accounts. Pakistani business and government people are not so scrupulous. American AID is an honest administration that winks at local corruption and at the corrupting of the local economy.

Pakistan is a country of many cities. In these cities there exist many small native handicraft and manufacturing enterprises in and around the bazaar. The Pakistani artisan in wood is often very good; the Pakistani metal worker has a reputation of being able to copy anything put before him. Even machine tools of various descriptions are made by local mechanics. The gun "copiers" in the tribal hills of West Pakistan are well known; it is also known that the beautiful replicas they make are not effective weapons. The metal used is so soft that if fired the weapon would explode. They are good for show but not for action. Sporting goods (tennis rackets, cricket bats) and stainless steel surgical instruments are well-known products of Pakistan handicrafts that have made their way into world markets.

Not so well known is the story of the tube wells and industry-producing diesel engines of primitive design that have developed without official encouragement in West Pakistan. The story is as follows:

As a result of many years of irrigation in the Punjab, the water table has risen. A high and rising water table brings salinity problems to the soil. It also makes it possible to draw water for irrigation purposes by pumping from the water table. During the past half-dozen years throughout the Punjab, a large number of private tube wells have been sunk. These tube wells are simple pipes plus filters with an attached pump and a source of power. The tube wells are much more efficient than the ancient open-well Persian-wheel irrigation system. They came about as a spontaneous market-generated reaction of the village landowners. Local industries (shops) have grown up manufacturing a simple, old-fashioned (obsolete by our standards) diesel engine, as well as the pumps and other equipment necessary for these wells. The estimate is that about 30,000 tube wells were being dug each year. The equipment, including the 30,000 diesel engines or electric motors, is being produced in tiny factories throughout the Punjab.

These tube wells are not as pretty or as efficient in the eyes of a Western advisor as deeper tube wells, dug by government agencies, capable of irrigating many more acres per well. However, the deep tube wells must use imported pumps and modern western diesel or electric engines. Thus there is a conflict between deep and shallow tube wells. There is also a conflict between indigenous enterprise and the large importing or "modern" firms, set up from the top with AID funds, granted monopoly positions by government and staffed with large-scale native promoters as middlemen and "profiteers." The deep tube well development is profitable for the dominant oligarchy in Pakistan, the shallow tube well is not.

It is obvious that in the indigenous tube well development—in the manufacturing of components, sales of equipment and the digging of the wells—there is the prospect of a dozen native "Fords" and "Firestones." There is no want of local enterprise in Pakistan; there is no lack of mechanical skills that could produce equipment that will expand output. There *is* a lack of an economic climate receptive to such a development, as well as a financial structure that could facilitate the growth of smaller enterprises. And for this the government and United States AID must be held responsible.

But what is wrong with the deep tube wells and the modern engines and pumps? The deep tube wells require replacement and maintenance parts which are beyond the capabilities of the Pakistan economy to produce. At Pakistan's stage of industrial development, equipment is not maintained very well. The life of modern equipment, of automobiles, etc., is shorter in Pakistan than in a developed country. Thus the imports required to maintain the AID gifts will be a recurring problem. What AID does is to stifle enterprise that should be promoted and impose upon the economy an import burden in future years. No program can be called a blessing, as AID is touted to be, when it in fact imposes an expensive industrial structure upon the recipient country.

The "route" to economic growth has been a matter of fashion: industrialization was Pakistan's preferred path, until, by the accident of the Ford and Rockefeller foundations' efforts in agriculture, agricultural output grew. During the past year or so, there arose the prospect for a great revolution in agriculture due to new seeds for wheat and rice, Mexi-pak and Irri-3 as they are called. These seeds are a real blessing, in the sense that they can, if used correctly, help increase production manyfold. They require nitrogen fertilizer of course, but the country is capable of producing nitrogen fertilizer from natural gas. They also require a controlled application of water. With the irrigation system and the development of tube wells this is possible. As a result, in West Pakistan it was possible to foresee the solution of the country's food problem.

But at the same time there was a sudden emphasis upon agricultural mechanization. The cry from the government leadership in the summer of 1968 was for the introduction of modern agricultural techniques into the country. Once again the techniques that were pushed by the foreign advisors and appealed to the ruling "elite" demanded sophisticated modern machinery whose production was beyond the capabilities of the economy. Moreover, with this kind of mechanization there inevitably arises a serious displacement of the peasants. But at the same time as they are being pushed off the land, there are no industrial jobs for them in the city. In addition there is a real question whether sophisticated mechanization would work in Pakistan.

There may be a rule that is worth postulating. An economy, such as Pakistan's, has a per capita income of, say, $80 a year. The least affluent economies of Western Europe have a per capita income of about $640 per year. This means that three doublings of per capita income, the first to $160, the second to $320 and the third to $640, stand between the threshold of affluence and poverty..

There are two ways, not mutually exclusive, to achieve a growth in income. One is to introduce parts of the $640 economy into an $80 economy. This enclave approach will yield a per capita income that depends upon the relative weight of the modern and the primitive parts of the economy. Presumably by making the affluent part a larger and larger fraction of the total, in time affluence will be achieved.

But long before this goal has been met, this path will have created large differences in the standard of life in the modern and the traditional sectors. Because of this, and because we live in an era when peasant unrest seems endemic, the enclave approach seems especially unstable politically. Another way is to attempt a broad front incremental strategy for improvement. It is my impression that a movement of $80 to $160 per capita income per year along a broad front is both more feasible economically and more humane socially and thus preferable to the enclave path. It is also my impression that the modernization drives fostered by American aid are enclave approaches. A little bit of the West can act as a barrier to further improvement and modernization, because of the dependence of what is modern upon foreign replacement parts and continuing aid.

In the Pakistan case, the movement toward agricultural industrialization was both premature and unwarranted. The simple improvement of the capabilities of the bullock by changing from an over-the-shoulder to a chest harness would perhaps double the horsepower per bullock and permit the substitution of a steel-tipped turning plow for the primitive forked-stick wooden plow. This could lead to substantial increase in output and would not require a specialized input that is beyond the production capabilities of the local economy.

The Japanese have been very ingenious in developing mechanized hand farrows, plowing devices and other things. Many of these could be readily copied and manufactured by a bazaar-type industry. Yet the AID "western" or "modernization" mentality scoffs at the feasibility of these incremental approaches. The Pakistanis who were most intrigued with the development of bazaar industries and the incremental additions to production capabilities in agriculture by deep plowing, by new harnesses and so forth, often called themselves Leninists.

There is no reason in economics or in culture for Bengal and West Pakistan to be the same country. Indeed, aside from the fact that it shares a common religion with the Bengals, much of West Pakistan is culturally underdeveloped compared to the East. We should not look upon it as a loss, as a defeat for American policy, if Pakistan divides. We should not look upon it as a great defeat for the West if either or both parts of Pakistan goes socialist or even "Maoist." In the power equation of the world, Pakistan is a cipher; any country foolish enough to conquer Pakistan, conquers a burden. We should turn our backs upon the policies of the past and substitute for the AID program a very simple and trivial foreign aid program—access to American markets.

One should be prepared, however, for serious divisive forces to erupt in India if East and West Pakistan should separate. For a Bengal state will be attractive to many who now live in India. There would be a great pressure to unite West Bengal, now part of India, and East Bengal. This would necessarily have to be a secular state; it would mean burying the communal and religious passions. It would mean giving Calcutta its hitherland again. It would mean the creation of a state with a Bengal cultural unity.

Separation of West Bengal from India could start a process of dissolution in the Indian nation. In terms of local capabilities for managing large-scale organizations, India is unmanageable. It is obvious that there is no reason for a unified Indian state to exist except for the possibility that if division occurs the subcontinent will be rent by innumerable and continuous local wars, as it was prior to the British conquest.

The best way to anticipate and mitigate the worst possibilities of this development would be for the United States and other nations to agree that India might be best governed as a most simple federation, with the national sovereign having very limited powers. A completely disarmed and pacified subcontinent should be our policy aim; it is criminal for a national state at the economic level of India and Pakistan to use resources on national defense.

There is a distinct prospect that the breaking up of India and Pakistan will see the emergence of left-wing governments. Even now I can hear cries for American intervention in, say, Bengal if division occurs. But intervention can only occur if we view the development of Indian states that call themselves communist as a threat. A "communist" Bengal state, or any other state on the subcontinent, would be a union of the poorest and a threat to no man. As I indicated earlier, many of the so-called communists in the subcontinent might in truth be more market oriented than our AID officials and the beneficiaries of American largesse, the 200 families of Pakistan.

February 1970

Gunboat Diplomacy
and
Colonialist Economics

FRANK CHURCH

Hope, Francis Bacon once commented, makes a good breakfast, but a lean supper. As Latin America enters the seventies, her governments tremble beneath the bruising tensions that separate hope from fulfillment.

"Here is a subcontinent," historian Arthur Schlesinger, Jr., observes, "where one-eighth more people than the population of the United States subsist on less than one-eighth of our Gross National Product, where 5 percent of the people receive a third of the income and 70 percent live in abject poverty, and where in country after country the political and social structures are organized to keep things that way. . . ."

As Germán Arciniegas of Colombia pointed out in a famous observation, there are two Latin Americas: the visible and the invisible.

Visible Latin America is the Latin America of

presidents, generals, embassies, newspapers, business houses, universities, cathedrals, *estancias* and *haciendas*. But in the shadows lies "mute, repressed" Latin America, a "vast reservoir of revolution . . . . Nobody knows what these . . . silent men and women think, feel, dream, or await in the depths of their being." In recent years, invisible Latin America has begun to stir. Workers and *campesinos* want three meals a day and a modicum of human recognition and dignity. Indians want to enter the national life of their countries. Intellectuals and students what social justice. Engineers and soldiers want modernization. Whatever the particular goal, the inherited condition of life is becoming every day more insupportable for more people.

Much of Latin America entered the twentieth century with a way of life inherited from sixteenth century Spain and Portugal. This is a way of life which in many respects is incompatible with a modern, industrialized society. Latin countries are plunging headlong into the twenty-first century with precious little time to make a transition that took generations in the United States and centuries in Western Europe.

Yet the imperative is clear. In countries whose per capita income currently ranges from $80 to $800 a year, only the fastest economic growth conceivable can possibly produce enough food, shelter, clothing and employment to match the spiraling requirements of the swelling population. This multitude, which now numbers 276 million souls, is growing at the rate of 3 percent a year, faster than any other population in the world; yet production, on a net per capita basis, is increasing at only half that rate. Inflation is endemic; foreign exchange is in short supply; export trade opportunities are restricted by barriers interposed by the already rich, developed nations; and overall economic growth is falling chronically short of satisfactory levels. The sixties did not bring the much heralded Decade of Development to Latin America. The euphoric expectation of bountiful blessings generated by the Alliance for Progress has receded, and widespread disillusionment has set in.

Still, economists know what is required within Latin America to move it into an era of adequate, self-sustaining economic growth. There is general consensus on the necessity for far-reaching agrarian and fiscal reform, for increasing internal savings and enlarging internal markets, for regional economic integration and for more favorable trading arrangements with the developed countries. Most of all, there is the need to bring into the national economic life the large numbers of Latin Americans, amounting in some countries to the greater part of the whole population, who are now, for all practical purposes, subsisting outside a money economy.

Obviously, if such profound internal changes can be accomplished at all, they can be brought about only by the Latin Americans themselves. The impetus must come from within. Success or failure may be marginally influenced, but it cannot be bestowed from without— either by the United States or any other foreign power.

It is also evident that the means adopted, the economic systems devised, the political forms chosen will likewise have to be homegrown. Neither the leisurely evolution of modern capitalism, as it matured in northern Europe and the United States, nor the differing brands of Marxism, as practiced in Russia or

China, offer models for Latin America that are really relevant to its cultural inheritance or its pressing needs. Even Cuban-style communism has found a meager market in other Latin lands. Che Guevara's romantic excursion to spread Castroism to the mountains of Bolivia ended in fiasco and death. For Latin America, steeped in the Christian tradition and prizing the individual highly, communism has little appeal. Indeed, those in the forefront of the struggle for radical reform, or even revolution, in Latin America today are more likely to be found wearing Roman collars than carrying Red banners.

In the seventies, therefore, we must anticipate turmoil and upheaval throughout Latin America, a decade of instability, insurrection and irreversible change. Each country will stake out and cultivate its own political and economic terrain. The spirit of nationalism will grow more fervent, and movement along the political spectrum will be generally toward the Left. Inflammable sensitivities will run high.

As for the United States, we would be well advised to practice an unaccustomed deference. The more gently we press our hemispheric neighbors, the greater our influence is likely to be. This will not be easy, for self-restraint is the hardest of all lessons for a great power to learn. The illusion of omnipotence is too seductive. Every great power would prefer to believe—and ascribe to itself—the tribute once paid by Prince Metternich to imperial France: "When Paris sneezes, Europe catches cold."

In casting our own weight about the Western Hemisphere, the United States has shown typically little self-restraint. Between 1898 and 1924, we directly intervened no less than 31 times in the internal affairs of our smaller neighbors. And we have yet to kick the habit, as our abortive Bay of Pigs invasion bears witness, not to speak of our military occupation of the Dominican Republic as recently as 1965.

In addition to its direct interventions, the United States has deeply penetrated the economy of Latin America with an immense outlay of private investment. By the end of 1968, American business interests had nearly $13 billion invested in Latin countries and the Caribbean, nearly three-fourths of which was concentrated in minerals, petroleum and manufacturing industries. The extent and growth of these holdings have inevitably—and not surprisingly—given rise to cries of "Yankee imperialism."

A recent study by the Council for Latin America, a United States business group, reports that in 1966, the total sales by all United States affiliates in Latin America amounted to 13.7 percent of the aggregate gross domestic product of all the countries of the region. If foreign-owned companies played the same proportionate role in the United States, their annual sales would exceed $130 billion.

Latin Americans have also begun to deny what was long taken as an article of faith—namely, that foreign investment promotes economic development. Foreign Minister Gabriel Valdés of Chile writes: "We can assert that Latin America is contributing to finance the development of the United States and other affluent nations. Private investments have meant, and mean today for Latin America, that the amounts that leave our continent are many times higher than those invested in it. Our potential capital is diminishing while the profits of invested capital grow and multiply at an enormous rate, not in our countries but abroad."

Minister Valdés is supported by the United Nations Economic Commission for Latin America which estimates the flow of private investment to Latin America in the period 1960-66 at $2.8 billion while the repatriation of profits and income amounted to $8.3 billion. This means that over this period foreign investment caused a net loss of $785 million a year in Latin America's balance of payments.

Working with later data on a somewhat different basis, the Council for Latin America makes the very opposite claim, putting the net positive contribution of United States investment to Latin America's balance of payments, during the 1965-68 period, at $8.5 billion a year.

Wherever the truth may lie, it is clear that the influence of United States business in Latin America is enormous and that its impact produces political as well as economic repercussions. Whether or not the Latin Americans are right in their analysis of the adverse effect of private foreign investment on their balance of payments, the important political point is that they think they are right about that analysis.

The United States' presence in Latin America is pervasive, culturally as well as economically. Latins listen to American music, go to see American movies, read American books and magazines, drive American cars, drink Coca-Cola and shop at Sears. The ubiquitous American tourist is to be seen on every hand, worrying aloud about the water and food and complaining about the difficulty of making himself understood in English.

The Latin reaction to all of this is somewhat ambivalent. Latins like the products of United States culture and United States business, but at the same time they feel a bit overwhelmed and fearful that Yankees may indeed be taking over their countries. One of the causes of internal resistance to proposals for a Latin American Common Market is the fear that United States companies would be able, through their sheer size, to benefit from it to the disadvantage of local entrepreneurs. Given this situation, it has to be expected that regardless of the policies we adopt, however enlightened and beneficial they may be, the United States will long remain a national target in Latin America for criticism, misgiving, suspicion and distrust.

The picture is not all that bleak, however. Millions of people in Latin America think well of the people of the United States. Certain of our leaders have been greatly admired—Franklin Roosevelt for his "Good Neighbor" policy and John F. Kennedy for the way he responded to the heartfelt aspirations of the dispossessed. No one can fault the sincerity of President Kennedy when he launched the Alliance for Progress in March of 1961, inviting the American republics to join in a "vast cooperative effort, unparalleled in magnitude and nobility of purpose, to satisfy the basic needs of the people for homes, work and land, health and schools." Since then, the United States has funneled in more than $10 billion in various forms of aid.

Given the magnitude of our effort during the sixties, we are left to wonder why it produced such disappointing results. We thought we were seeding the resurgence of democratic governments; instead, we have seen a relentless slide toward militarism. We thought we could remodel Latin societies, but the reforms we prescribed have largely eluded us. We thought our generosity would meet with gratitude, but we have seen antagonism toward us grow as our involvement in their problems has deepened. We pledged ourselves to objectives that could never be within the reach of any program of external aid; by promising more than we could deliver, we have made ourselves a plausible scapegoat for pent-up furies and frustrations for which we bear little or no responsibility.

Worse still, the kind of aid we have extended has tended to aggravate rather than mitigate these difficulties. Bilateral in character, administered on a government-to-government basis, our foreign aid program is embroiled in the internal politics of both the donor and recipient countries. The program's very nature makes this unavoidable, but the consequences are contributing to a steady deterioration in relations.

First, let us consider what has happened to the foreign aid progam, due to the pressure of domestic politics within the United States. What began (back in the days of the Marshall Plan for Western Europe) as principally a grant-in-aid undertaking has been transformed by the outcry against "foreign giveaways" into what is now primarily a loan program. Furthermore, with respect to accomplishing our foreign policy objectives, hindsight indicates we have gone about foreign aid backwards. The Marshall Plan should have been administered mainly on a loan instead of a grant basis, and the ready return of our investment would have done much to solve our balance-of-payments problems in the 1960s. In Latin America, the formula should have been reversed, with the emphasis on grants instead of loans.

Now the accumulation of these loans, and others as well, by Latin American governments is creating serious debt-service problems. The Rockefeller Report notes:

> Heavy borrowings by some Western Hemisphere countries to support development have reached the point where annual repayments of interest and

amortization absorb a large share of foreign exchange earnings. Within five years, a number of other nations in the Western Hemisphere could face the same situation. Many of the countries are, in effect, having to make new loans to get the foreign exchange to pay interest and amortization on old loans, and at higher interest rates. This debt service problem is a major concern. If countries get into a position where interest and amortization payments on foreign loans require a disproportionately large share of available foreign exchange, then the general pace of development will be slowed by the inability to maintain imports of the capital equipment needed to support economic growth.

Of course, in fairness it should be pointed out that our foreign aid program is not the sole contributor, by any means, to this mounting debt service problem. From 1962 through 1969, the Export-Import Bank lent $1.7 billion to Latin America at commercial interest rates and generally shorter maturities than Agency for International Development (AID) loans. Various European governments and banks (as well as United States banks) have made substantial loans, frequently at rates of 6 to 8 percent and for maturities of no more than three to five years. It is clear that both we and the Europeans are going to have to review our lending policies and explore ways for stretching out repayment schedules. Joint action between the lending nations, the international lending institutions and debtor nations is necessary. The Peterson Task Force on Latin America appointed by President Richard Nixon has suggested that we put this strategy "into effect now to prevent an emergency—not to deal with one after it has arisen."

Not only did the pressures of domestic politics change our aid to loans, but concern over our chronically adverse balance of payments led the Congress to insist upon tying these loans to the purchase of goods and services in the United States. Thus our aid—so-called—became an ill-disguised subsidy for American exports. While it undeniably constitutes an addition to Latin American economic resources, it can only be used for purchases in the United States or, under the new presidential directive, within the hemisphere, where prices are often above European or Japanese levels. Moreover, still another politically motivated restriction requires that half the goods financed by the United States must be transported in American bottoms. It has been estimated that this provision alone reduces the effectiveness of each $100 of United States loan assistance by as much as $20, furnishing another irritant to developing countries.

But the worst political consequence of all has been the inability of Congress to resist the temptation to use the aid program as both carrot and stick to reward or punish recipient governments, depending on how we may regard their behavior. Since 1961, the punitive sections of the Foreign Assistance Act have increased from four to 21. The most notorious of the provisions is the Hickenlooper Amendment. Although it has proved useless as a deterrent to the confiscation of American-owned businesses abroad, this amendment will remain on the books. Few congressmen would relish explaining to their consituents why they voted to repeal a provision that prohibits giving further aid to a foreign government that has expropriated an American-owned business and failed to pay adequate compensation.

Yet the Hickenlooper Amendment is only the most

prominent of a whole series of penalties written into our Foreign Assistance Act. There are, for instance, the amendments designed to enforce the American view of fishing rights. On occasion, United States fishing boats have been seized by Ecuador or Peru for fishing in what we regard as the high seas but they regard as territorial waters. If a fine is imposed, our law provides that military sales and assistance must be suspended; it also provides that the amount of the fine must be subtracted from the economic aid we are furnishing the guilty government. This provision was solemnly adopted as an appropriate punishment to put an end to any further meddling with American boats. Alas, it has not worked that way. We tie so many strings to our "aid" that some governments have preferred to take their money in fines. The trouble with attaching such penalties to the aid program is that, although they might give us some emotional satisfaction, they do not stop the behavior against which they are aimed. What is worse, they provoke a series of diplomatic showdowns that corrode, weaken and eventually destroy good relations.

Peru is a textbook case. The deterioration of our relations with that country began in 1964, when the State Department, on its own initiative, started to drag its heels on extending aid to Peru as a tactic to force the government to settle the International Petroleum Company (IPC) case. The tactic was not successful and resulted in some bitterness on the part of the Peruvian government, then headed by Fernando Belaúnde Terry, a man who otherwise qualified as a true Alliance for Progress president.

The bitterness increased when we refused to sell the Peruvians F-5 aircraft. But then, when they decided to buy Mirage aircraft from France, the State Department reversed itself and offered F-5s. At this point, Congress decreed that foreign aid should be withheld from countries buying sophisticated weapons abroad. The net result is that Peru now has Mirages, a plane aptly named for the contribution it makes to Peruvian security.

Finally, a military government more radical than the reformist Belaúnde came to power and promptly expropriated IPC. The new Peruvian government has not only failed to pay compensation, it has actually presented IPC with a bill of $694 million for its alleged past transgressions. And through all of this, there has been the continuing wrangle over fishing boats.

This sketchy review is necessarily oversimplified. The story of United States-Peruvian relations in the last five years contains ample mistakes on both sides. The point is that each successive stage in the deterioration has been provoked, in one way or another, by some aspect of the United States aid program. Indeed, more than one United States ambassador to Latin America has said privately that his difficulties stemmed directly from our aid program. One can scarcely imagine a more damning indictment.

Let us now consider the political impact of a bilateral, government-to-government aid program upon the recipient countries. They are naturally interested in putting the money into places of immediate advantage, where the political payoff is greatest. Heavy emphasis falls on program loans rather than project loans, for in the first lump sum transfers of dollar credits augment a given government's foreign exchange reserves. This is an indirect method of lending budgetary support. The reserves, of course, are available to be purchased with local currency by importers who desire to buy, let us say, machine tools in Cincinnati or perfume in Paris.

Since it was never a part of the rationale of a program loan that its proceeds should be used to finance the purchase of French perfume, AID early limited the purposes for which program loans could be used. But money is interchangeable, and restrictions applied solely to the loan do not insure that the borrowing government will not use its other resources for the purchase of frivolous luxury items, while relying on the United States to finance necessities. Little if any net economic gain would be made in these circumstances.

It became necessary, therefore, to make program loans contingent on agreement by the borrowing government to regulate its imports generally in such a way as to insure that its total foreign exchange reserves were used with optimum efficiency from our point of view.

Further, the question arose as to what to do with the local currency generated by the program loan. In the absence of agreements to the contrary, this currency can be used in ways that would undermine, neutralize or offset the intended purpose of the loan. Therefore, to insure that these local currency proceeds are used in ways that meet with our approval, AID made agreement on this point a condition of program lending. As in the case of foreign exchange reserves, it followed, of course, that this agreement had to encompass the government's fiscal and monetary policies across the board.

All of this inevitably involves the United States in the most intimate areas of another country's sovereignty, its tax policies and its monetary system. Program loans are disbursed in installments, usually quarterly, and each disbursement is preceded by the most detailed review by our AID mission of the recipient country's economic performance for the prior quarter. Why has the government's tax program not been enacted? The central bank is letting the local money supply increase too fast. Recent wage settlements have been inflationary. The currency is overvalued. These and a hundred other similar questions and complaints typically come up in a program review. It is done with the best of motives, but at an exorbitant political price.

Our aid technicians must sit as advisers and overseers at the highest levels in the finance ministries of various Latin American governments. Inescapably, this places us in a patronizing position which is demeaning to our hosts. The large colony of our AID administrators, meanwhile, living in conspicuous luxury in every Latin capital, cannot help but feed popular resentment against the United States. If a militant nationalism directed against the gringos is now on the rise, it is quite possible that our own policies, largely connected with AID, have given it the spur.

One is left to wonder how so cumbersome and self-defeating an AID program has lasted so long. Again, I suggest, the answer can be found by examining the politics involved on Capitol Hill. The analysis, I assure you, is a fascinating one.

Year after year, in order to get the needed votes in Congress, a package of contradictory arguments is assembled. The package contains something for everyone, with the result that the life of the AID program has been prolonged by a hybrid coalition of both liberal and conservative members. Let us explore how this artful strategy has worked with respect to the two main categories of AID, military and economic assistance. *Military Assistance.* Conservative members of Congress have been wooed to support this kind of aid on the ground that bolstering indigenous armies and police forces furnishes us with a shield against the spread of communism in the hemisphere. Furthermore, it is argued, strengthened military power within Latin America is to be welcomed as a force for internal stability favorably disposed toward local American interests. For the most part these arguments are accepted as articles of faith, even though events discredit them. In Cuba it was demonstrated that once a regime has lost minimum essential support, no army will save it. Castro didn't walk over Batista's army; he walked through it. In Peru and Bolivia, however, where the government's army seized the governments, the new military regimes galvanized public support behind them not by favoring but by grabbing local American interests. Each confiscated a major American-owned business—the Gulf Oil Corporation in Bolivia, the IPC in Peru.

Liberals in Congress have been lured to support military assistance by quite different though equally flimsy arguments. They have been told that our subsidy brings us into close association with the military hierarchy, thus enabling us to exert a tempering influence on the politically ambitious generals, while assuring ourselves of their friendship in case they do take over. Again argument and fact are mismated. The 1960s were marked by an unprecedented shift toward military dictatorship in Latin America. Hardly more than half a dozen popularly chosen democratic governments remain alive south of our borders. I wouldn't call that much of a tempering influence.

Furthermore, once a military junta has installed itself behind its American-furnished tanks, guns and planes, there is no assurance that the United States will be benignly regarded. In fact, the new Nasserist regimes of Peru and Bolivia, among all governments of South America, are the most aggressively hostile toward us.

Meanwhile, the military missions we have installed in no less than 17 Latin capitals add to the debilitating image of the United States as a militaristic nation. Even the Rockefeller Report which gave its blessing to military assistance looks with disfavor upon "our permanent military missions in residence," since they "too often have constituted too large and too visible a United States presence."

That puts it mildly. Ralph Dungan, our former ambassador to Chile, testified before the Senate Foreign Relations Subcommittee on Western Hemisphere Affairs: "I believe there is no shaking the prevailing Latin conception of the United States as a society dominated to a very large measure by 'the Pentagon.' This perception is widely shared across the political spectrum." Dungan went on to say that "perhaps no single action which the United States has taken in recent years, including the Bay of Pigs fiasco, was so significant in confirming the view of Latin America of the United States as a nation willing and ready to use its vast military power unilaterally . . . as the unfortunate invasion of the Dominican Republic." Other friendly hemisphere observers have noted that we will never know whether the Alliance was a success or failure because the program stopped the minute United States Marines landed in Santo Domingo in the spring of 1965.

Economic Assistance. Here again congressional support has been secured on the basis of false and conflicting doctrines. Conservative votes have been solicited upon the theory that economic assistance is good for business, that it can shore up the status quo in Latin America and thus proves an effective deterrent to revolution. It is argued that our input of dollars will promote stability and thwart the anticapitalists. Oddly enough this proposition is widely believed even though Cuba, the only country in the hemisphere that has gone Communist, enjoyed a relatively high per capita income along with a highly concentrated investment of American capital.

Liberals in Congress have accepted the need for economic assistance on the weakness of the opposite argument, namely that far from preserving the status quo, our financial aid is meant to promote necessary economic and social change. But as our experience with the Alliance for Progress bears out, external aid does not produce internal change. Because the money has been channeled through existing governments, it has mainly been spent for the benefit of the governing elites. It has perhaps helped in some instances to modernize Latin economies, but not to restructure them. In short, the liberals have also been taken in.

The conclusion I must reach is that our AID program as administered in Latin America has proved to be—on balance—a net loss. As our meddling has increased, resentment has grown. It lies at the root of an alarming deterioration in inter-American relations—a deterioration that has led to the assassination of one of our ambassadors, the kidnapping of another plus a labor attaché; the riotous receptions given Governor Nelson Rockefeller as President Nixon's personal emissary, indeed, the refusal of some countries even to receive him; and most recently, the unruly student demonstrations following the arrival of our assistant secretary of state for Latin American affairs on an orientation visit to Bolivia.

This does not mean that we should throw up our hands in despair or turn our backs on the hemisphere. What is necessary is that we first get off the backs of our neighbors. We must learn to hold ourselves at arms length; we must come to terms with the inevitable, letting changes take place without insisting upon managing or manipulating them. We must begin to show some self-restraint.

Here, then, are some guidelines I would favor for a new United States policy toward Latin America in the seventies:

First of all, we should begin to adopt trade regulations that give the developing countries in Latin America a better break. We should listen closely to the growing unified Latin complaint on this score and give the most serious consideration to their urgent appeals for preferential treatment. The political hurdles to such a course are high, the strongest presidential leadership will be necessary; but for too long we have avoided biting this particular bullet with the palliative of the AID program.

The great independence hero of Cuba, José Martí, once warned his countrymen that "a people economically enslaved but politically free will end by losing all freedom, but a people economically free can go on to win its political freedom." To achieve the latter, which Latin Americans believe they are now fighting for, Latin products must not be squeezed from the world's markets.

Next, we must start to observe, as well as praise, the principle of nonintervention. It was José San Martín, one of Latin America's legendary figures, who said that we are as we act. If we are to act in accordance with the principle of nonintervention, we must not only accept Latin governments as they come, but we must also refrain from the unilateral use of our military power in any situation short of one involving a direct threat to the security of the United States. Such was the case in our showdown with the Soviet Union when the Russians tried in the fall of 1962 to obtain a nuclear foothold in Cuba. But let there be no more military interventions 1965-style in the Dominican Republic or elsewhere.

We should bring home our military missions, end our grant-in-aid and training programs and sever the intimate connections we have sought to form with the Latin military establishments. After all, it was we who made possible in large part the recent war between El Salvador and Honduras by our gift of arms and training eagerly extended to both sides. This is a shabby business for us to mix in.

We should begin to liquidate our bilateral government-to-government economic AID program, as the recent Peterson Task Force Report recommends, effecting at the same time a corresponding shift of economic assistance to the World Bank, the Inter-American Development Bank and other multilateral institutions. Such a transfer could be cushioned by phasing out our bilateral program in the following manner:

1. The United States naturally should fulfill those loan commitments already in the pipeline, but the money should be untied so that the recipients may put it to the most efficient use. This can be done by presidential action, which has thus far been limited to the freeing of only those markets within the hemisphere.

2. The State Department should open negotiations for the reservicing of debt repayment in those instances where the burden unduly restricts necessary economic growth. This too lies within the authority of the president and accords with the recommendations of both the Rockefeller Report and the Peterson Report. We should seek also to involve European creditors in this process. I would oppose stretching out debts to the

United States so that debts to other creditors can be paid on time.

3. Financial assistance from the United States for public housing projects, schools, hospitals, family-planning programs and other social work should in the future be funneled through the newly established Inter-American Social Development Institute. If this institute is administered properly, it will emphasize the use of matching grants instead of loans, and it will deal not directly with Latin governments but with private groups, trade unions, rural cooperatives and charitable foundations.

The Social Development Institute should be staffed with personnel ready to try a wide variety of new experiments, willing to refrain from sending another horde of North American directors into Latin countries and who will share with Latin Americans the real experience of innovating and initiating new programs. In short, if the Social Development Institute is to succeed, it must be divorced entirely from the old ways of AID.

4. As for technical assistance, the remaining part of AID, it somehow remains as much overrated in the United States as it stands discredited in Latin America. The program's present weakness was perhaps best summed up in an excellent study by a Senate Government Operations Subcommittee on the American AID program in Chile. Speaking for the subcommittee, former Senator Ernest Gruening concluded that our technicians were "too far advanced technically . . . for what is required in underdeveloped countries. They are also too ignorant of local conditions and customs and serve periods too short to make a significant impact." These faults are endemic to our technical assistance program throughout Latin America.

The limiting factor on the amount of technical

assistance we have extended has never been money; it has always been people. The technician not only has to be professionally qualified; he should also know the language and the culture. He should be accomplished at human relations as well as in his technical specialty. There just are not many people like this to export abroad, and it is better not to send technicians at all than to send the wrong kind.

Yet there remains a need to transfer technology as well as capital to Latin America. This can best be done through expanding the exchange-of-persons program to enable more Latin Americans to study in the United States and through selective grants to a few outstanding Latin American universities. The role of shirt-sleeve diplomat, the concept which underlay the original Point Four program, can best be played by Peace Corps volunteers.

Another promising agency has been created by last year's Foreign Assistance Act, the Overseas Private Investment Corporation, more commonly known as OPIC. Its purpose is to encourage through a liberalized program of investment guarantees a larger flow of American private capital into developing countries. In Latin America, OPIC could play a useful role if it encourages the right kind of investment, directing it away from the sensitive resource areas and pointing it toward joint ventures in which Latin Americans will share largely in both ownership and management. Here again everything depends on the way OPIC is administered. The use of joint ventures deserves emphasis. I am well aware that joint ventures are distasteful to many—not all—American companies. But in the long run this may be the only way United States business interests can survive in Latin America.

Finally let me just add one warning. Private foreign investment is not economic cooperation and assistance; it is business, and most Latin leaders are willing to treat it in a businesslike manner. What Latin Americans are telling us is, "if the United States wants its investors to prosper in the region, then it is incumbent on the United States to make sure that investors are 'development-oriented.' "

Whether the public or private sectors are involved, it is essential for the United States to lower its profile in Latin America. Our national interests can best be served not by helping Latin America less but by loosening our embrace. We should keep a decent distance away from their internal affairs, from their military apparatus and their revolving-door governments. This would be best for us and best for them.

It would also disengage the United States from its unseemly courtship of governments that are living contradictions to our traditional values as a nation. When we pour our money into budgetary support for a notoriously authoritarian government, when we supply it with riot guns, tear gas and Mace, intelligent young Americans who still want to believe in our professed ideals ask some elementary questions. "If we are not against such dictatorships," they ask, "then what is it we are for that really matters?"

In the final analysis, each country must live by the ideals it prizes most highly. That is the basis upon which governments turn to their people for loyalty and support. A crisis of spirit arises when our foreign policy comes unhinged from the historic values we hold dear as a people and when the role of the United States in the world becomes inexplicable to its own young citizens. This is happening to us. Its occurrence is of more fundamental importance than any question of economic theory, investment policy or diplomatic tactics.

Devising the right role for the United States in its own hemisphere and the world at large, a role consistent with the admirable ideals of its origins, would go far toward restoring our country to the unique position it once held in the community of man.

June 1970

ARMS AND WAR

The Failure of
Fail-Safe

JOHN R. RASER

We have defiled our intellect by the creation of such scientific instruments of destruction that we are now in desperate danger of destroying ourselves. Our plight is critical and, with each effort we have made to relieve it by further scientific advances, we have succeeded only in aggravating our peril. As a result, we are now speeding inexorably toward a day when even the ingenuity of our scientists may be unable to save us from the consequences of a single rash act or a lone reckless hand upon the switch of an uninterceptible missile

General of the Army Omar N. Bradley, Nov. 5, 1957

Every man—whether poet or pimp, philosopher or philanderer—likes to believe that the work to which he applies his energies is of some value. He may define that value in any number of ways: It uplifts the spirit of man, it serves basic human cravings, it increases man's comprehension of the universe, or it fulfills his own indisputable drives. Most of us, lauding consistency more than living it, claim all of the above things at some

127

time, and rationalize our work in terms of any or all of the named values. And like Jeremy Bentham, or like Max Spielman in John Barth's novel *Giles Goat Boy*, we are likely to measure our work by "examining each moment whether what we are doing just now is likely to add to, or detract from, the sum of human misery." It's a tricky and uncertain rule, but it may be the best we can find.

Students of human behavior—behavioral scientists—have special problems in these areas, both because what we study (humankind) is the most precious and volatile element in our world, and because what we discover in our studies can have such a potent effect on the destiny of the very object of study—human beings. Because the study of human behavior is so crucial, and so poorly understood, I should like to outline what behavioral scientists do.

Briefly, we try to understand how human beings act in a variety of situations, by studying them in laboratories and clinics, by using interviews and questionnaires, and by examining historical cases. Some of us go a step further. We interpret what we have learned and apply it to problems of human existence—child-rearing, marital relations, racial tensions, poverty, the population explosion, educational policy or war.

It is this last—war—that is my major interest, and that I wish to discuss. I should like to report on several studies of what happens to human beings in a crisis, then apply the findings of those studies to some aspects of modern warfare. In doing so, I have two objectives. First, I hope to demonstrate that those of us who engage in these difficult and frequently maligned analyses of human behavior sometimes have good reason to believe that our work *is* of value and *does* contribute to the alleviation of human misery; and second, I hope to furnish insights into the crucial role that various assumptions about human behavior can have upon questions of the design of weapons and upon modern military strategy.

I should like to begin by summarizing the findings of several research projects. The first, by James A. Robinson, a professor of political science at Ohio State University, is "Simulating Crisis Decision-Making." The second, "Crises in Foreign Policy Making: A Simulation of International Politics," is by Charles F. Hermann of Princeton University. The third, written at Stanford by Ole R. Holsti, is "Perceptions of Time and Alternatives as Factors in Crisis Decision-Making." The last is a book by physiological psychologist Walter Cannon, *Bodily Changes in Pain, Hunger, Fear and Rage.*

Now, these are jawbreaking titles and it is obvious from just listing them—without reference to their contents, which are larded with graphs, tables and formulas—that this is not the type of literature that one keeps on one's coffee table for light reading. Nor are they the kind of document likely to be found in a congressman's briefcase, a president's chambers, or a general's quarters. But they *are* worth knowing about.

The first two, by Robinson and Hermann, are reports of a complicated laboratory experiment in which military officers acted out the roles of national and military decision-makers in "games" of international affairs. The experimenters introduced crises into the games at various stages—crises that suddenly confronted the officers with intense threats to the achievement of their goals. In studying the officers' behavior in such crises, the experimenters were able to determine that, as a crisis became more intense, the men lost some of their ability to evaluate information, were able to consider fewer alternative courses of action, and tended to be less flexible. In short, as threat increased and time for response decreased, their ability to cope with the situation was lessened.

Holsti's study applied a sophisticated technique of computer analysis to the six-weeks'-long period preceding the outbreak of World War I. His study of the pattern of message flow, and his analysis of the contents of the messages, shows plainly that as the crisis intensified, the key governmental and military decision-makers of Austria-Hungary, Germany, England, France and Russia responded in the same manner as the officers in Robinson and Hermann's laboratory experiment. The decision-makers saw fewer alternatives, they distorted their position in relationship to others, their messages became more stereotyped, and they began to lose the ability to think in long-range terms, focusing their attention instead on extricating themselves from the current problem—and damn the long-range consequences. Thus, as threat intensified, their ability to think and act rationally degenerated, as was true of the officers in the laboratory study.

These studies are among the most recent analyses of the effects of a crisis on decision-making in international relations. Other studies indicate that in most areas of human concern—child-rearing, domestic relations, driving, business and, indeed, all human activity—conditions of crisis generate similar effects. Panic, terror, hysteria, confusion, anger, and even merely "being rattled" or "upset" can produce these lapses in a person's mental ability. According to the late Harry Stack Sullivan, even the mildest forms of a crisis create
. . . a considerable degree of imperception, an

arrest of constructive, adaptive thinking, and a high degree of suggestibility to almost anything that seems simple and a way out of the difficult situation. There is complete insensitivity to elaborate, difficult suggestions; but the person is relatively impotent to ward off or to resist any simple idea that is given to him.

The point to keep in mind from these three studies, then, is that in times of crisis one is just not able to function as well mentally as one normally does.

The book by Walter Cannon records over 40 years of research on people from several races and cultures. When fear or anger are aroused, he reports, our bodies change. Adrenaline shoots into the bloodstream, the heart speeds up and pumps faster, the muscles expand, the nerves and muscles in the back tense, blood sugar increases, and strength becomes measurably greater. In brief, when faced with a sudden threat, people become—physically—superb fighting machines, far more capable of meeting that threat than otherwise—*if the threat is immediate and physical, and if physical violence is needed to counter it!* Like a cornered rat suddenly transformed into a screeching bundle of fury, launching itself with bared teeth at a man 100 times its size, a desperate and afraid human being turns into a frightening engine of destruction. But as Cannon also points out, while the body gorges itself with strength on account of fear, the mind loses its focus. We think less clearly, we lose our perspective, vision becomes centered on the source of our fear—we are "in a blind rage." Like the rat, we may launch ourselves against an overwhelming adversary, only to go down in "glorious" defeat.

These studies, then, give us a picture supported by

much other research. Threat, fear and rage (crises) *stimulate* us physically but *impair* our mental powers. That's the way we are built, that's how the evolutionary process has coded our glands to operate.

Now I want to change the subject momentarily and discuss the nature of war. Not its value or morality, but its nature. I simply want to describe what it has been like to fight in a war, and how this has changed as we have created sophisticated weaponry to serve our dreams and fears.

Centuries ago, men fought on foot or from horseback, from behind walls and towers. They fought with clubs, knives, spears, swords, bows and arrows, slings and axes. The Greek or the Hun charged into battle with his every cell inflamed with rage, his heart pounding, adrenaline surging through his veins, his muscles bulging. The defender, too, crouching in his fortress or dashing for his weapon, was suddenly hit with terror and then rage as he saw the slaughter begin, and he too was transformed into a madly fighting animal. For both, their physiological responses served them well, and their heroic actions became the stuff of epic literature.

More recent developments in weapons mean that the combatants often face one another with guns and flaming jellies. When the man in the trench is suddenly shaken by an exploding shell, or watches his friend's face shattered by a well-placed bullet, rage hits him, his body responds, and his thinking blanks. Screaming vengeance, he may charge suicidally into a hail of machine-gun fire, or dash to toss a grenade into a gunnery nest, or singlehandedly disarm a tank with stones or Molotov cocktails. Again, occasional success is the result. More often, on account of such new death-dealing devices, the outcome is horrible death.

Man's instinctual reactions are beginning to conflict with his own cleverness in creating weapons—and are serving him less well. But usually only a few die, so such incidents, while sad, are probably not important in the scheme of the universe.

But with some types of modern weapons, infinitely greater power has been placed in the hands of the individual. The strategic-bomber pilot over Germany or North Vietnam with his load of TNT or napalm, winging towards his industrial or military target, consults a hundred instruments, a dozen charts, groggily remembers a morning briefing, coordinates his crew. Now the defenders react—fighters dive from above, flak and missiles ascend from below. Fear clutches the pilot's heart, rage clouds his vision, he is less able to think clearly, he forgets his information, he tries desperately to get out of trouble—his pounding heart, pulsing veins and tense muscles are not an aid to him at all, but a hindrance, while his impaired mental power makes him a less, not more, effective fighting man. The result may be, and often is, a blanket of death dumped in fury or error on an innocent hamlet, an empty field, or on the pilot's own troops. No longer is the man whose reasoning power collapses in a crisis the only one to suffer; now others must pay the price. And if the man whose judgment falters under pressure is not a bomber pilot but a chief of state, as in 1914, the world might be plunged into war and several million people might die. But again, in a limited war using conventional weapons, the destruction is nowhere near total. Fifty years after the armistice, the war has lost its sharp outlines, new problems have plagued the world, and the race of man goes on.

When untold nuclear firepower is added to the

equation, however, the outcome is different. In our preoccupation with jungle and paddy war in Vietnam, we have let this fact recede to the backs of our minds, but there is another—and all-encompassing—spectre of violence dominating our world. That spectre consists of arsenals of nuclear destruction designed to deter the very holocaust they render possible. To the brains and judgments of individual men has been coupled the power of the suns. Belligerents confront one another across the world—hostile, angry, fearful, threatening and being threatened—and the world is always on the brink of crisis. No longer does the nuclear warrior face his enemy man to man; now he is tangled in a vast complex of gadgets. He is expected to be a servomechanism to electronic devices, a brain plugged into a vast machine, a single circuit in an endlessly complex chain of command. He has been physically emasculated and intellectually extended. His is the brain, the decision unit; but the mechanical extensions of his senses and of his muscles embrace the globe.

Having now reported some behavioral-science research findings on human reactions to threat and crisis, and having sketched the changing nature of man's role in warfare, I should like to combine the two discussions. In doing so, I hope to show how these human reactions may confound the intent and functioning of these weapons systems. I will use just one example—that of the nuclear submarine, usually considered the most reliable deterrence instrument in the American arsenal.

Forty-one of these Polaris submarines prowl the depths of the oceans, each carrying more explosive power than has been expended in the history of warfare. Each is linked to headquarters by radio waves. Each is commanded by officers chosen for their reliability. In

1964 some strategists began to question that reliability, suggesting that it might be safer if there were some kind of electronic lock-up of the missiles, a lock-up that could be released only by radio signal from headquarters—a Permissive Action Link, as it was designated. The Navy's response was an outraged assertion that these officers had been carefully selected, painstakingly trained and continually tested, and that they could be totally trusted to behave responsibly—*never* to fire unless ordered to and *always* to fire if ordered to. And the admirals won the dispute. The PAL proposal was dropped and, following a large-scale rescreening program of the Strategic Air Command and Navy personnel who occupied key positions, the assumption was "bought" that the men were a totally reliable component in the decision system.

As we have seen, this very assumption may have been wrong. It may be wrong even with the safeguard of the most sophisticated selection and testing programs. Bruno Bettelheim, a psychiatrist who spent two years in Dachau and Buchenwald, reports of his fellow-prisoners that:

> The way a person acted in a showdown could not be deduced from his inner, hidden motives, which, likely as not, were conflicting. Neither his heroic nor his cowardly dreams, his free associations or conscious fantasies permitted correct predictions as to whether, in the next moment, he would risk his life to protect the life of others, or out of panic betray many in a vain effort to gain some advantage for himself.

The same is true of military officers. Roy Grinker and John Spiegel, psychiatrists who conducted studies of aircraft combat crews during World War II, reported the results of interviews, as well as the results of their intensive testing program. They concluded:

> ... no matter how "normal" or "strong" an individual is, he may develop a neurosis if crucial stress impinging on him is sufficiently severe. ... Furthermore, it has been learned that the important psychological predispositions to "operational fatigue" are usually latent and therefore difficult to detect until they are uncovered by catastrophic events. It must be concluded that for the vast majority the *only test for endurance of combat is combat itself.*

They go on to state that military-security regulations prohibit their giving statistics as to how often soldiers collapse during combat!

Surely, you might say, the skills of selection boards and psychiatric procedures have been improved in the more than 20 years since the end of World War II. But not according to two of the men responsible for the Navy's selection and testing program. Captain R.L. Christy and Commander J.E. Rasmussen write that:

> ... the information which is available suggests that the present-day program is not nearly as effective as it was during World War II. ... Moreover, the general training and experience level of psychiatrists and clinical psychologists assigned to these activities has generally decreased since the end of the Korean War.

They point out that "the program is least effective with high-level personnel where the examiner is faced with complex personality structures and sophisticated defense mechanisms," and conclude that:

> In simplest terms, it is unrealistic to expect any examiner to identify a reasonably well integrated

individual's Achilles' heel and the unique combination of emotional and situational factors which could render him ineffective in the unforeseeable future.

What are the implications of this for nuclear weapons systems and their control personnel? The authors state that:

When the manpower supply is plentiful, it well may be wise to adopt rather high and rigid psychiatric assessment standards for use with men assigned to nuclear weapons. *Some adjustment of the standards becomes necessary during periods of critical manpower shortage.* [Emphasis added.]

And finally:

Isolated instances exist, such as those recently reported in the press releases on the human-reliability problem, where obviously unfit individuals have been assigned to nuclear-weapons systems and subsequently have been responsible for potentially disastrous situations. There is no question that the majority of these individuals would have been disqualified for such an assignment if they had undergone psychiatric assessment prior to assuming their duties in a nuclear-weapons system. However, it has been the authors' experience that *the most potentially dangerous situations in the Navy have involved personnel who demonstrated no evidence of psychiatric disturbance at the time of their initial assignment to militarily sensitive duties.* Moreover, as a rule these individuals function in a highly effective fashion for a considerable length of time prior to developing psychiatric illness. Quite frequently, in retrospect, one could not have anticipated that the illness would have developed in this particular group of patients even though the presence of certain underlying psycho-pathology might have been recognized.

This, then, is the reality behind the military public-relations programs that would persuade us that we can "sleep tight tonight" since our fates are in the hands of infallibly reliable guardians. But behind the public facade, the military has also apparently recognized the frailty of man, for most weapons systems have been hedged with some sort of "fail-safe" arrangement. With the Polaris, for example, only after receiving a sequence of radio signals may a submarine commander fire his missiles at predetermined targets. And this firing requires that several men perform coordinated tasks. The captain and his crew are *never* supposed to decide on their own to fire those missiles. They *can*—it's technically possible—but they aren't supposed to. The captain must *coordinate* the efforts of a group of subordinates in order to fire the missiles, the assumption being that if the captain loses his judgmental ability, the others will retain theirs and thus prevent a mistaken firing.

Yet this assumption, too, is probably wrong. These are men who are chosen for compatibility, who have worked and thought and reasoned together. Chances are very good that they will react in the same way to any crisis. Grinker and Spiegel discuss the intense emotional bonds that grow among combat crews and the almost mystical sense of trust and interdependence that develops, concluding that "From a psychological point of view, the combat leader is a father and the men are his children." And even if the subordinates have doubts, there is research showing that they will most probably obey their captain's order. Paul Torrance has conducted research on B-26 crews and finds that when there is disagreement among them on a correct solution to a problem, the captain nearly always carries the others with him, regardless of whether his decision is "objectively" right or wrong. German officers obeyed, almost to the last man, even though many of them could not have truly accepted Hitler's doctrines. Laboratory subjects will obey an experimenter's instructions to the point of inflicting (so they think) intense electrical shocks on another subject, simply because an experimenter instructs them to do so "for the purposes of the research." When asked later why they did it, the subjects responded, with surprise at the question, "Why, we were told to." The drive to obey an authority seen as legitimate is almost overwhelming—even among students! How much stronger it must be for a military man not to behave mutinously when the "authority" is his senior officer.

My main point, however, is that these men control immense destructive power—and that they alone can check its use. Nothing but the sanity and cool judgment of *all* such key men in the world keep us alive today. Not only submarine commanders, but heads of state, secretaries of defense, radar observers, generals, and bomber-wing and missile-complex commanders must be able to think rationally, interpret information correctly and act responsibly—keep cool heads in crisis after crisis and wait patiently and soberly during times of calm. And it must be *all* of them.

This is the way the world is—poised on the brink of destruction because of the assumption that we can rely on the wisdom and cool judgment of these men at all times. Let me sketch a playlet demonstrating the possible consequences of our having failed to make an examination of that assumption before we acted on it.

Both the Soviet Union and the United States (not to mention France, Great Britain, China, and a dozen other countries that may soon join them) have long-range bombers, intercontinental missiles, shorter-range bombers and missiles, and fleets of submarines, all carrying arsenals of nuclear weapons and all under the control of men who must use their good judgment about striking or holding. Let's place our cast of actors on the submarines, since we started with them and since they are often touted as the most error-proof weapons system. If it's *conceivable* that an accident could occur with Polaris, leading to a decision that leads to an unintended war, then the danger is even greater with B-52s, Minuteman missile complexes, and short-range strike forces operating in the European corridors.

The United States and the Soviet Union also have been trying very hard to find ways of detecting these submarines so they cannot remain invulnerable in war. Suppose that in about 1975—in the midst of a Pueblo-like crisis—the Soviet Union responds by asserting that its own intelligence efforts are not inferior to those of the United States, that it has just perfected a radical new means of detecting submerged Polaris submarines. The United States, unwilling to believe this and afraid of domestic and allied reaction, denies that the Soviet Union has succeeded. The Soviet leaders, facing internal critics of the country's unaggressive stance over Vietnam, decide to demonstrate their military potency to the United States, the power of their technology to the world, and their vigorous leadership to their own people. They daringly plan to knock out one Polaris in such a way that everyone will be pretty certain they they did it, but no one could prove it. (Recall the Thresher incident if you like.) They track a submarine with one of their location ships (a fishing trawler); they find its range in the depths of the Indian ocean; they launch a salvo of long-range torpedoes. What they don't know is that the United States has made some recent sonic advances of its own. The submarine detects the oncoming torpedoes and takes evasive action, so it is not the "clean kill" upon which the attacker had relied, but a "near miss." The torpedoes explode, the submarine's hull is damaged, water begins to flood in, panic hits the crew. All is chaos. The men know they will die in a few minutes. The officers, on the basis of instrument readings, are certain that the Polaris has been hit by the Russians, but due to the damage, the depth at which they are cruising, and the attacker's jamming, they cannot establish radio contact with headquarters. Visions of mushroom clouds turning their families into ashes, visions that have haunted their minds for months, suddenly well to the surface; rage explodes in their bodies. Their hearts begin to pound, adrenaline shoots into their blood streams, their muscles expand, their breathing rates accelerate, their blood-sugar levels increase, their muscular strength nearly doubles—but . . . to what end? There is no charging foe, no soul-curdling yell to let out; there are only rows of cold buttons to push. Their reasoning falters, they can't think of alternatives, their memories function inadequately, they can't accurately process information coming in over their meters, they lose track of the long-term perspective and begin to act reflexively. The captain gives the command—"We must accomplish our mission. We will not die in vain." The crew, stunned and equally irrational, obey.

The final act thus begins. The submarine is desperately trimmed for firing. The missiles lift from their capsules. Suddenly every decision level is in crisis, from radar observer to premier, and reflexes replace reflection. The Soviet Union, now under real attack, despairingly begins to retaliate; the United States orders its counterforce strike; the macabre dance of death unfolds, and in a few hours the world has been reduced to radioactive rubble. There are survivors, but the final curtain of dust does its work well; in a few generations the genetic key has been cruelly twisted, the race of man retreats into mutant extinction, the insects begin their rule of the next geological epoch.

This particular scenario is dramatic and unlikely. It is also tragic and possible. Five nations have thousands of separate weapons systems spread over the world, each with individual command units. As early as 1960, an authoritative report indicated that U.S. nuclear systems had already suffered 10 major accidents and about 50 minor ones—and this, of course, did not include the Thresher incident, the U-2 crashes, Vietnam activities, or nuclear bombs dropped off Spain and Greenland. Premier Khrushchev reportedly told Richard Nixon about an erratic Soviet missile that was destroyed by a signal from the ground as it headed toward Alaska, and on another occasion he implied that military commanders, on their own initiative, could order an attack on American U-2 bases. And these realities obtain in only a short period of time, and with the most "responsible" and sophisticated nuclear powers! In a few years there will be many more such nations. How much compounded will the chance of such crises be when Indonesia, Egypt, Israel or South Africa have their own primitive nuclear complexes to reinforce their local quarrels? And we may be sure that the experience and technology of every other country will not match the expertise that provides the safeguards incorporated into a Polaris.

Coupling the individual human being to the power of the suns has meant that man's physiological response to crisis may no longer be functional—it may be a tragic flaw. He has become an unwitting victim of his own clever machinations. Now that we have attached our brains to intricate machines of near limitless power, and swaddled our tumescent bodies in frustrating physical inaction, even in the thick of warfare, man may become a self-destroying misfit.

This conceivable scenario with even the relatively foolproof Polaris highlights two basic assumptions on whose accuracy the fate of the world may rest: (1) that carefully selected men will retain cool judgment in an intense crisis, and (2) that even if one man fails, others will act as a "fail-safe" device. Yet, as I have demonstrated, *behavioral-science research shows that both assumptions are almost certainly false.*

We have been trapped, trapped by our egos, into believing that under any conditions we human beings can control both ourselves and the limitless machines to which we attach ourselves. This belief grew out of seventeenth-century rationalism, and has been reinforced by our spectacular success in mastering our environment. And we *are* good—damned good—at creating a world in our image and in controlling that world. But there are little foxes, fragile seams, weak links, Achilles' heels, endemic to the human condition, and it well behooves us to lower our ego defenses enough to hear the voices of those who have examined human behavior at its extremes—the kind of extremes that can face decision-makers upon whose infallibility we rely. Sometimes these voices can tell us not only where we are making mistakes, but how we might rectify them.

In 1965 I suggested that the Polaris submarines retain their 1200-mile range missiles rather than getting 2500-mile range missiles; and that they be kept "off-station" or out of range of their targets by several hours' sailing time. This would mean that they *could* be used as retaliatory threats (which is what we claim they are for), but that they would *not* be in the provocative position of being able to strike first without warning, and that they could *not* cause a terrible escalation of the kind of incident I have just described. The responses from military and governmental personnel were that this was an intriguing idea, but since it would mean that Polaris could not be used in a "counterforce" role, the idea could not be taken seriously (as if the use of Polaris in counterforce targeting were somehow decreed by God, or as if counterforce strategies themselves had been proven desirable); or that it was "too late," since the long-range missiles were already in production; or that it would be pointless unless all of our weapons systems could receive the same treatment. In short, the reaction was one of unwillingness to cope with the really difficult problems, a response of fatalistic resignation to the uncontrollability of our destinies, and of detachment from the horror that we may be hastening.

National decision-makers must decide how to build weapons systems; they must decide whether to rely on "nuclear deterrence" or some other strategy. They must make endless assumptions (often unconsciously) about what people are like, how people will respond to crisis, to threat, to rage, to boredom, to too much or too little information, and so on and on. But it is not their business to read endless and often badly written research reports; it is beyond their scope to understand the complex scientific methods used in exposing the intricate dynamics of human behavior. Thus, these decision-makers often act in ignorance—they make false assumptions.

The scholar—the serious student of human behavior, like Robinson, Hermann, Holsti, Cannon and myself—believes that someone must be responsible for examining policy in the light of the things we are learning about how human beings function. We believe we are failing in our mission unless we tap the policy-maker on the shoulder and tell him we have reason to believe that he is making an unjustified assumption or an erroneous decision. And if he fails to respond to the tap, some of us believe we need to use whatever skills we can generate to collar and shake him, to shout in his ear—to *make* him listen. Otherwise, we are being irresponsible in our role as scholars.

What I have said in the last few pages is just one "minor" illustration of the kind of contribution we can make. Polaris *has* been improved over the years, on the basis of the designers' better understanding about the complexities of human behavior. It is far more difficult to devise a credible "accidental war" scenario now than it was in 1960—or 1965.

But many issues—from other, less stable weapons systems to negotiating strategies, from our policy towards China or in Vietnam, to race relations or population growth—are crying for analysis and understanding. We behavioral scientists are not simply teaching industry how to administer personality tests better, or teaching the Defense Department how to design a bomber cockpit better, or teaching the Peace Corps how to train a volunteer better.

In many instances we are digging up information that

is revolutionary—information that may suggest that a radical revision is necessary in the basic policy assumptions of our nation's decision-makers, and of decision-makers throughout the world.

January 1969

FURTHER READING

Arms Control for the Late Sixties (Princeton, N.J.: Princeton University Press, 1967) by James E. Dougherty and J. F. Lehman, Jr.

Sanity and Survival: Psychological Aspects of War and Peace (New York: Random House, 1968) by Jerome D. Frank.

Nuclear Weapons, Missiles, and Nuclear War: Problems for the Sixties (San Francisco: Howard Chandler, 1960) by Charles A. McClelland.

The Price of War

BRUCE M. RUSSETT

"Peace" stocks are up; "war" stocks are down; congress-men scrutinize Pentagon expenditures with newly jaun-diced eyes. Any (New Left) schoolboy can rattle off a list of the top ten defense contractors: General Electric, Boeing, General Dynamics, North American Avia-tion. . . . Scholars and journalists have worked hard lately, and now almost everyone knows who profits from defense spending. But who knows who pays for it?

Nothing comes free, and national defense is no exception. Yet curiously little attention has been paid to the question of which segments of American society and its economy are disproportionately sacrificed when defense spending rises. Despite some popular opinion to the contrary, our economy is a good deal less than infinitely expansible. Something has to give when military expenditures take larger bites out of the pie. But when this happens, what kinds of public and private expenditures are curtailed or fail to grow at previously established rates? What particular interests or pressure groups show up as relatively strong or relatively weak in maintaining their accustomed standards of living? And which of them are better able to seize the opportunities offered when international conflict cools off for awhile?

The questions, of course, are implicitly political, and they are important. But the answers have to be sought within economic data. What we want, in a sense, is a "cost-benefit" analysis of war or the preparations for war, an analysis that will tell us not only who most profits from war, but who most bears its burden. Apart from the direct costs in taxation and changes in wages and prices, which I will not go into here, there are the equally significant costs in social benefits, in opportunities foregone or opportunities postponed.

What I want to do here is to examine expenditures—by categories of the Gross National Product, by their function and by governmental unit—to see what kinds of alternative spending suffer under the impact of heavy military spending. The necessary data are available for the period 1939-1968, and they allow us to see the effects of two earlier wars (World War II and the Korean War) as well as the burdens of the current Vietnam venture.

First, however, an overview of the changing level of defense expenditures may be helpful. For 1939, in what was in many ways the last peacetime year this nation experienced, defense expenditures were under $1.3 billion. With the coming of war they rose rapidly to a still unsurpassed peak of $87.4 billion in 1944. The 1968 figure was by contrast around $78.4 billion, reflecting a buildup, for the Vietnam war, from levels of about $50 billion in the first half of this decade. The raw dollar figures, however, are deceptive because they reflect neither inflation nor the steady growth in the economy's productive capacity that makes a constant defense budget, even in price-adjusted dollars, a diminishing burden.

The graph shows the trend of military expenditures as a percentage of Gross National Product (GNP) over the past 30 years.

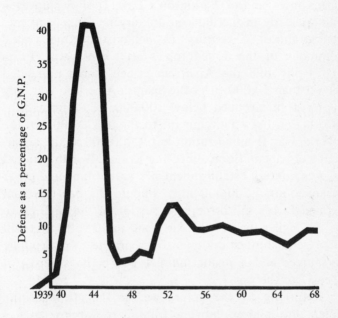

We immediately see the great burdens of World War II, followed by a drop to a floor considerably above that of the 1930s. The Cold War and particularly the Korean action produced another upsurge in the early 1950s to a level that, while substantial, was by no means the equal of that in the Second World War. This too trailed downward after the immediate emergency was past, though again it did not retreat to the previous floor. In fact, not since the beginning of the Cold War has the military accounted for noticeably less than 5 percent of this country's GNP; not since Korea has it had as little as 7 percent.

This repeated failure to shrink the military establishment back to its prewar level is a phenomenon of some interest to students of the dynamics of international arms races and/or Parkinson's Law. It shows up even more clearly in the data on military personnel and goes back almost a century to demonstrate the virtual doubling of the armed forces after every war. From 1871 to 1898 the American armed forces numbered fewer than 50,000; after the Spanish-American War they never again dropped below 100,000. The aftermath of World War I saw a leveling off to about 250,000, but the World War II mobilization left 1,400,000 as the apparent permanent floor. Since the Korean War the United States military establishment has never numbered fewer than about 2,500,000 men. Should the post-Vietnam armed forces and/or defense portion of the GNP prove to be higher than in the early and mid-1960s, that will represent another diversion from private or civil public resources and a major indirect but perhaps very real "cost" of the war.

Returning to the graph, we see the effect of the Vietnam buildup, moving from a recent low of 7.3 percent in 1965 to 9.2 percent in 1968. This last looks modest enough, and is, when compared to the effects of the nation's two previous major wars. At the same time, it also represents a real sacrifice by other portions of the economy. The 1968 GNP of the United States was well in excess of $800 billion; if we were to assume that the current war effort accounts for about 2 percent of that (roughly the difference between the 7.3 percent of 1965 and the 9.2 percent of 1968) the dollar amount is approximately $16 billion. That is in fact too low a figure, since some billions were already being devoted to the war in 1965, and direct estimates of the war's cost are typically about $25 to $30 billion per year. The amounts in question, representing scarce resources which might be put to alternative uses, are not trivial.

I assume that defense spending has to come at the expense of something else. In the formal sense of GNP proportions that is surely true, but it is usually true in a more interesting sense as well. Economics is said to be the study of the allocation of scarce resources; and, despite some periods of slack at the beginning of wartime periods (1940-41 and 1950), resources have generally been truly scarce during America's wars. Major civilian expenditures have not only lost ground proportionately (as would nevertheless happen from a military spending program financed entirely out of slack) but they have also failed to grow at their accustomed rates, they have lost ground in constant dollars as a result of inflation, or they have even declined absolutely in current dollars. During World War II, for example, such major categories as personal consumption of durable goods, all fixed investment, federal purchases of non-military goods and services, and state and local expenditures all declined sharply in absolute dollar amounts despite an inflation of nearly 8 percent a year.

Some observers argue that high levels of military spending are introduced to take up the slack and maintain demand in an otherwise depression-prone economy. If this were the case, opportunity costs would be minimal. But there is little evidence for that proposition in the American experience of recent decades. Certainly the Vietnam experience does not support it. I assume, *pace* "Iron Mountain," that with the demonstrable public and private needs of this society, and with modern tools of economic analysis and manipulation, full or near-full employment of resources would be maintained even in the face of major cuts in military spending. Because of the skill with which economic systems are now managed in modern economies, defense expenditures are much more likely to force tradeoffs than they were some 30 years ago. Hence the point of my original question, "Who pays for defense?"

I do not argue that defense expenditures are necessarily without broader social utility. Spending for military research and development produces important (if sometimes overrated) technological spillovers into the civilian sector. The education, skills and physical conditioning that young men obtain during service in the armed forces are likely to benefit them and their society when they return to civilian life. Nevertheless the achievement of such benefits through spillovers is rarely the most efficient way to obtain them. While scientific research may be serendipitous, the odds are far better that a new treatment for cancer will come from medical research than from work on missile systems. Therefore we must still consider as real costs the tradeoffs that appear when defense cuts deep into the GNP, though they are not quite so heavy as a literal interpretation of the dollar amounts would imply.

One must also recognize that some civilian expenditures—for health, for education and for research—have been stimulated by Cold-War and ultimately military requirements. Such were various programs of the 1950s, when a greater need was felt for a long-run girding of the loins than for more immediate military capabilities. Still, to concede this is far from undercutting the relevance of the kind of question we shall be asking. If civilian and military expenditures consistently compete for scarce resources, then the one will have a negative effect on the other; if both are driven by the same demands, they will be positively correlated. If they generally compete but are sometimes viewed as complementary, the negative correlation will be fairly low.

An evaluation of the relationship of defense and alternative kinds of spending in this country requires some explicit criteria. There is room for serious argument about what those criteria should be, but I will suggest the following:

1. It is bad to sacrifice future productivity and resources for current preparation for war or war itself; insofar as possible such activities should be financed out of current consumption. Such an assumption might be easily challenged if it were offered as a universal, but for the developed countries of North America and Western Europe in recent years it seems defensible. All of them are now, relative to their own past and to other nations' present, extremely affluent, with a high proportion of their resources flowing into consumption in the private sector. Furthermore, for most of the years 1938-1968, the demands of defense have not been terribly great. Since the end of World War II, none of these countries has had to devote more than about 10 percent of its GNP to military needs, save for the United States during the Korean War when the figure rose to just over 13 percent. It is surely arguable that such needs rarely require substantial mortgaging of a nation's future.

a) By this criterion one would hope to see periodic upswings in defense requirements financed largely out of personal consumption, with capital formation and such social investment in the public sector as health and education being insensitive to military demands.

b) Another aspect of this criterion, however, is that one would also anticipate that in periods of *declining* military needs the released resources would largely be *kept* for investment and education rather than returned to private consumption. In a strong form the criterion calls for a long-term increase in the proportion of GNP devoted to various forms of investment, an increase that would show up on a graph as a fluctuating line made up of a series of upward slopes followed by plateaus, insensitive to rising defense needs but responsive to the opportunities provided by relaxations in the armament pace.

2. Another point of view, partially in conflict with the last comment, would stress the need for a high degree of insulation from political shocks. A constant and enlarging commitment to the system's social resources is necessary for the most orderly and efficient growth of the system, avoiding the digestive problems produced by alternate feast and famine. Some spending, on capital expenditures for buildings for instance, may be only temporarily postponed in periods of fiscal stringency, and may bounce back to a higher level when the pressure of defense needs is eased. To that degree the damage would be reduced, but not eliminated. In the first place, school construction that is "merely" postponed four years will come in time to help some students, but for four years a great many students simply lose out. Secondly, boom and bust fluctuations, even if they do average out to the socially-desired dollar level, are likely to be inefficient and produce less real output than would a steadier effort.

Calculation of a nation's GNP is an exercise in accounting; economists define the GNP as the sum of expenditures for personal consumption, investment or capital formation, government purchases of goods and services and net foreign trade (exports minus imports). Each of these categories can be broken down. Private consumption is the sum of expenditures on durable goods (e.g., automobiles, furniture, appliances), nondurables (e.g., food, clothing, fuel) and services (airline tickets, haircuts, entertainment); investment includes fixed investment in nonresidential structures, producers' durable equipment (e.g., machinery), residential struc-

Table 1 — THE EFFECT OF DEFENSE SPENDING ON
CIVILIAN ACTIVITIES IN THE UNITED STATES, 1939-68

	% of Variation	Regression Coefficient	Index of Proportionate Reduction
PERSONAL CONSUMPTION			
TOTAL	84	−.420	−.041
Durable Goods	78	−.163	−.123
Nondurable Goods	04	−.071	−.014
Services	54	−.187	−.050
FIXED INVESTMENT			
TOTAL	72	−.292	−.144
Nonresidential Structures	62	−.068	−.140
Producers' Durable Equipment	71	−.110	−.123
Residential Structures	60	−.114	−.176
Exports	67	−.097	−.115
Imports	19	−.025	−.037
Federal Civil Purchases	38	−.048	−.159
State & Local Gov't Consumption	38	−.128	−.105

tures and the accumulation or drawing down of stocks (inventories); government purchases include both civil and military expenditures of the federal government and spending by state and local units of government. Except for inventories (which fluctuate widely in response to current conditions and are of little interest for this study) we shall look at all these, and later at a further breakdown of public expenditures by level and function.

In the table, the first column of figures—the percentage of variance explained—tells how closely defense spending and the alternate spending category vary together—how much of the changes in the latter can be "accounted for" by defense changes. The regression coefficient tells the amount in dollars by which the alternate spending category changes in response to a one-dollar increase in defense. The proportionate reduction index shows the damage suffered by each category relative to its "normal" base. It assumes for illustration a total GNP of $400 billion, an increase of $25 billion in defense spending from the previous period, and that the alternative expenditure category had previously been at that level represented by its mean percentage of GNP over the 1946-67 period. This last measure is important for policy purposes, since the impact of the same dollar reduction will be far greater to a $100 billion investment program than to a $500 billion total for consumer spending.

Looking at the table, one can see that, in general, the American experience has been that the consumer pays most. Guns do come at the expense of butter. Changes in defense expenditures account for 84 percent of the ups and downs in total personal *consumption*, and the regression coefficient is a relatively high -.420. That is, a one-dollar rise in defense expenditures will, all else being equal, result in a decline of $.42 in private consumption.

Of the subcategories, sales of consumer durables are most vulnerable, with 78 percent of their variations accounted for by defense. Spending on services is also fairly vulnerable to defense expenditures, with the latter accounting for 54 percent of the variance. But the negative effect of defense spending on nondurables is not nearly so high, with only 4 percent of the variance accounted for. This is not surprising, however, as needs for nondurables are almost by definition the least easily postponed. Moreover, during the World War II years new consumer durables such as automobiles and appliances were virtually unavailable, since the factories that normally produced them were then turning out war material. Similarly, due to manpower shortages almost all services were expensive and in short supply, and long-distance travel was particularly discouraged ("Is this trip necessary?"). Hence, to the degree that the consumers' spending power was not mopped up by taxes or saved, an unusually high proportion was likely to go into nondurables.

Investment (fixed capital formation) also is typically hard-hit by American war efforts and, because it means a smaller productive capacity in later years, diminished investment is a particularly costly loss. Defense accounted for 72 percent of the variations in investment, which is only a little less than that for defense on consumption, and the reduction of $.292 in investment for every $1.00 rise in defense is substantial. The coefficient is of course much lower than that for defense and consumption (with a coefficient of -.420) but that is very deceptive considering the "normal" base from which each starts. Over the 30 years for which we have the figures, consumption took a mean percentage of GNP that was typically about five times as great as investment. Thus in our hypothetical illustration a $25 billion increase in defense costs in a GNP of $400 billion would, *ceteris paribus*, result in a drop in consumption from approximately $256 billion to roughly $245 billion or only a little over 4 percent of total consumption. Investment, on the other hand, would typically fall from $51 billion to about $44 billion, or more than 14 percent. Proportionately, therefore, investment is much harder hit by an expansion of the armed services than is consumption. Since future production is dependent upon current investment, the economy's *future* resources and power base are thus much more severely damaged by the decision to build or employ current military power than is current indulgence. According to some rough estimates, the marginal productivity of capital in the United States is between 20 and 25 percent; that is, an additional dollar of investment in any single year will produce 20 to 25 cents of annual additional production in perpetuity. Hence if an extra billion dollars of defense in one year reduced investment by $292 million, thenceforth the level of output in the economy would be permanently diminished by a figure on the order of $65 million per year.

This position is modified slightly by the detailed breakdown of investment categories. Residential structures (housing) vary less closely with defense spending than do nonhousing structures or durable goods for producers, but its regression coefficient is the strongest and shows that it takes the greatest proportionate damage. Within the general category of investment, therefore, nonresidential structures and equipment usually hold up somewhat better proportionately than does housing. Doubtless this is the result of deliberate public policy, which raises home interest rates and limits the availability of mortgages while trying at the same time to maintain an adequate flow of capital to those firms needing to convert or expand into military production.

The nation's international *balance of payments* is often a major casualty of sharp increases in military expenditures; the present situation is not unusual. Some potential exports are diverted to satisfy internal demand, others are lost because domestic inflation raises costs to a point where the goods are priced out of the world market. Imports may rise directly to meet the armed forces' procurement needs—goods purchased abroad to fill local American military requirements show up as imports to the national economy—and other imports rise indirectly because of domestic demand. Some goods normally purchased from domestic suppliers are not available in sufficient quantities; others, because of inflation, become priced above imported goods. If the present situation is "typical," the Vietnam war's cost to the civilian economy would be responsible for a loss of more than $1.5 billion dollars in exports.

The import picture is more complicated. According to the sketch above, imports should rise with defense spending, but in the table the percentage of variance explained is very low and the regression coefficient is actually negative. This, however, is deceptive. The four years of World War II show unusually low importation due to a combination of enemy occupation of normal sources of goods for the United States, surface and submarine combat in the sea lanes and the diversion of our allies' normal export industries to serve their war needs. To assess the impact of defense expenditures on imports in a less than global war one must omit the

World War II data from the analysis. Doing so produces the expected rise in imports with higher defense spending, on the order of +.060. This suggests that the current effect of Vietnam may be to add, directly and indirectly, over $1 billion to the nation's annual import bill. Coupled with the loss of exports, the total damage to the balance of payments on current account (excluding capital transfers) is in the range $2.5-$3.0 billion. That still does not account for the entire balance of payments deficit that the United States is experiencing (recently as high as $3.4 billion annually) but it goes a long way to explain it.

In the aggregate there is no very strong impact of defense on *civil public expenditures*. The amount of variation accounted for by defense is a comparatively low 38 percent; the regression coefficients are only -.048 for federal civil purchases and -.013 for state and local governments. During the four peak years of World War II changes in federal civil expenditures were essentially unrelated to changes in defense spending. Samuel P. Huntington, however, notes, "Many programs in agriculture, natural resources, labor and welfare dated back to the 1930s or middle 1940s. By the mid-1950s they had become accepted responsibilities of the government," and hence politically resistant to the arms squeeze. If so, the overall inverse relationship we do find may be masking sharper changes in some of the less well-entrenched subcategories of central government budgeting. Further masking of the impact on actual programs may stem from the inability of government agencies to reduce costs for building maintenance and tenured employees, thus forcing them in dry times to cut other expenses disproportionately.

When relating state and local government expenditures to defense, some restraint is required. There really is no relationship except between the points above and below the 15-percent mark for defense. During World War II state and local government units did have their spending activities curtailed, but overall they have not been noticeably affected by defense purchases. Quite to the contrary, spending by state and local political units has risen steadily, in an almost unbroken line, since 1944. The rise, from 3.6 percent of the GNP to 11.2 percent in 1968, has continued essentially heedless of increases or diminution in the military's demands on the economy.

When we look at the breakdowns by function, however, it becomes clear that the effect of defense fluctuations is more serious, if less distinct than for GNP categories. I have chosen three major items—education, health and welfare—for further analysis, on the grounds that one might reasonably hypothesize for each that expenditure levels would be sensitive to military needs, and, for the first two, that a neglect of them would do serious long-term damage to the economy and social system of the nation.

All three are sensitive to defense spending, with *welfare* somewhat more so than the others, which is not surprising. In most of this analysis reductions in expenditure levels that are forced by expanded defense activities represent a cost to the economic and social system, but welfare is different. Insofar as the needs for welfare, rather than simply the resources allocated to it, are reduced, one cannot properly speak of a cost to the economy. Rather, if one's social preferences are for work rather than welfare, the shift represents a gain to the system. Heavy increases in military pay and procurement do mean a reduction in unemployment, and military cutbacks are often associated with at least temporary or local unemployment. The effect seems strongest on state and local governments' welfare spending. In fact, the inverse relationship between

Table 2 — THE EFFECT OF DEFENSE SPENDING ON PUBLIC
CIVIL ACTIVITIES IN THE U.S., FISCAL YEARS 1938-67

	% of Variation	Regression Coefficient	Index of Proportionate Reduction
EDUCATION—TOTAL	35	−.077	−.139
Institutions of Higher Ed.	12	−.013	−.146
Local Schools	34	−.053	−.125
Other Ed.	19	−.014	−.265
Federal Direct to Ed.	16	−.013	−.309
Federal Aid to State & Local Gov'ts for Ed.	08	−.004	−.140
State & Local Gov't for Ed.	24	−.060	−.124
HEALTH & HOSPITALS—TOTAL	32	−.017	−.113
Total Hospitals	30	−.014	−.123
Fed. for Hospitals	25	−.004	−.130
State & Local for Hospitals	29	−.011	−.120
OTHER HEALTH—TOTAL	22	−.003	−.087
Fed. for Health	06	−.001	−.101
State & Local for Health	45	−.002	−.078
WELFARE—TOTAL	54	.019	−.128
Fed. Direct for Welfare	13	.003	−.493
Fed. Aid to State & Local Gov'ts for Welfare	17	−.005	−.087
State & Local for Welfare	30	−.011	−.134

defense and welfare at most spending levels is understated at 54 percent on the chart. At all but the highest levels of defense spending achieved in World War II, the inverse relationship is very steep, with small increases in military needs having a very marked dampening effect on welfare costs. But manpower was quite fully employed during all the years of major effort in World War II, so ups and downs in defense needs during 1942-45 had little effect.

Both for education and for health and hospitals, the relationship to the immediate requirements of national defense is less powerful (less variance is explained), but nonetheless important. Furthermore, the regression coefficient is quite high for education, and since the mean share of GNP going to education is only 3.5 percent for the period under consideration, the proportionate impact of reductions is severe.

A widespread assumption holds that public expenditures on *education* have experienced a long-term secular growth in the United States. That assumption is correct only with modifications. The proportion of GNP devoted to public education has increased by three-quarters over the period, from 3.0 percent in 1938 to 5.3 percent in 1967. But it has by no means been a smooth and steady upward climb. World War II cut deeply into educational resources, dropping the educational percentage of GNP to 1.4 in 1944; only in 1950 did it recover to a level (3.6 percent) notably above that of the 1930s. Just at that point the Korean War intervened and education once more suffered, not again surpassing the 3.6 percent level before 1959. Since then, however, it has grown fairly steadily without being adversely affected by the relatively modest rises in defense spending. Actually, educational needs may have benefitted somewhat from the overall decline in the military proportion of the economy that took place between the late 1950s and mid-1960s. The sensitivity of educational expenditures to military needs is nevertheless much more marked on the latter's upswings than on its declines. Education usually suffers very immediately when the military needs to expand sharply; it recovers its share only slowly after defense spending has peaked. Surprisingly, federal educational expenditures are less related (less variance explained) than is spending by state and local units of government; also, local schools at the primary and secondary levels are more sensitive than are public institutions of higher education, whose share has grown in every year since 1953.

Public expenditures for *health* and hospitals are only a little less sensitive to the pressures of defense than are dollars for education. Here again the image of a long-term growth deceptively hides an equally significant pattern of swings. Health and hospitals accounted for a total of .77 percent of GNP in 1938; as with education this was sharply cut by World War II and was not substantially surpassed (at 1 percent) until 1950. Once more they lost out to the exigencies of defense in the early 1950s, and bounced back slowly, at the same rate as did education, to recover the 1950 level in 1958. Since then they have continued growing slowly, with a peak of 1.23 in 1967. Thus, the pattern of health and hospitals is almost identical to that for education—some long-term growth, but great cutbacks in periods of heavy military need and only slow recovery thereafter. In detail by political unit the picture is also much the same—despite reasonable a priori expectation, federal spending for this item is less closely tied to the defense budget than is that by state and local governments. It should also be noted that the impact of defense on health and hospitals is slightly less severe than on education.

It seems fair to conclude from these data that America's most expensive wars have severely hampered the nation in its attempt to build a healthier and better-educated citizenry. (One analyst estimates that what was done to strengthen education accounted for nearly half of the United States per capita income growth between 1929 and 1957.) A long-term effort has been made, and with notable results, but typically it has been badly cut back whenever military needs pressed unusually hard.

It is too soon to know how damaging the Vietnam war will be, but in view of past patterns one would anticipate significant costs. The inability to make "investments" would leave Americans poorer, more ignorant and less healthy than would otherwise be the case. We have already seen the effect of the war on fixed capital formation. Consumption absorbed a larger absolute decline in its share of GNP between 1965 and 1968 than did fiscal investment—from 63.3 to 62.1 percent in the first instance, from 14.3 to 13.8 percent in the second; but given the much smaller base of investment, the proportionate damage is about twice as great to investment as to consumption. In most of the major categories of public social "investment," nevertheless, the record is creditable. Despite a rise from 7.6 to 9.1 percent in the defense share between 1965 and 1967, the total public education and health and hospitals expenditure shares went up 4.5 to 5.3 percent and from 1.17 to 1.23 percent respectively. And even federal spending for education and health, though not hospitals, rose. There are of course other costs involved in the inability to initiate needed programs—massive aid to the cities is the obvious example. But on maintaining or expanding established patterns of expenditure the score is not bad at all.

The pattern of federal expenditures for *research and development* indicates some recent but partially hidden costs to education and medicine. From 1955 through 1966 R & D expenditures rose spectacularly and steadily from $3.3 billion to $14.9 billion. Obviously such a skyrocketing growth could not continue indefinitely; not even most of the beneficiary scientists expected it to do so, and in fact the rate of increase of expenditures fell sharply as early as 1966—the first year since 1961 when the defense share of GNP showed any notable increase.

Finally, we must note a very important sense in which many of these cost estimates are substantially underestimated. My entire analysis has necessarily been done with expenditure data in current prices, that is, not adjusted for inflation. Since we have been dividing each expenditure category by GNP in current dollars that would not matter providing that price increases were uniform throughout the economy. But if prices increased faster in, say, education or health, than did prices across the board, the real level of expenditure would be exaggerated. And as anyone who has recently paid a hospital bill or college tuition bill knows, some prices have increased faster than others. From 1950 through 1967 the cost of medical care, as registered in the consumer price index, rose by 86.2 percent. Thus even though the health and hospital share of public expenditure rose in current prices, the real share of national production bought by that spending fell slightly, from 1 percent to about .99 percent. Presumably the difference has been made up in the private sector, and benefits have been heavily dependent upon ability to pay. Comparable data on educational expenses are less easy to obtain, but we do know that the average tuition in private colleges and universities rose 39 percent, and in public institutions 32 percent, over the years 1957-1967. This too is faster than the cost of living increase over those years (not more than 20 percent) but not enough to wipe out a gain for government education expenditures in their share of real GNP.

In evaluating the desirability of an expanded defense effort, policy-makers must bear in mind the opportunity costs of defense, the kinds and amounts of expenditures that will be foregone. The relationships we have discovered in past American experience suggest what the costs of future military efforts may be, although these relationships are not of course immutable. Should it be concluded that certain new defense needs must be met, it is possible by careful choice and control to distribute the burdens somewhat differently. If costs cannot be avoided, perhaps they can be borne in such a way as to better protect the nation's future.

October 1969

FURTHER READING

Public Expenditures in Communist and Capitalistic Nations (Homewood, Ill.: Irwin, 1969) by Frederic L. Pryor.

The Common Defense (New York: Columbia, 1961) by Samuel P. Huntington.

What Price Vigilance? The Burdens of National Defense (New Haven: Yale, 1970) by Bruce M. Russett.

ABM and the Arms Race

MARVIN KALKSTEIN

In recent months there has been extensive discussion and debate of the ABM issue, and it has been generally recognized as one of the key issues presently facing the nation. On Friday, March 14, 1969, President Nixon announced the administration's decision with regard to ABM. Now it remains for Congress and the public to determine where we go from here.

With the President's announcement, we now have a set of specific recommendations and arguments upon which to focus our attention. The President suggested that the proposed deployment is designed to fulfill three objectives:

1. protection of our land-based retaliatory forces against direct attack by the Soviet Union

2. defense of the American people against the kind of nuclear attack that Communist China is likely to be able to mount within the decade

3. protection against the possibility of accidental attack from any source.

Let us first look at the question of protecting our land-based retaliatory forces. The President has said that "the imperative that our nuclear deterrent remains secure beyond any possible doubt requires that the United States must take steps now to insure that our strategic retaliatory forces will not become vulnerable to Soviet attack." It should be recognized that our present deterrent is comprised of a mix of nuclear-weapons systems including, according to Defense Department figures as of September 1968, 1,054 land-based intercontinental ballistic missiles, 656 sea-based Polaris missiles on 41 nuclear powered submarines and 646 strategic air bombers. This force then consists of 1,710 ballistic missiles and 646 bombers capable of delivering a total of 4,200 nuclear weapons against an enemy. The same source indicates that the Soviet Union possesses 900 land-based ICBMs, 45 sea-based ballistic missiles and 150 strategic air bombers capable of carrying a total of about 1,200 nuclear warheads. According to Defense Department estimates, even as few as 200 delivered warheads could cause 50 million Soviet fatalities and destroy 70 percent of their industry. Thus, it should be obvious that present Soviet forces do not pose a credible threat to our retaliatory forces. Concern for the security of our retaliatory forces seems to stem from the fact that the Soviet Union reached its present level of ICBMs through a large buildup in the past two or three years.

The main argument supporting this contention that the Soviet Union is striving to achieve a first-strike capability has been the recent disclosure by Secretary of Defense Melvin Laird of intelligence information regarding the Soviet deployment of the SS-9 missile, thought to be capable of carrying nuclear warheads with a yield as large as 20 or 25 megatons. Other estimates put the size of the warhead at five-ten megatons. Since the main advantage in using high-yield warheads would be to attack hardened missile sites rather than cities, Laird has cited their deployment as evidence of Soviet first-strike intentions. However, the number of SS-9 missiles currently deployed is given as 200 and on the basis of the recent rate of deployment, it is predicted that the number will reach 500 in 1975.

Neither of these numbers represents a credible first-strike potential; indeed, what is truly incredible is the suggestion that the United States deterrent force is suddenly to become wholly inadequate. Even equipping the SS-9 with Multiple Independently Targetable Re-entry Vehicles (MIRVs) will not change this picture, as I will discuss later. Furthermore, former Secretary of Defense Clark Clifford was aware of the same intelligence at the time of his January 15, 1969 defense-posture statement, and he was neither unduly alarmed nor as prone to predict so many Soviet SS-9 weapons in 1975. He felt that their deployment would probably soon level off. The recent buildup, he stated, was most likely motivated more from a desire to achieve parity with United States forces rather than an attempt to arrive at a first-strike capability against our forces.

Apart from the SS-9, there appears to be further concern in the Administration based upon the Soviets' having achieved a capability of producing a sizeable number of submarines equipped with ballistic missiles. At the indicated rate of seven submarines a year, however, it will be many years before this force equals ours. They may be regarded as a threat to our land-based bombers, since they might afford a shorter warning time. But the Perimeter Acquisition Radar (PAR) would be to some extent helpful as a means of affording early warning.

Another factor cited by the President in the buildup of Soviet strategic forces is their development of the Fractional Orbital Bombardment System (FOBS). FOBS are recognized as having very low accuracy and therefore cannot properly be regarded as a threat to our hardened land-based missiles. They may, however, represent a threat to our bomber forces. By using a low orbit, it is possible that they could reduce the warning time that we would have from our Ballistic Missile Early Warning System (BMEWS), thus making it more difficult to get our aircraft airborne before their bases are struck. However, according to former Secretary Clifford, it would not reduce the possibility of early detection by our planned Over-the-Horizon (OTH) and satellite-borne missile warning systems. He suggested as an additional available option that we can increase from 40 to 60 percent the proportion of bombers held on 15-minute ground alert, assuring us of the survival of at least 385 planes capable of delivering more than 10,000 megatons of nuclear explosives.

Probably the most secure component of our retaliatory force is the Polaris submarine fleet. Secretary Laird in his testimony before the Senate Armed Services Committee and the Disarmament Subcommittee of the Foreign Relations Committee on March 20 and 21, 1969, intimated that this security may be threatened by the mid-1970s. However, in no way did he substantiate this possibility. The nation's leading technical experts for years have regarded the Polaris submarine as invulnerable and none as yet have indicated any change in this opinion. The most recent public information is that detection and tracking of these submarines at any substantial distance is still beyond the realm of present technical capability and is likely to remain so for a considerable time into the future. It is obvious that unforeseen developments might negate any weapons system we might have, including an ABM system, but such consideration cannot be used as a major basis for defense policy. At least, not if we wish to pursue sound policies.

In discussing our capability against "Greater-Than-Expected Threats," former Secretary Clifford regarded only an extensive, effective Soviet ABM defense as a counter to our submarine-launched missiles. Apparently, he was not as impressed as Secretary Laird with potential Soviet threats to our Polaris submarines. Of our additional available options, one of which allows the expansion of Sentinel to include defense of our Minutemen sites, he stated that, "We need not take any of these steps until we have some evidence that the threat is actually beginning to emerge." Obviously, his assessment of our intelligence information was quite different from Laird's. Or, quite possibly, Secretary Laird's position is based on reasons he has been unwilling to discuss. Clifford concluded that "taking our strategic posture as a whole, we have an ample margin of safety and we can afford to proceed with due deliberation on very costly new programs."

In ruling out increasing the number of sea- and land-based missiles and bombers as a means to insure the survival of our retaliatory forces, the President argued that such a course provides only marginal improvement of our deterrent. This seems indeed to be true but can only be regarded as such by recognizing the fact that our present forces represent an overwhelmingly large deterrent. Quite rightly, with such an overwhelming deterrent, any increase at this time would be of marginal value.

A second option rejected by the President would be to further harden our ballistic missile forces by putting them in more strongly reinforced underground silos. Harold Brown, former Secretary of the Air Force, has described new harder silos as "a form of ABM defense." Increasing the hardness by about a factor of ten would reduce the probability of one SS-9 destroying a Minuteman missile from 90 percent to about 20 percent. To regain a 90 percent destruction capability, the Soviet Union would need ten times as many such weapons as would presently be the case. Converting their SS-9 missiles to MIRVs would not appreciably affect the situation. The probability of destroying a Minuteman with three five-megaton warheads is not much greater than with one 25-megaton warhead. The introduction of superhard silos would, in fact, have a number of advantages for protecting our ICBMs. Since concrete is a main ingredient, it would be much cheaper and far more reliable. I have a high expectation that concrete would do what it is expected to do, whereas the highly complex ABM system could fail for a variety of reasons. Finally, such an approach would not give rise to a new round in the arms race. At the very least, moving to superhard silos should allow us to delay an ABM deployment for a number of years.

Finally, the economics of attempting to provide an effective defense of our land-based missiles should not be overlooked. The present proposed figures for the Safeguard system will allow the deployment of only a relatively small number of Spartan and Sprint missiles at each site. (The Spartan has a 400-mile to 500-mile range and can afford defense coverage to a very large area; the Sprint is a 25-mile to 30-mile range missile that can provide protection against an incoming missile around the terminal point.) The first two ABM sites to be deployed by 1973 are planned to protect our Malmstrom, Montana, and Grand Forks, North Dakota, Minuteman bases, each of which have about 150 Minuteman missiles. On the basis of 700 Spartan missiles in the original Sentinel system, we can expect that 60 to 70 Spartans will be allotted per ABM base. The increased cost for the Safeguard system suggests that a similar number of Sprints may be assigned to each base. The reason for rejecting the Sentinel defense of our cities against Soviet attack is that area defense based only on Spartan will not work against a sophisticated and large attack of the sort that the Soviet Union can launch. Thus the protection of our missiles will depend upon the hardpoint defense provided by the Sprint missiles. Sixty to 70 Sprints can at best provide protection against an equal number of Soviet warheads. Obviously, in 1973 only a handful of our Minuteman missiles will be protected, and it won't be until several years later that the Safeguard system will encompass our full Minuteman force. Even then, its capability to cope with a Soviet first-strike will be questionable.

Should the Soviet Union contemplate a first-strike attack, they would have to use at least as many warheads as we have Minuteman missiles. With less than half as many Sprints as Minutemen, more than half our Minutemen would be virtually unprotected. To protect all our Minutemen (which admittedly may not be a necessary aim), we would need at least as many Sprints. If, as is likely, an attacker would assign more than one warhead per Minuteman to insure himself of a high probability of destroying our Minuteman, we would have to increase the number of Sprints accordingly. Furthermore, if we desire a high probability of destroying an incoming missile, we would have to assign several Sprints for each warhead in their force. Even if our objective is to assure ourselves of the survival of a few hundred Minuteman missiles after an enemy first-strike, the number of Sprints needed may range into the several thousands, requiring the expenditure of tens of billions of dollars for Sprints alone.

Greatly increased expenditures would undoubtedly be required for the radar and computer components of the system if the system is even to suggest the survival of an adequate retaliatory force. At present, our Missile Site Radars are not sufficiently hardened to withstand the effects of a high-yield airburst. Several incoming warheads targeted on the MSR would stand a good chance of destroying or incapacitating it. Once this has occurred, all the remaining Sprints dependent upon that MSR will have become useless. To avoid this, in addition to greater hardening for the MSRs, considerable expenditures will be required for more MSRs. We would thus be talking about spending tens of billions of dollars just to make it possible that Safeguard has some chance of providing the protection that the President desires.

The President's second proposed objective for his ABM was to protect the American people from a nuclear attack by Communist China. The first line of defense against such an attack is prevention, and that is precisely what our deterrent forces are meant to accomplish. If our deterrent forces can be relied upon to prevent a nuclear attack by a large strategic force of the Soviet Union, they should be more than adequate against the virtually nonexistent strategic nuclear forces of Communist China. In spite of the militant talk by the Chinese and about them, former Secretary of Defense Robert S. McNamara in his September 18, 1967, speech announcing the previous Sentinel decision acknowledged that "China has been cautious to avoid any action that might end in a nuclear clash with the United States—however wild her words—and understandably so.

We have the power not only to destroy completely her entire nuclear offensive forces but to devastate her society as well." Furthermore, should China be so "insane and suicidal" as to contemplate an attack upon the United States, there would be means available to her for which an ABM defense would be inadequate. There are many ways of overcoming such a defense. An ABM system would be ineffective against attack by means other than ICBMs—for example, low-flying aircraft, cruise missiles, missiles launched from offshore submarines, and missiles smuggled into ports from other locations and then detonated. In addition, there are a number of easy and inexpensive means by which an ICBM can penetrate an area defense such as the proposed system would provide for our cities. These penetration aids include fragmentation of the missile's booster rocket, chaff, decoys, electronic jamming and radar blackout produced by the predetonation at high altitude of an incoming missile. All of these are relatively simple and at least some would be likely to be incorporated by an enemy whose initial ICBM deployment would be faced with an ABM. It would be naive to assume that a nation capable of the effort to produce an ICBM system would not add some such minor extra effort to its initial ICBM system if it is aware that it will be faced with an ABM system such as the proposed one.

The third stated objective was protection against the

possibility of accidental attacks. An accidental attack is, by definition, an unintentional attack, and one might reasonably presume that a nation whose missile was accidentally fired would prefer to prevent its warhead from exploding upon an enemy target. A number of mechanical means are employed by the United States to reduce the likelihood of accidents, and it is reasonable to expect that safety measures are employed by other nations as well. Since the prevention of accidental attack is in the mutual interest of all nations involved, an exchange of the independent safety features employed by each nation should be possible, perhaps leading to a weapons-safety conference of the nuclear-weapon nations. An obvious additional desired feature would be to have provisions for the destruction or disarming of an accidentally fired missile by the nation to whom it belongs before such missile could reach its target. Senator Stuart Symington at the hearings before the disarmament subcommittee of the Senate Foreign Relations Committee suggested that we already can do this with our missiles. At the time of these hearings, both Secretary Laird and his deputy, David Packard, concurred in the view, but the Pentagon has since asked that their public testimony be changed to deny the possibility of disarming the missiles once fired. The difficulty with a destruct capability may be that one cannot prevent the nation under attack from triggering such a mechanism and so, for the purposes of having an assured deterrent, this destruct capability could present problems. Although I am generally not inclined to suggest purely technological solutions, it would seem that a tamper-proof destruct mechanism should be in the realm of technical feasibility. Along these lines, a suggestion to prevent unintentional or irrational firing of the Polaris submarine weapons could also safeguard against accidental firings as well. In 1964, a Permissive Action Link was suggested that would have provided a kind of electronic lockup of the missiles, a lockup that could be released only by radio signal from headquarters. This proposal was evidently dropped but might well be worth renewed consideration.

It is encouraging to note from the remarks in his announcement that the President is aware of some of the problems and dilemmas of the present arms balance. He noted that "there is no way that we can adequately defend our cities without a loss of life," stating in his announcement, "the heaviest defense system we consider, one designed to protect our major cities, still could not prevent a catastrophic level of United States fatalities from a deliberate all-out Soviet attack." At his press conference, he concluded that the only way we can save lives is to prevent war.

A significant point in the President's announcement was his continued emphasis on his desire to avoid programs that might be regarded as provocative to the Soviet Union. Under the present system of deterrence, this is a crucial point and one that we must not lose sight of. For most of the 1960s, we and the Soviet Union have maintained a strategic weapons relationship that can be characterized as one of stable deterrence. Under this relationship, both sides are assured that a nuclear attack by one side will be returned by a second-strike attack causing unacceptable damage to the initial attacker. This is so because both sides have sufficiently large and secure forces that even after being hit by a first-strike, significant residual retaliatory forces will remain. The recognition of this condition and the experience gained in living for several years under this condition have contributed to the stability of United States-Soviet Union military relations and to the relaxation of strategic tensions between the two superpowers. Anything that might threaten to alter this condition would be destabilizing and a cause for increased tension. It is for this reason that provocative acts are to be avoided. This is as true for the Soviet Union as it is for the United States and should be as well recognized by their leaders as it seems to be by ours. We would be doing ourselves as well as the Soviet Union a disservice to act on the supposition that they are being so foolhardy as to pursue a first-strike capability.

The proposed Safeguard system, whether regarded as provocative or not in its present form, leaves the door open to more provocative ABM steps on our part in the future. Unfortunately, the proposed "thin" ABM system with the annual review and evaluations suggested by the President can still be regarded as most likely a first step toward the construction of a thick system. What has happened in the past two months is that the Army was caught trying to take a giant step toward the thick system and has had to settle for presidential permission to take a small step instead.

In addition, there are other critical weapons decisions facing the President now. The most destabilizing strategic-weapons development in recent years has been the development of the Multiple Independently Targetable Re-entry Vehicle (MIRV), which will be ready for deployment within a few years. The deployment of MIRV in the absence of an extensive ABM on the other side would raise the specter of first-strike intentions. It is the ability to destroy with one of your missiles more than one of an opponent's missiles that puts a premium on striking first and hence is destabilizing. If the

President sincerely wishes to avoid extreme provocation, he should make the decision now to refrain from testing, procurement and deployment of MIRV. Continuing with MIRV cannot help but provoke the Soviet Union to expand both its offensive and defensive forces.

The President has put considerable emphasis in his announcement on prospective arms-limitation talks with the Soviet Union. If we are to move to an era of negotiation, as has been the President's pledge, it should be more fruitful if we do not use the tactics of confrontation as a bargaining ploy. If both sides are truly interested in halting the arms race, as seems to be the case, meaningful negotiations should proceed without introducing extraneous complicating factors, such as the Safeguard ABM Program. If we are to avoid proceeding beyond a point of no (or difficult) return, we must begin *now* to seek agreements. It is recognized that negotiations, of necessity, tend to be difficult and complex. However, once MIRV is fully developed and ready to deploy, the problems of controlling a strategic arms limitation agreement become more severe. Therefore, it would be highly desirable to seek an *immediate* joint moratorium on the procurement and deployment of new strategic-weapons systems. This would include ABM, MIRV and strategic bomber systems. The moratorium should also include range testing of new missile systems, so as to stop MIRV before it is too late. Such a moratorium would afford the time and the atmosphere for achieving a more comprehensive agreement.

In the final analysis, the only permanent solution to the ABM and MIRV questions is a negotiated agreement limiting both defensive and offensive weapons systems. This must become the President's and the country's prime objective.

I would like now to discuss the areas of public concern and the ways in which ABM has become a public issue. The shifts of the Defense Department in their attempts to sell the nation on ABM has brought into serious question their credibility, which already had been brought into doubt as a result of the Vietnam war. The obvious reason for the Army's attempt to locate Sentinel sites near cities, when, under the concept of a thin area defense, the sites could have just as well been located several hundred miles from the cities, was that it would afford them an easier opportunity to proceed to a thick system, which appears to be their ultimate objective. The one-month period of review of the ABM question appears to have been used mainly as an attempt to cool public concern and outrage and to seek means by which a modified system could be made more palatable to the American public and Congress.

The shifting arguments and somewhat conflicting testimony of Secretaries Laird, Packard and Rogers have done little to restore confidence in the administration's handling of this vital defense issue. The annual review of the ABM that the President proposes assures the proponents of an expanded ABM system ample opportunity to push their case on a regular and continuing basis. The history with regard to the ABM has shown that appropriate intelligence to support the Army position can be found or manufactured almost on demand. Thus, intelligence that the Soviets are continuing to increase their numbers of offensive weapons deployed will be the basis for demands to extend the number of ABMs protecting our land-based missiles, and any intelligence, regardless of how little substance, suggesting sophistication in the developing Chinese ICBMs will be used as strong arguments for expanding to a thick system around many of our cities. It is hard to imagine that the President would be able to withstand such future pressures since, in deciding to support an ABM system, he found it expedient to yield to military pressures even when there were strong Congressional and public forces operating in the opposite direction. It remains for the public to question and to apply pressure in order to contain Pentagon interests.

A second and perhaps most obvious reason for public interest is the huge amounts of money involved. At a time when our cities are deteriorating, people are going hungry, and our educational system is near collapse, tens of billions of dollars are spent on military systems without question of value or need. The threat to our country is not from foreign missiles but from a breakdown of our society from within. If there is to be a re-ordering of our national priorities, the public must take a hand. The ultimate aspect of public concern should be the arms race. The ABM issue may represent a final breakthrough in public awareness that the arms race must be a vital concern for everyone. It is hard to believe that we have lived with the threat of nuclear annihilation for more than 20 years and only now does the public seem to be aware and concerned about it. Previous issues of arms policy were never viewed in relation to the arms race but rather in terms of personal concerns with regard to fallout in the case of nuclear test-ban considerations and personal responses to the fallout-shelter program. For the first time, the arms race itself has become a matter of public concern and will have to remain so until it is ended or de-escalated.

I would like to conclude by discussing briefly the public role on these issues. If we consider the decision-making process in this country, we find that on defense issues the decision making takes place at a corporate level or above. Basically, a few large industrial concerns, the Pentagon, members of Congress and the administration are involved and the public takes no or little part in such decisions. If there is a re-ordering of national priorities, the issues that would become important would include housing, welfare, education and transportation. These are "people" issues and "people" would have to be involved in the decisions relating to them. However, unless we get this reordering of priorities, there will be little opportunity to address ourselves to these issues. It is, therefore, necessary that defense be made a "people" issue too.

June 1969

FURTHER READING

ABM: Yes or No? (Santa Barbara, Calif.: Center for the Study of Democratic Institutions, 1969) by Donald Brennan, William O. Douglas, Leon Johnson, George S. McGovern, and Jerome Wiesner, with an introduction by Hubert H. Humphrey.

American Scientists and Nuclear Weapons Policy (Princeton, N.J.: Princeton University Press, 1965) by Robert Gilpin.

Debate the Antiballistic Missile (Chicago: Bulletin of the Atomic Scientists, 1967) edited by Eugene Rabinowitch and Ruth Adams.

The Future of the Strategic Arms Race (New York: Carnegie Endowment for International Peace, 1969) by George W. Rathjens.

Responsibility and Response (New York: Harper & Row, 1967) by Maxwell D. Taylor.

ABM: An Evaluation of the Decision to Deploy an Antiballistic Missile System (New York: Harper & Row, 1969) by Jerome B. Wiesner, Abram Chayes et al.

Pentagon Bourgeoisie

SEYMOUR MELMAN

Military industry in 1970 employed about 3 million persons on work directly traceable to the Department of Defense (DOD). In addition, 3.4 million men and women served in the uniformed armed forces and about one million civilians were employed by the Department of Defense, mostly on military bases engaged in research, development, testing, prototype manufacture and supporting activities, and base maintenance. All told, about 22,000 enterprises have been linked to the Department of Defense as performers of contracted work.

People tend to assume that the firms serving the Department of Defense are like other enterprises. But the 25 years of experience enjoyed by these firms has

This essay originally appeared as Chapter 1 of the *War Economy of the United States*, Seymour Melman (ed.), St. Martin's Press, Inc., 1971. Copyright © by St. Martin's Press, Inc., Macmillan & Co., Ltd.

created a new type of enterprise that is basically different in many operating characteristics from the entrepreneurial firm of industrial capitalism. Moreover, the combined effect of this network of enterprises has modified the economy as a whole because of the character and the size of military expenditures.

The autonomous capitalist firm has operated to extend the decision power of its management by keeping costs down and profits coming. Success has been characteristically measured in terms of percentage of a market, percent of capital investment, or change in the proportion of employees in a given industry. For this extension of decision power, profitability has been calculated and accumulated as a vital source of fresh capital for investment. Thus, during the last half century, firms have become increasingly self-financed, relying increasingly on themselves for accumulation of capital for further investment.

Managing includes decisions on what products to produce; how to accumulate capital; how to design and organize production; the quantity of the product; the price to be charged; and the mode of distribution of the product. Together, these functions constitute management. The autonomy of the private firm rests on the fact that the final veto power over these decisions is in the hands of its own management. This central characteristic has been altered in the military-industrial firm.

From 1946 on, industrial firms were increasingly linked with military research institutes and with the Department of Defense in conformity with a policy regulation issued by the then Chief of Staff of the United States Army, General Dwight D. Eisenhower. Following that policy memorandum, the Pentagon arranged durable connections between nominally private firms, nominally private research laboratories (profit, university and other non-profit) and the military establishment. Through this period, the Department of Defense proceeded to act in ways that are characteristic of a large, monopolistic buyer—intervening in the internal affairs of the supplying firms to suit its convenience.

The relationship of the Defense Department to these firms is like that of large automotive firms to parts suppliers, or the relation of department stores or mail-order houses to suppliers of products, very often under brand names selected by the buyer. Eisenhower effectively founded the market network he later named the "military-industrial complex," but within the industrial side of the complex, management's decisions were increasingly subject to the official *Armed Services Procurement Regulations.*

In 1961, Robert McNamara established, under the Office of the Secretary of Defense, a central administrative office, functionally similar to the type of unit that has operated in central-office-controlled, multidivision, major manufacturing firms. The key element here was the concentration of control in new institutions, like the Defense Supply Agency also set up by McNamara, the impact of which induced a qualitative change in the character of military-industrial enterprise: Final decision power over the main components of managerial control was vested in the new state management apparatus.

Top management at the DOD formally rendered decisions on products. Only the most minor decisions were left to the individual firm. Moreover, the government-based management provided capital, not only by making available land, buildings or machinery, but also by guaranteeing loans obtained from private sources. The extension of the scope and intensity of the state management's control proceeded in every sort of decision-making; on how to produce, on quantity, price and shipment. The net effect was to establish the state management as the holder of the final decision power and also to limit the scope of decision left to the managements of the defense contractors, the subdivisions of the state management.

Within industrial capitalism, subfirms frequently operate under central office control. In the military-industrial system, however, the central office is located in the executive branch of the federal government. It is unprecedented in size, and so is the number of submanagements. By 1968, the Department of Defense industrial system supplied $44 billions of goods and services. This exceeded the combined net sales (in billions) of General Motors ($22.8), General Electric ($8.4), U.S. Steel ($4.6) and DuPont ($3.4). Altogether, this constitutes a form of state capitalism operating under the Department of Defense—hence, the designation "Pentagon capitalism." Internally, the military-industrial complex differs also from the entrepreneurial business; this is best illustrated by the role of profit and cost minimization.

Profit and loss statements are computed in military industry, and a profit category is shown. However, this profit is not a reward for entrepreneurial risk-taking, which is the conventional justification for the profit taken in industrial capitalism. Under conditions of assured (by contract) price and quantity of goods to be delivered to the Department of Defense, there is no risk of the ordinary sort. There may be residual "risk" of not getting further business, but that is another matter. Moreover, profits for a subunit can be readily regulated by the state management which is inclined to regard "profits" of its subunits as a cost to the top controllers.

Within the new military-industrial enterprise, then,

the self-correcting mechanisms that characterize the private firm are altered, if not dissolved. When major managerial functions are poorly performed in the ordinary firm, it is the entrepreneurial obligation to correct the malfunction. In the military-industrial firm, this may not be feasible insofar as final decision-making is in the hands of the state management. Thus unusually high costs, or problems in the design of the product, or problems in acquiring sufficient capital are not, in a military-industrial enterprise, necessarily problems for that management.

In the private firm, high costs become important pressures to modify industrial practice. For unduly high cost, as against the cost of alternative methods, can translate into competitive disadvantage and limited profits which means limited options for further capital investment and hence, limited options for further production decision-making by the management. Therefore, the manager of the classic industrial firm is moved to act to minimize costs. This logic operates except where managements, either singly or in concert with others, restrict market competition and shift cost increases to price, while maintaining an acceptable profit margin for all. However, it is ordinarily understood that the latter practice is an alteration of the more characteristic cost-minimizing calculus of the private firm. In the military-industrial firm, cost increases or unusually high costs are dealt with mainly by raising price. The record shows that on the average, the final price of major weapons systems has been about 3.2 times the initial estimate.

Finally, the conventional firm can move among markets when it finds that its products are not well accepted. No options of this sort exist for the military-industrial firm. For the Department of Defense is the market and the firm may not sell to anyone else except with permission of the Department of Defense—as, for example, to a politically allied foreign military establishment.

These modifications in the self-correcting mechanisms of the classic business firm substantially alter the characteristics of that model entity, distinguishing the military-industrial firm and its controlling state management from the private and autonomous entrepreneurial enterprise.

So much for the complex itself, but the operation of the military-industrial firms also produces a series of unique effects for the economy as a whole. These include distortions of national growth, as well as missed opportunities in terms of depleted industries, services and occupations. From 1945 to 1970, $1,100 billions were expended by the U.S. government for military purposes. This exceeds the 1967 value of all business and residential structures in place on the surface of the United States. However, the prime effects of the military-industrial activity stem from its economic functional nature.

Ordinarily, in national income accounting, all money-valued goods and services are included in the category Gross National Product (GNP). However, because of the character and size of military economic activity, it is important to make an economic-functional differentiation between economic growth that is productive and economic growth that is parasitic.

Productive growth includes goods and services that make up part of what we mean by the standard of living or can be used for further production of whatever sort. Parasitic economic growth refers to goods and services that are not part of the standard of living or cannot be used for further production. Plainly, military goods and services are overwhelmingly in the latter class.

Each year, from 1960 to 1970, 8 to 10 percent of the U.S. Gross National Product has been used for the military. The men and women who did the work were paid, but their products were, upon completion, withdrawn from market exchange. Whatever worth may be attributed to military products on other than economic-functional grounds, it is apparent that you cannot live in, wear or ride an intercontinental missile or an antipersonnel bomb. Neither can such products be used for further production. What seemed a small portion, 10 percent or less, of each year's GNP accumulated to an immense sum from 1945 to 1970.

The full cost to a society of parasitic economic growth is twofold: First, there is the value of the man-hours, materials and whatever goes into making nonproductive goods or services; second, there is the economic use-value that is lost for standard of living or for further production (as against possible military use-value). Such economic use-value is ordinarily equivalent to the price paid for making nonproductive (or productive) goods. *Therefore, the social cost of parasitic economic growth is that of the resources used up directly plus the productive use-value foregone, or double the price nominally paid.* Thus, the $1,100 billion military outlay by the United States from 1945 to 1970 actually cost the nation $2,200 billion, or the value of total reproducible wealth of the nation (excluding only the land).

A collateral effect of sustained parasitic economic activity in the United States has been to jeopardize the international and the domestic value of the dollar. For the payments made to people for parasitic economic growth are made for goods and services that are not purchasable thereafter. The payments for such goods and services are not "sterilized" economically and are used as claims on those goods that do reach the marketplace. There is no gainsaying the importance of military economic activity as a cause of price instability in today's American society. The 20 percent drop in the purchasing power of the dollar from 1964 to 1970 places its future value in doubt. This means, of course, that the value of money income, savings, insurance and pension funds was diminished by a similar amount; that is, the drop in the value of the dollar saw a corresponding destruction of capital.

The value of the dollar, relative to other currencies, is critically affected by another mechanism. In 1950, the United States Treasury possessed $24 billions in gold bullion. By August, 1970, this had diminished to $11.8 billions. The reason for the drain, despite a sustained favorable balance of trade, was due primarily to the heavy overseas outlays for military and allied purposes during the period 1950 to 1970. The net result was an accumulation of dollars abroad that was not used for purchases from the American economy. Some of these dollars were presented to the U.S. Treasury for redemption in gold. As against $11.8 billions in gold bullion held by the Treasury in August 1970, there were $42 billions of short-term claims by foreigners against the United States reported by American banks. It is plausible to expect that if foreign claimants on United States gold were to attempt massive cashing-in of their short-term claims this country would embargo the shipment of gold abroad. The world monetary system would collapse.

It is significant that the annual portion of GNP used for parasitic economic growth is not an average, homogeneous 8 to 10 percent of U.S. goods and services. For example, the military-related institutions and military industry have been using more than half of the nation's technical research talent. Since a missile designer cannot be designing railroad equipment or civilian electronics at the same time, the country has had more missiles but less railroad equipment, civilian electronics and kindred goods.

Only insofar as we understand the consequence of applying half and more of the country's technical research talent to parasitic economic growth can we explain what is otherwise an anomaly: the appearance of technological and economic depletion in many sectors of American industry and services—together with a growth in GNP. The principal industries that are deteriorating now include steel, house-building, ship-building and machinery production of many classes. Deterioration or grossly unsatisfactory performance in services afflicts the telephone and postal systems, the supply of electricity (notably in the northeastern states during the last period) and the performance of medical services.

In 1967, 40.7 percent of the young men examined by Selective Service for military induction were rejected on grounds of physical or educational incapacity. This means that the American economy, with a GNP of one trillion dollars a year, has been shortchanging the young men and women of this society in education and health care. That is inexplicable, except as we appreciate that $1,100 billion was expended for military and related parasitic purposes over 25 years, and the quality of the manpower was concentrated in military and allied work.

Opportunity cost, the value of something foregone, is

one way of assessing the value of goods or services. In the present case, what has been the opportunity cost to American society of expending $1,100 billion for military purposes? Consider that over a period of 20 years this meant a foregone expenditure of $50 billion a year for alternative purposes.

Perhaps even more important than depletion of industries is the depletion of occupations and regions in the economy. Depleted occupations refer, for example, to an unknown but large number of engineers who functioned for many years on behalf of the military and thereby acquired a trained incapacity for functioning in a civilian industrial environment. Depleted regions refer to states, cities and counties which have had a preponderance of military industry and related activity, especially during the decade 1960-1970. By 1970, a slowdown in the rate of military-industrial expenditures, notably in research and development, created depressed areas in regions like the suburbs of Los Angeles, the San Francisco Bay area, Seattle, eastern Long Island and the area around Route 128 in Boston.

The opportunity cost of the military system includes the inability of the United States to provide economic development at home for the 30 million Americans who need it. They need it because of a high infant mortality rate and limited life span, a high incidence of certain epidemic diseases, and limited education and, hence, limited productivity and income. The process that alters this condition is called economic development. It requires investment in human capital and in physical productive facilities.

In the United States, a process of economic development would require an outlay of about $50,000 for a family of four. Considering 30 million possible candidates, about 60 percent of them white and 40 percent black, the requirement for 7.5 million "equivalent family units" would entail an expenditure of $375 billions over a period of, say, 10 years, or $37.5 billions per year. That sum, it should be noted, compares with estimates of the full annual cost of the Vietnam war at its peak. Obviously, expenditures of $37.5 billions per year for economic development are not conceivable while military budgets use up $70 to $80 billions per year.

The prime limits on the capability of the United States economy are most critically defined in terms of the availability and the use of skilled manpower. To accomplish economic development we need an investment of skilled manpower in the work of enhancing the human capital and productive skills of persons who are economically underdeveloped. The same consideration constrains American participation in economic development in other areas of the world.

The officially budgeted costs of the war in Vietnam include the incremental costs as distinguished from an estimate of the total costs of that war. Thus for 1967, $20 billions; for 1968, $26 billions; for 1969, $29 billions; and for 1970, it is estimated at $23 billions. In 1962, in my book *The Peace Race* I calculated that the total cost of economic development for the populations of Africa, Asia and Latin America. My reckoning indicated that an annual capital investment of $22 billions was the cost worldwide for accelerating an economic development process.

Evidently, the incremental military costs—by themselves—to the United States for the war in Vietnam, from 1967 to 1970, used up a capital sum approximately equal to what I calculated would be required for accelerating economic development in Asia, Africa and Latin America.

For the United States, the policy issue involved in changing from a military-priority economy is not restricted to having a military security system of the present sort as against no military security at all. In fact, many alternatives are conceivable in place of the military security goal of preparing to fight 2½ wars at once, which is the policy that dominated in the 1960s. For example, the United States could conceivably define its foreign policies so as to require a military security force to operate a plausible nuclear deterrent, to guard the shores of the United States and to have a capability for participating in international peace-keeping. The total manpower required to operate such a force, including supporting staffs and functions, would comprise about one million men, and the cost of operation would be about one-third of the 1970 military budget of $75 billions. A military security concept of this sort opens up the possibility of alternative uses of about $50 billions a year of money and manpower now employed for military and related purposes.

The state management that controls the military-industrial system has applied its considerable influence to counter legislative and other kinds of preparations for conversion of military-industrial employees and facilities to civilian work. By September 1970 Senator Abraham Ribicoff summarized the results of an inquiry by his Subcommittee on Executive Reorganization into the status of capability for conversion to civilian economy among military-industrial firms:

In general, the responses indicated that private industry is not interested in initiating any major attempts at meeting critical public needs. Most industries have no plans or projects designed to apply their resources to civilian problems. Furthermore, they indicated an unwillingness to initiate such actions without a firm commitment from the government that their efforts will quickly reap the financial rewards to which they are accustomed. Otherwise, they appear eager to pursue greater defense contracts or stick to proven commercial products within the private sector . . . . After carefully examining the letters as a whole, we found that the need for serious thought and action on conversion has largely been disregarded by most of the business community. . . . For the business units of industrial capitalism, the development of military industry has meant a transformation from the autonomous entrepreneurial firm to the military-industrial enterprise functioning under a state management. For the economy as a whole, the formalization of Pentagon capitalism and the outlays on its behalf have involved parasitic growth on a large scale and at a large opportunity cost. The economy and society as a whole bear the unknown cost of an array of depleted industries, occupations and industrial areas, and the cost of sustaining an economically under-developed population of 30 million among 200 million Americans.

March/April 1971

FURTHER READING

What Price Vigilance? The Burdens of National Defense (New Haven: Yale University Press, 1970) by Bruce Russett.
The War Profiteers (Indianapolis: Bobbs-Merrill, 1971) by Richard Kaufman.

Road to Oblivion (New York: Simon & Schuster, 1970) by Herbert York.

Our Depleted Society (New York: Holt, Rinehart & Winston, 1970) by Seymour Melman.

Pentagon Capitalism (New York: McGraw-Hill, 1970) by Seymour Melman.

A CASE STUDY OF
THE MORAL COSTS
OF INTERVENTION:
MYLAI

Vietnam: Betrayal and Self-Betrayal

ROBERT JAY LIFTON

The Vietnam War, in its general social impact, has entered a new phase. It has become both boring and unmentionable. It is boring because practically everything that can be said about it has already been said many times over. It is unmentionable because, at least from the standpoint of the young, it is still insoluble.

The students I talk to no longer seem inclined to explore the larger ethical or historical issues of the war. They are absorbed in the question of how they can pursue their own lives without being consumed or destroyed, whether physically or psychically, by this evil. As they confront this problem, betrayals and self-betrayals build upon one another in the most vicious of circles. It is this theme of betrayal—a psychologically devastating one, I think—that I want to focus on here.

There is the sense of being betrayed by a nation, a

government, by specific political leaders, or by the older generation in general, all of whom, the young feel, have imposed on them the obligation to murder or be murdered. For that is what war comes down to when its rationale is punctured and it stands revealed, as the Vietnam War does, as morally wrong and an expression of deception. But there is also a sense of self-betrayal as the young must choose among the various options available to them: to submit to active or reserve military service, to embark upon a particular form of study or work that one would not otherwise seek if it did not offer the possibility of deferment, to emphasize some physical or psychological disability as another path to deferment which, if successful, leaves one with a sense of stigma as well as relief.

Even if one is among the relatively few, though still impressive number of those who are committed to going to jail or into exile rather than enter military service, he may still at least to some degree internalize society's message that he is betraying his country, that he is an outcast or a criminal. And there is little doubt that this message is reinforced and disturbingly complicated by the experience of two or more years in an American prison, or even longer in enforced exile.

But what of the many thousands of young men who do become participants in this war? The psychiatrist Peter Bourne, who has studied the basic training process, compares it to my own observations on Chinese thought reform. In basic training draftees experience a direct assault upon their previous identities and beliefs, followed by a protracted period of environmental shock in which they are made to feel profoundly inadequate and unworthy. They are shamed and made to feel guilty until they become convinced that they have no value except in their potential to become a soldier. Only then can the draftee be reborn with a new identity—that of a soldier—an identity that depends on the acquisition of all the appropriate skills of self-defense and of killing. This does not mean that military values are held without inner conflict, or that upon discharge soldiers do not become angry at their former masters, but rather that whatever combination of attitudes the veteran emerges with, he is likely to retain an element of identification with the military which may cause him to feel, as Bourne puts it, "that any limitation of military power is an incursion on his own influence."

Should the individual trainee go on to Vietnam, and particularly if he goes into combat there, his military experience takes on a new dimension. He kills, sees others killed, defends himself against being killed and (if he lives) emerges as a special kind of survivor. Like all survivors, he retains an image of the deaths he has known, what I call the death imprint. But in his case the death imprint is infused with absurdity, an absurdity that something in him has perceived from the very beginning. It has to do with the lack of an acceptable rationale or justification for his particular encounter with death in Vietnam other than the very narrow and often ambivalently held military ethos that was im- planted in him in basic training. The result is that the death encounter in Vietnam, and the imprint he retains from it, are associated with confusion, with treachery and with hate. In his exposure to a people and to an environment that he cannot grasp or trust and in his painful inability to distinguish friend from foe, he is rendered more vulnerable to anxiety about death in general. But he may also come to exhibit that paradox- ical survivor reaction which has been observed in other kinds of survivors: a residual love of the death encounter and even an attraction to related forms of violence.

The combat veteran also retains complicated forms of guilt associated with the death encounter—guilt over having survived while so many of his buddies died, or for having killed in order to survive, guilt also for having participated in the killing of farmers, women and children whose designation as "the enemy" he can never accept with complete conviction. Like the Hiroshima survivors I interviewed he is likely to retain a vague but disturbing form of guilt simply through having participated in evil. This form of guilt is always associated with war, but it is especially unresolvable when the war cannot be inwardly justified. He is likely also to retain some of the psychic numbing—the desensitization to suffering and brutality, to death and killing—that he had to call upon in combat, but which is a dangerous commodity to bring back to our present society.

The overall problem of the survivor of combat in Vietnam, like that of any survivor, is the search for significance, the problem of formulating what he has seen and done there in a way that can give it meaning or justification so that he can find meaning and justification for his subsequent life. How does the veteran solve this problem?

One way is to embrace what former Marine Commandant David M. Shoupe has called "the new American militarism." This, says General Shoupe, is "a powerful creed" composed of anticommunism and patriotism, whose highest priority is national defense and whose most important attitudes are "a pugnacious and chauvinistic tendency toward expanding military influence and toward military solutions in general." The new militarism has found its way into many parts of our society and veterans can join together with a variety of groups to share in the nightmare military vision evoked by General Shoupe: "Standing in front, adorned with service caps, ribbons and lapel emblems is a nation of veterans—patriotic, belligerent, romantic and well-intentioned—finding a certain sublimation and excitement in their country's latest military venture."

What I've been trying to show here is that the psychological emanations from the war in Vietnam and from associated experiences in military service perpetuate exactly this dangerous but all too appealing image. And just as the veteran of combat in Vietnam may join in that jingoistic vision as a means of justifying his own survival, so can American society in general join in it out of anxious justification of its own increasingly tenuous survivals, survivals of military adventures abroad and of rebellions at home.

Where are we to look for a countervailing vision? There is another, more unusual type of veteran who can find his significance by candid formulation of just the absurdity and evil he has witnessed in Vietnam. Though such men are in a minority we are fortunately seeing more and more of them, and their capacity to make their experience heard is of enormous importance to all peace movements. Whether they will be heard depends importantly on the encouragement they get from the pockets of resistance to the war and to militarism appearing throughout American society and especially, of course, among young people.

But in speaking of the young, we return to the theme with which I began, the theme of betrayal. Psychologically, betrayal and self-betrayal represent both loss and injury: loss of trusting connection with one's world, injury to self-esteem and above all to individual integrity. I do not think it is too much to say that one of the chief consequences of the war in Vietnam has been that a whole generation, indeed the whole nation, has suffered precisely this form of psychological loss and injury. And under such conditions people are likely to try to replace that which has been lost and to retaliate for injuries sustained.

The rebellion of the young cannot be laid solely to the war. But one must remember that Vietnam raises many issues with disturbing reverberations in our larger society and the rest of the world: the mass destruction by a white nation of a nonwhite people and of their country, the blindly excessive use of a destructive technology, the economic and social power of the military and industrial forces so active in the war, the political myths of anticommunism and the universal applicability of American-style democracy. It is not surprising that the young and the blacks connect the war with every grievance they feel, with every critical assessment they make of this country and its institutions. The connections are very much there.

I am afraid that the Vietnam War has so divided our society, so intensified its impulses toward violence and dehumanization that they now threaten to undermine what is most constructive and truly innovative in the youth rebellion and to contribute significantly to destructive forms of polarization and combat whether between young and old, right and left, black and white, or, for that matter, between blacks and blacks, the young and the young, and the left and the left. The end of the war in Vietnam will still leave America in deep trouble. But the sooner it is ended, the better our chances for avoiding the final realization of General

Shoupe's nightmare vision and for altering the atmosphere of betrayal and self-betrayal pervading the country.

October 1969

FURTHER READING

Crimes of War (New York: Random House, and Vintage paperback, 1971) edited by Richard A. Falk, Gabriel Kolko and Robert Jay Lifton.

In the Service of Their Country: War Resistors in Prison (New York: Viking, 1970) by Willard Gaylin.

No Victory Parades: The Return of the Vietnam Veteran (New York: Holt, Rinehart & Winston, 1971) by Murray Polner.

Boundaries: Psychological Man in Revolution (New York: Random House, and Vintage paperback, 1970) by Robert Jay Lifton.

War Crimes and
Individual Responsibility

RICHARD A. FALK

The dramatic disclosure of the Mylai massacre has led to a public concern over the commission of war crimes in Vietnam by American military personnel. Such a concern is certainly appropriate, but insufficient if limited to inquiry and prosecution of the individual servicemen involved in the monstrous events that apparently took the lives of over 500 civilians in the No. 4 hamlet of Mylai village on March 16, 1968. The Mylai massacre itself raises a serious basis for inquiry into the military and civilian command structure that was in charge of battlefield behavior at the time.

The evidence now available suggests that the armed forces have made efforts throughout the Vietnam War to suppress, rather than investigate and punish, the commission of war crimes by American personnel. The evidence also suggests a failure to protest or prevent the manifest and systematic commission of war crimes by the armed forces of the Saigon regime in South Vietnam.

The scope of proper inquiry is even broader than the prior paragraph suggests. The official policies developed for the pursuit of belligerent objectives in Vietnam appear to violate the same basic and minimum constraints on the conduct of war as were violated at Mylai. B-52 pattern raids against undefended villages and populated areas, "free bomb zones," forcible removal of civilian populations, defoliation and crop destruction and "search and destroy" missions have been sanctioned as official tactical policies of the United States government. Each of these tactical policies appears to violate the international laws of war binding upon the United States by international treaties ratified by the U.S. government with the advice and consent of the Senate. The overall conduct of the war in Vietnam by the U.S. armed forces involves a refusal to differentiate between combatants and noncombatants and between military and nonmilitary targets. Detailed presentation of the acts of war in relation to the laws of war is available in a volume bearing the title *In the Name of America* published under the auspices of the Clergy and Laymen Concerned about Vietnam in January 1968, or several months before the Mylai massacre took place. Ample evidence of war crimes has been presented to the public and to its officials for some time without producing an official reaction or rectifying action. A comparable description of the acts of war that were involved in the bombardment of North Vietnam by American planes and naval vessels between February 1965 and October 1968 is available in a book by John Gerassi entitled *North Vietnam: A Documentary*.

The broad point, then, is that the United States

government has officially endorsed a series of battlefield activities that appear to constitute war crimes. It would, therefore, be misleading to isolate the awful happening at Mylai from the overall conduct of the war. It is certainly true that the perpetrators of the massacre at Mylai are, if the allegations prove correct, guilty of the commission of war crimes, but it is also true that their responsibility is mitigated to the extent that they were executing superior orders or were even carrying out the general line of official policy that established a moral climate in which the welfare of Vietnamese civilians is totally disregarded.

I. Personal Responsibility: Some Basic Propositions

The U.S. prosecutor at Nuremberg, Robert Jackson, emphasized that war crimes are war crimes no matter which country is guilty of them. The United States more than any other sovereign state took the lead in the movement to generalize the principles underlying the Nuremberg Judgment that was delivered against German war criminals after the end of World War II.

At the initiative of the United States, in 1945 the General Assembly of the United Nations unanimously affirmed "the principles of international law recognized by the Charter of the Nuremberg Tribunal" in Resolution 95(I). This resolution was an official action of governments. At the direction of the membership of the United Nations, the International Law Commission, an expert body containing international law experts from all of the principal legal systems in the world, formulated the Principles of Nuremberg in 1950.

These seven Principles of International Law are printed below in full to indicate the basic standards of international responsibility governing the commission of war crimes. These principles offer the most complete set of guidelines currently available on the relationship between personal responsibility and war crimes.

PRINCIPLES OF INTERNATIONAL LAW recognized in the Charter of the Nuremberg Tribunal and in the judgment of the Tribunal as formulated by the International Law Commission, June-July, 1950.

Principle I

Any person who commits an act which constitutes a crime under international law is responsible therefor and liable to punishment.

Principle II

The fact that internal law does not impose a penalty for an act which constitutes a crime under international law does not relieve the person who committed the act from responsibility under international law.

Principle III

The fact that a person who committed an act which constitutes a crime under international law acted as Head of State or responsible government official does not relieve him from responsibility under international law.

Principle IV

The fact that a person acted pursuant to order of his Government or of a superior does not relieve him from responsibility under international law, provided a moral choice was in fact possible for him.

Principle V

Any person charged with a crime under international law has the right to a fair trial on the facts and law.

Principle VI

The crimes hereinafter set out are punishable as crimes under international law:

a. Crimes against peace:

(i) Planning, preparation, initiation or waging of a war of aggression or a war in violation of international treaties, agreements or assurances;

(ii) Participation in a common plan or conspiracy for the accomplishment of any of the acts mentioned under (i).

b. War crimes:

Violations of the laws or customs of war which include, but are not limited to, murder, ill-treatment or deportation to slave-labour or for any other purpose of civilian population of or in occupied territory, murder or ill-treatment of prisoners of war or persons on the seas, killing of hostages, plunder of public or private property, wanton destruction of cities, towns, or villages, or devastation not justified by military necessity.

c. Crimes against humanity:

Murder, extermination, enslavement, deportation and other inhuman acts done against any civilian population, or persecutions on political, racial or religious grounds, when such acts are done or such persecutions are carried on in execution of or in connexion with any crime against peace or any war crime.

Principle VII

Complicity in the commission of a crime against humanity as set forth in Principle VI is a crime under international law.

Neither the Nuremberg Judgment nor the Nuremberg

Principles fixes definite boundaries on personal responsibility. These boundaries will have to be drawn in the future as the circumstances of alleged violations of international law are tested by competent domestic and international tribunals. However, Principle IV makes it clear that superior orders are no defense in a prosecution for war crimes, provided the individual accused of criminal behavior had a moral choice available to him.

The Supreme Court upheld in *The Matter of Yamashita* 327 U.S. 1 (1945) a sentence of death against General Yamashita imposed at the end of World War II for acts committed by troops under his command. The determination of responsibility rested upon the obligation of General Yamashita for the maintenance of discipline by troops under his command, which discipline included the enforcement of the prohibition against the commission of war crimes. Thus General Yamashita was convicted even though he had no specific knowledge of the alleged war crimes, which mainly involved forbidden acts against the civilian population of the Philippines in the closing days of World War II. Commentators have criticized the conviction of General Yamashita because it was difficult to maintain discipline under the conditions of defeat during which the war crimes were committed, but the imposition of responsibility sets a precedent for holding principal military and political officials responsible for acts committed under their command, especially when no diligent effort was made to inquire, punish and prevent repetition. *The Matter of Yamashita* has an extraordinary relevance to the failure of the U.S. military command to secure adherence to minimum rules of international law by troops serving under their command. The following sentences from the majority opinion of Chief Justice

Stone in *The Matter of Yamashita* have a particular bearing:

> It is evident that the conduct of military operations by troops whose excesses are unrestrained by the orders or efforts of their commands would almost certainly result in violations which it is the purpose of the law of war to prevent. Its purpose to protect civilian populations and prisoners of war from brutality would largely be defeated if the commands of an invading army could with impunity neglect to take reasonable measures for their protection. Hence the law of war presupposes that its violation is to be avoided through the control of the operations of war by commanders who are to some extent responsible for their subordinates. [327 U.S. 1, 15]

The Field Manual of the Department of the Army, FM 27-10, adequately develops the principles of responsibility governing members of the armed forces. Sect. 3 (b) makes it clear that "the law of war is binding not only upon States as such but also upon individuals and, in particular, the members of their armed forces." The entire manual is based upon the acceptance by the United States of the obligation to conduct warfare in accordance with the international law of war. The substantive content of international law is contained in a series of international treaties that have been properly ratified by the United States. These include 12 Hague and Geneva Conventions.

These international treaties are listed in the Field Manual and are, in any event, part of "the supreme law of the land" by virtue of Article VI of the U.S. Constitution. Customary rules of international law governing warfare are also made explicitly applicable to the obligation of American servicemen in the manuals issued to the armed forces.

It has sometimes been maintained that the laws of war do not apply to a civil war, which is a war within a state and thus outside the scope of international law. Some observers have argued that the Vietnam War represents a civil war between factions contending for political control of South Vietnam. Such an argument may accurately portray the principal basis of the conflict, but surely the extension of the combat theater to include North Vietnam, Laos, Thailand, Cambodia and Okinawa removes any doubt about the international character of the war from a military and legal point of view. Nevertheless, even assuming for the sake of analysis that the war should be treated as a civil war, the laws of war are applicable to a limited extent, an extent great enough to cover the events at Mylai and the commission of many other alleged war crimes in Vietnam. Sect. 11 of the Field Manual recites Article 3 common to all four Geneva Conventions on the Law of War (1947) and establishes a minimum set of obligations for civil war situations:

> In the case of armed conflict not of an interna-tional character occurring in the territory of one of the High Contracting Parties, each Party to the conflict shall be bound to apply, as a minimum, the following provisions:
> 1) Persons taking no active part in the hostilities, including members of armed forces who have laid down their arms and those placed *hors de combat* by sickness, wounds, detention or any other cause, shall in all circumstances be treated humanely,

without any adverse distinction founded on race, colour, religion or faith, sex, birth or wealth, or any other similar criteria.

To this end, the following acts are and shall remain prohibited at any time and in any place whatsoever with respect to the abovementioned persons:

(a) violence to life and person, in particular murder of all kinds, mutilation, cruel treatment and torture;

(b) taking of hostages;

(c) outrages upon personal dignity, in particular, humiliating and degrading treatment;

(d) the passing of sentences and the carrying out of executions without previous judgment pronounced by a regularly constituted court, affording all the judicial guarantees which are recognized as indispensable by civilized peoples.

2) The wounded and sick shall be collected and cared for. An impartial humanitarian body, such as the International Committee of the Red Cross, may offer its services to the Parties to the conflict.

The Parties to the conflict would further endeavor to bring into force, by means of special agreements, all or part of the other provisions of the present Convention.

Such a limited applicability of the laws of war to the Vietnam War flies in the face of the official American contention that South Vietnam is a sovereign state that has been attacked by a foreign state, North Vietnam. This standard American contention, repeated in President Nixon's speech of November 3, 1969, would suggest that the United States government is obliged to treat the Vietnam conflict as a war of international character to which the entire law of war applies.

Several provisions of the Field Manual clearly establish the obligation of the United States to apprehend and punish those committing war crimes:

Sect. 506. Suppression of War Crimes

a. *Geneva Conventions of 1949.* The Geneva Conventions of 1949 contain the following common undertakings:

The High Contracting Parties undertake to enact any legislation necessary to provide effective penal sanctions for persons committing, or ordering to be committed, any of the grave breaches of the present Convention defined in the following Article.

Each High Contracting Party shall be under the obligation to search for persons alleged to have committed or ordering to be committed, such grave breaches, and shall bring such persons, regardless of their nationality, before its own courts. It may also, if it prefers, and in accordance with the provisions of its own legislation, hand such persons over for trial to another High Contracting Party concerned, provided such High Contracting Party has made out a *prima facie* case.

Each High Contracting Party shall take measures necessary for the suppression of all acts contrary to the provisions of the present Convention other than the grave breaches defined in the following Article.

In all circumstances, the accused persons shall benefit by safeguards of proper trial and defense, which shall not be less favourable than those provided by Article 105 and those following of the Geneva Convention relative to the treatment of Prisoners of War of August 12, 1949. (GWS art. 49; GWS Sea, art. 50; GPW, art. 129; GC, art. 146).

b. *Declaratory Character of Above Principles.* The principles quoted in *a*, above, are declaratory of the obligations of belligerents under customary international law to take measures for the punishment of war crimes committed by all persons, including members of a belligerent's own armed forces.

c. *Grave Breaches.* "Grave breaches" of the Geneva Conventions of 1949 and other war crimes which are committed by enemy personnel or persons associated with the enemy are tried and punished by United States tribunals as violations of international law.

If committed by persons subject to United States military law, these "grave breaches" constitute acts punishable under the Uniform Code of Military Justice. Moreover, most of the acts designated as "grave breaches" are, if committed within the United States, violations of domestic law over which the civil courts can exercise jurisdiction.

Sect. 507. Universality of Jurisdiction

a. *Victims of War Crimes.* The jurisdiction of United States military tribunals in connection with war crimes is not limited to offenses committed against nationals of the United States but extends also to all offenses of this nature committed against nationals of allies and of cobelligerents and stateless persons.

b. *Persons Charged with War Crimes.* The United States normally punishes war crimes as such only if they are committed by enemy nationals or by persons serving the interests of the enemy State. Violations of the law of war committed by persons subject to the military law of the United States will usually constitute violations of the Uniform Code of Military Justice and, if so, will be prosecuted under that Code. Violations of the law of war committed within the United States by other persons will usually constitute violations of federal or state criminal law and preferably will be prosecuted under such law (see pars. 505 and 506). Commanding officers of United States troops must insure that war crimes committed by members of their forces against enemy personnel are promptly and adequately punished.

Sect. 508. Penal Sanctions

The punishment imposed for a violation of the law of war must be proportionate to the gravity of the offense. The death penalty may be imposed for grave breaches of the law. Corporal punishment is excluded. Punishments should be deterrent, and in imposing a sentence of imprisonment it is not necessary to take into consideration the end of the war, which does not of itself limit the imprisonment to be imposed.

Sect. 509. Defense of Superior Orders

a. The fact that the law of war has been violated pursuant to an order of a superior authority, whether military or civil, does not deprive the act in question of its character of a war crime, nor does it constitute a defense in the trial of the accused individual, unless he did not know and could not reasonably have been expected to know that the act ordered was unlawful. In all cases where the order is held not to constitute a defense to an allegation of a war crime, the fact that the individual was acting pursuant to orders may be considered in mitigation of punishment.

b. In considering the question whether a superior order constitutes a valid defense, the court shall take into consideration the fact that obedience to lawful military orders is the duty of every member of the armed forces; that the latter cannot be expected, in conditions of war discipline, to weigh scrupulously the legal merits of the orders received; that certain rules of warfare may be controversial; or that an act otherwise amounting to a war crime may be done in obedience to orders conceived as a measure of reprisal. At the same time it must be borne in mind that members of the armed forces are bound to obey only lawful orders (e.g. UCMJ, Art. 92).

Sect. 510. Government Officials

The fact that a person who committed an act which constitutes a war crime acted as the head of a State or as a responsible government official does not relieve him from responsibility for his act.

Sect. 511. Acts Not Punished in Domestic Law

The fact that domestic law does not impose a penalty for an act which constitutes a crime under international law does not relieve the person who committed the act from responsibility under international law.

These provisions make it amply clear that war crimes are to be prosecuted and punished and that responsibility is acknowledged to extend far beyond the level of the individuals who performed the physical acts that inflicted harm. In fact, the effectiveness of the law of war depends, above all else, on holding those in command and in policy-making positions responsible for the behavior of the rank-and-file soldiers on the field of battle. The reports of neuropsychiatrists, trained in combat therapy, have suggested that unrestrained behavior by troops is an expression almost always of tacit authorization, at least, on the part of commanding officers, a form of authorization that conveys to the rank-and-file soldier the absence of any prospect of punishment for the outrageous behavior. It would thus be a deception to punish the triggermen at Mylai without also looking further up the chain of command to identify the truer locus of responsibility.

II. Some Comments on the Mylai Massacre

The events took place on March 16, 1968. The Secretary of Defense admitted knowledge of these events eight months before their public disclosure. The disclosure resulted from the publication in the *Cleveland Plain Dealer* in November 1969 of a photograph of the massacre taken by Ronald Haeberle. The lapse of time, the existence of photographs, the report of the helicopter pilot, the large number of American personnel (approximately 80 men of Company C, First Battalion, 20th Infantry Division) involved in the incident creates a deep suspicion that news of the massacre was suppressed at various levels of command and that its disclosure was delayed at the highest levels of military and civilian government. The numerous other reports of atrocities connected with the war have also not been generally investigated or punished with seriousness. In fact, other evidence of atrocities has been ignored or deliberately suppressed by military authorities at all levels of the U.S. command structure.

The massacre at Mylai exhibits a bestiality toward the sanctity of civilian lives that exceeds earlier atrocities that took place at Lidice or Guernica. At Lidice, Czechoslovakia, on June 10, 1942, the male population of the town was shot, women were taken off to concentration camps, and the children sent off to schools and families. At Mylai women and children were not spared. At Guernica bombs were dropped on an undefended Spanish village, terrorizing and killing the inhabitants, a scene made universal by Picasso's mural commemorating the horrifying events. Such military tactics are daily employed by American forces in Vietnam. At Mylai civilians were systematically chosen; they were the intended victims of the act, not the uncertain, random victims of an air attack.

The Mylai massacre is the culmination of the policies of counterinsurgency warfare in South Vietnam. It is not, however, an isolated atrocity, as many other occurrences in South Vietnam have revealed a brutal disregard of Vietnamese civilians and have disclosed little or no effort by military commanders to punish and prevent this behavior. In addition, the Mylai massacre is consistent with the overall effort to "deny" the National Liberation Front its base of support among the civilian population of Vietnam, by the assassination of civilians alleged to be NLF cadres (from December 1967 to December 1968, 18,393 such civilians were killed in the Phoenix Operation), by fire-bomb zone attacks against villages in NFL-held territory, defoliation and crop destruction, and by search-and-destroy missions that involved the destruction of the homes and villages of many thousand Vietnamese civilians. It is estimated by the U.S. Senate Subcommittee on Refugees, chaired by Senator Edward Kennedy, that over 300,000 South Vietnamese civilians have been killed since the beginning of the war, mainly by U.S. air strikes and artillery. Such a figure represents a number six times as great as American war dead and suggests the indiscriminate use of weapons against the very people that the U.S. government contends it is fighting the war to protect.

The massacre at Mylai stands out as a landmark atrocity in the history of warfare, and its occurrence represents a moral challenge to the entire American society. This challenge was summarized by Mrs. Anthony Meadlow, the mother of David Paul Meadlow, one of the soldiers at Mylai, in a simple sentence: "I sent them a good boy, and they made him a murderer" (*New York Times*, November 30, 1969). Another characteristic statement about the general character of the war was attributed to an army staff sergeant: "We are at war with the ten-year-old children. It may not be humanitarian, but that's what it's like" (*New York Times*, December 1, 1969).

III. Personal Responsibility in Light of Mylai

The massacre at Mylai raises two broad sets of issues about personal responsibility for the commission of war crimes: The legal scope of personal responsiblity for a specific act or pattern of belligerent conduct and the extralegal scope of personal responsibility of citizens in relation to war crimes and to varying degrees of participation in an illegal war.

1) The War Criminal: Scope of Responsibility. We have already suggested that evidence exists that many official battlefield policies relied upon by the United States in Vietnam amount to war crimes. These official policies should be investigated in light of the legal obligations of the United States and if found to be "illegal" then these policies should be ceased forthwith and those responsible for the policy and its execution should be prosecuted as war criminals by appropriate tribunals. These remarks definitely apply to the follow-

ing war policies, and very likely to others: 1) the
Phoenix Program, 2) aerial and naval bombardment of
undefended villages, 3) destruction of crops and forests,
4) "search-and-destroy" missions, 5) "harassment and
interdiction" fire, 6) forcible removal of civilian population, 7) reliance on a variety of weapons prohibited by
treaty. In addition, allegations of all war atrocities
should be investigated and reported upon. These atrocities—committed in defiance of declared official policy—should be punished. Responsibility should be imposed upon those who inflicted the harm, upon those
who gave direct orders, and upon those who were in a
position of command entrusted with overall battlefield
decorum and with the prompt detection and punishment of war crimes committed within the scope of their
authority.

Finally, political leaders who authorized illegal battlefield practices and policies, or who had knowledge of
these practices and policies and failed to act are
similarly responsible for the commission of war crimes.
The following paragraph from the Majority Judgment of
the Tokyo War Crimes Tribunal is relevant:

A member of a Cabinet which collectively, as
one of the principal organs of the Government, is
responsible for the care of prisoners is not absolved
from responsibility if, having knowledge of the
commission of the crimes in the sense already
discussed, and omitting or failing to secure the
taking of measures to prevent the commission of
such crimes in the future, he elects to continue as a
member of the Cabinet. This is the position even
though the Department of which he has the charge
is not directly concerned with the care of prisoners. A Cabinet member may resign. If he has

knowledge of ill-treatment of prisoners, is power-less to prevent future ill-treatment, but elects to remain in the Cabinet thereby continuing to participate in its collective responsibility for pro-tection of prisoners he willingly assumes responsi-bility for any ill-treatment in the future.

Army or Navy commanders can, by order, secure proper treatment and prevent ill-treatment of prisoners. So can Ministers of War and of the Navy. If crimes are committed against prisoners under their control, of the likely occurrence of which they had, or should have had knowledge in advance, they are responsible for those crimes. If, for example, it be shown that within the units under his command conventional war crimes have been committed of which he knew or should have known, a commander who takes no adequate steps to prevent the occurrence of such crimes in the future will be responsible for such future crimes.

The United States government was directly associated with the development of a broad conception of criminal responsibility for the leadership of a state during war. A leader must take affirmative acts to prevent war crimes or dissociate himself from the government. If he fails to do one or the other, then by the very act of remaining in a government of a state guilty of war crimes, he becomes a war criminal.

Finally, as both the Nuremberg and the Tokyo Judgments emphasize, a government official is a war criminal if he has participated in the initiation or execution of an illegal war of aggression. There are considerable grounds for regarding the United States involvement in the Vietnam War—wholly apart from the conduct of the war—as involving the violation of the

United Nations Charter and other treaty obligations of
the United States. If U.S. participation in the war is
found illegal, then the policy-makers responsible for the
war during its various stages would be subject to
prosecution as alleged war criminals.

2) Responsibility as a Citizen. The idea of prosecuting
war criminals involves using international law as a sword
against violators in the military and civilian hierarchy of
government. But the Nuremberg Principles imply a
broader human responsibility to oppose an illegal war
and illegal methods of warfare. There is nothing to
suggest that the ordinary citizen, whether within or
outside the armed forces, is potentially guilty of a war
crime merely as a consequence of such a status. But
there are grounds to maintain that anyone who believes
or has reason to believe that a war is being waged in
violation of minimal canons of law and morality has an
obligation of conscience to resist participation in and
support of that war effort by every means at his
disposal. In this respect, the Nuremberg Principles
provide guidelines for citizens' conscience and a shield
that can and should be used in the domestic legal system
to interpose obligations under international law between
the government and the society. Such a doctrine of
interposition has been asserted in a large number of
selective service cases by individuals refusing to enter
the armed forces.

The issue of personal conscience is raised for everyone in the United States. It is raised more directly for
anyone called upon to serve in the armed forces. It is
raised in a special way for parents of minor children
who are conscripted into the armed forces. It is raised
for all taxpayers whose payments are used to support
the cost of the war effort. It is raised for all citizens who

in various ways endorse the war policies of the government. The circle of responsibility is drawn around all who have or should have knowledge of the illegal and immoral character of the war. The Mylai massacre puts every American on notice as to the character of the war. The imperatives of personal responsibility call upon each of us to search for effective means to bring the war to an immediate end.

And the circle of responsibility does not end at the border. Foreign governments and their populations are pledged by the Charter of the United Nations to oppose aggression and to take steps to punish the commission of war crimes. The cause of peace is indivisible, and all those governments and people concerned with Charter obligations have a legal and moral duty to oppose the continuation of the American involvement in Vietnam and to support the effort to identify, prohibit and punish the commission of war crimes. The conscience of the entire world community is implicated by inaction, as well as by more explicit forms of support for U.S. policy.

IV. Final Questions

Some may say that war crimes have been committed by both sides in Vietnam and, therefore, prosecution should be evenhanded, and that North Vietnam and the Provisional Revolutionary Government of South Vietnam should be called upon to prosecute their officials guilty of war crimes. Such a contention needs to be understood, however, in the overall context of the war, especially in relation to the identification of which side is the victim of aggression and which side is the aggressor. More narrowly, the allegation of war crimes by the other side does not operate as a legal defense against a war crimes indictment. This question was clearly litigated and decided at Nuremberg.

Others have argued that there can be no war crimes in Vietnam because war has never been "declared" by the U.S. government.

The failure to declare war under these circumstances raises a substantial constitutional question, but it has no bearing upon the rights and duties of the United States under international law. A declaration of war is a matter of internal law, but the existence of combat circumstances is a condition of war that brings into play the full range of obligations under international law governing the conduct of a war.

V. Conclusion

This is a very tentative statement of some implications of the Mylai disclosures. These disclosures suggest wider responsibilities in relation to Mylai, in relation to other war practices in Vietnam, and in relation to the war itself. These responsibilities include the clarification and identification of what sorts of behavior make one subject to prosecution as a potential war criminal. These responsibilities also range beyond the idea of criminal liability to encompass all Americans and, indeed, all peoples and governments in the world. We call upon people everywhere to investigate the actions of the United States in Vietnam and to relate their conscience to these actions. Such is the full call to responsible action in the wake of the Mylai disclosures.

January 1970

FURTHER READING

Nuremberg and Vietnam: An American Tragedy (Chicago: Quadrangle, 1970) by Telford Taylor.

Against the Crime of Silence: Proceedings of the Russell International War Crimes Tribunal (Flanders, N.J.: O'Hare, 1968) edited by John Duffett.

Vietnam and International Law (Flanders, N.J.: O'Hare, revised edition 1968) by John H. E. Fried, Rapporteur, Consultative Council, Lawyers Committee on American Policy Towards Vietnam.

Crimes of War (New York: Random House, 1971) edited by Richard A. Falk, Gabriel Kolko and Robert Jay Lifton.

Lessons of Mylai

EDWARD M. OPTON, JR. and NEVITT SANFORD

Revelation of the Mylai massacre caused widespread initial shock and bewilderment. The public, the press and our colleagues have found this event very difficult to comprehend. War crimes are not something we have associated with Americans. The psychological tension caused by the poor fit between the facts and the expectations Americans have of themselves makes it possible that out of the charnel heap we may learn some lessons about ourselves. But if anything is to be learned, social scientists must have the moral courage both to learn and to teach.

We claim no unique knowledge about Mylai, but we do believe that facts long on record permit some reasonably certain elementary conclusions.

First, most of the explanations so far advanced are seriously lacking in credibility. They explain away rather than explain; they say in one way or another that

Mylai doesn't really count rather than acknowledge its significance.

Second, the most important fact about the massacre is that it was only slightly different from, and only a minor step beyond, standard, official, routine United States practices in Vietnam.

Third, the major responsibility and guilt for the massacre lie with the elected officials who make U.S. policy in Vietnam, and with the high military officials who have misled both elected officials and the general public as to what they have been doing under the name of those policy directives.

Fourth, America's citizens share in the responsibility for Mylai, for there has been available to all ample evidence that the United States has been committing large-scale war crimes in Vietnam. A will to disbelieve, a self-serving reluctance to know the truth, just plain indifference, as well as failings in our ethics and our educational system, have prevented our electorate from influencing politicians whose policies allow for crimes against humanity.

Fifth, little is to be gained, and perhaps much lost by attempts to force recognition of responsibility on those who now completely wash their hands of the blood of Mylai. But if we were to assume that no one can be stirred to action by atrocities such as Mylai, or if we fail to press for full and frank application of social science investigation of Mylai and other American war crimes, we would participate by passivity in the horror of America's Mylais, past and future.

Almost all public speculation on the massacre has begun with the assumption that Mylai was an isolated, uncharacteristic incident. The speculation therefore has been on what exceptional circumstances could have resulted in such a deviation from normality. "They must have gone beserk" is the most oversimplified of these kinds of speculation.

Explanations in terms of the hard fighting and casualties the men had experienced fall into this category. The facts are that many units have fought harder and longer, suffered more casualties, and lived under worse conditions than Company C, 1st Battalion, 20th Infantry, both in this and other wars. Uncomfortable and dangerous as the war in Vietnam is for our men, it is a great deal less uncomfortable and a great deal less dangerous for the typical soldier than was the Korean War, the Second World War or the First World War.

Efforts to find an explanation of the massacre in the personalities of the officers and enlisted men involved are likewise misdirected. Undoubtedly these men have their quirks and oddities, but so do all of us. No one has reported behavior of the officers or enlisted men before or after Mylai that smacks of abnormality. Parents of the men have rarely complained that their sons returned from Vietnam in any abnormal psychic state. The men are reported to have gone about their gruesome work for the most part with cool efficiency and tragic effectiveness. The fact that the accused officers and men did nothing to draw special attention to themselves in the months before and after the massacre indicates that they were not remarkably different from the run-of-the- -mill soldier. Genuine explanations of Mylai will require us to pay attention to the factors that lead ordinary men to do extraordinary things. The American tradition is to locate the source of evil deeds in evil men. We have yet to learn that the greatest evils occur when social systems give average men the task of routinizing evil.

Another kind of speculation on the causes of Mylai is

the reverse of those discussed above. "This kind of thing happens in war," it is said; "It's terrible, but you have to expect excesses in combat." Not so. There have been excesses in combat in every war, but we know of no direct parallel to the Mylai massacre by American troops in any recent war except the war in Vietnam. American troops characteristically have not lined up old men, old women, mothers, children and babies in front of ditches and shot them down. The massacre is most emphatically not the "kind of thing that happens" in recent American wars. The question for investigation is: In what ways is Mylai like the kinds of things that are done as a matter of routine in Vietnam?

The pattern of violence at Mylai does not resemble a riot or a mass psychosis. But it does have its counterparts in certain American history: genocidal attacks on American Indians in the nineteenth century and mass lynchings which persisted until the 1930s. Scientific studies of lynch mobs have shown that the members of such mobs are by no means berserk; rather theirs is an all-too-rational response to the encouragement, spoken or unspoken, of their community leaders. The attitudes of elected officials and leading members of the community are crucial in permitting lynchings; rarely if ever has a mob carried out a lynching when the community leadership truly opposed it. It is important that at Mylai, as at the mass lynchings of blacks and the genocide of the native Americans, the victims were of a different race.

It is official United States policy in Vietnam to obliterate not just whole villages, but whole districts and virtually whole provinces. At first, efforts were made to remove the inhabitants before "saving" the regions by destroying them, but the pressure of the vast numbers of refugees thus created (at least one-fourth of the entire rural population of South Vietnam) has led to policies even more genocidal. Jonathan and Orville Schell, writing in the *New York Times* of November 26, 1969, note:

... Experience in the Quang Ngai Province as journalists has led us to write this letter in hopes of dispelling two possible misapprehensions: that such executions are the fault of men like Calley and Mitchell alone, and that the tragedy of Mylai is an isolated atrocity.

We both spent several weeks in Quang Ngai some six months before the incident. We flew daily with the FACs (Forward Air Control). What we saw was a province utterly destroyed. In August 1967, during Operation Benton, the "pacification camps" became so full that army units in the field were ordered not to "generate" any more refugees.

The army complied. But search-and-destroy operations continued. Only now peasants were not warned before an air strike was called in on their village. They were killed in their villages because there was no room for them in the swamped pacification camps. The usual warnings by helicopter loudspeaker or air-dropped leaflets were stopped. Every civilian on the ground was assumed to be enemy by the pilots by nature of living in Quang Ngai, which was largely a free fire zone.

The pilots, servicemen not unlike Calley and Mitchell, continued to carry out their orders. Village after village was destroyed from the air as a matter of de facto policy. Air strikes on civilians became a matter of routine. It was under these circumstances of official acquiescence to the destruction of the countryside and its people that the massacre of Mylai occurred. Such atrocities were and are the logical consequences of a war directed against an enemy indistinguishable from the people.

The genocidal policy is carried out in other ways as well. One of us, Opton, has personally accompanied a routine operation in which Cobra helicopters fired 20-mm. cannons into the houses of a typical village in NLF-controlled territory. They also shot the villagers who ran out of the houses. This was termed "prepping the area" by the United States lieutenant colonel who directed the operation. "We sort of shoot it up to see if anything moves," he explained, and he added by way of reassurance that this treatment was perfectly routine.

It is official United States policy to establish "free fire zones" and "kill zones" where anything that moves is fired upon. Although in the original theory these were zones from which civilians had been removed, it has long been well known that "free fire zones" now include very wide areas of the country, areas that include many inhabited villages. It is official United States policy to destroy the Vietnamese people's stockpiles of rice in NLF-influenced areas, thus starving the women and children (the armed men, we may be sure, provide themselves with the undestroyed portion of the rice harvest), and it is official, though secret, policy to destroy rice and other crops with chemical defoliants.

Official United States policy long ago gave up the idea of gaining the allegiance of the people of Vietnam. "Winning the hearts and minds" is now maintained only as a public relations product for consumption on the home market. In Vietnam itself the policy is, as explained to one of us by a Marine officer, "If you've got them by the balls, the hearts and minds will follow." Getting the villagers by the balls means bombing and shelling them from their villages, assassinating their leaders, breaking up their families by removing the men and removing the rural population to concentration camps euphemistically called "refugee camps." All these official policies involve killing, and killing on a large scale. It is routine policy to talk about what we are doing in euphemisms like "population control," "prepping the area" and so forth. And it is standard practice to talk about the Vietnamese people in depersonalized terms, like "gooks," "slopes" and "dinks." This makes it easier to kill civilians—knowingly, routinely and massively.

The euphemisms and the depersonalization may enable headquarters personnel, the politicians above them and the American public to pretend that large-scale killing of civilians does not occur, but the troops in the field know better. The furor over the Mylai massacre must seem to them grimly illogical. As the satirist Art Hoppe puts in in the *San Francisco Chronicle*, "The best way [to kill civilians], it's generally agreed, is to kill them with bombs, rockets, artillery shells and napalm. Those who kill women and children in these ways are called heroes. . . ." How is it, the foot soldier must wonder, that "to kill women and children at less than 500 paces is an atrocity; at more than 500 paces, it's an act of heroism"?

The official policy that results in large-scale killing of civilians through impersonal, long-distance weapons is matched by an official practice of inaction to reduce the cumulatively large-scale killing of civilians in thousands of individual, personal atrocities: dropping civilians out of helicopters and killing civilians by torture during interrogations, picking off civilians in their rice paddies in the large areas where anything that moves is "officially" considered an enemy, killing civilians for sport, "plinking" at them from passing air and land vehicles, and so on. These small-scale war crimes have become so common that our reporters have stopped reporting them; they are no longer "news." They have become routine to many of our soldiers, too; and the soldiers, to preserve their equilibrium, have developed the classical psychological methods of justifying what they see happening. The soldier comes to think of the Vietnamese not as a human like himself, nor even, as the army charge against Lt. Calley puts it, an "Oriental human being," but as something less than human. It is only a small further step to the conclusion that "the only good dink is a dead dink," as Specialist 4 James Farmer, Company C, Fourth Battalion, Third Infantry, 198th Infantry Brigade, American Division, expressed it to the *New York Times* (as reported in the *San Francisco Chronicle* of December 1, 1969).

The foot soldier in Vietnam sees Specialist Farmer's conclusion acted out daily—by air, by artillery, by quick death in a napalm holocaust, by slow death in a foodless, waterless "refugee camp" and by the unpunished examples of his fellow soldiers cutting down a civilian here, a family there. "The only good dink is a dead dink" is in the wind in Vietnam, and the soldier doesn't need to be a weatherman to know which way the wind blows. In that official and quasi-official "climate" the Mylai massacre logically represents no major deviation. The massacre was a minor embellishment on established policy and practice. We believe it would be hypocritical self-righteousness to condemn the men who committed a minor embellishment without condemning those who set the criminal policy itself.

Our elected officials and their appointed advisors

have special knowledge and considerable freedom of choice, and they have taken it upon themselves to act as our leaders; we therefore have the right and the duty to hold them personally responsible for the ignorance, insensibility, lack of human understanding and poor judgment they have displayed in shaping our Vietnam policy. Especially deserving of blame are those officials who knew that policies were wrong but found it expedient to remain silent, rather than endanger their careers or risk the ill will of their "teammates." This, discouragingly enough, might hold for the great majority of senators who voted for the Tonkin Gulf resolution. The very one-sidedness of that vote was enough to indicate that senators were not using their heads in our behalf but were more or less automatically displaying their anti-Communist valor. That vote by itself was clear evidence that we were embarking on a crusade of the totally good, peace-loving people—ourselves—against the totally evil.

There is ample evidence that high officials in our government have participated fully in the practice of portraying the "other side" as an aggregate of evil demons. This imagery has become so prominent and routine in official pronouncements, and in the media, that only people with some determination to think for themselves can resist adopting it as a matter of course. Among high officials, as among the general public, the dehumanization of "the enemy" tends to spread, so that now those who dare to demonstrate against our Vietnam policy are called "parasites," "goats" and "creeps" by the vice president.

Readers of *The Authoritarian Personality* recognized in Mr. Agnew's "impudent snob" speech a textbook manifestation of modern totalitarianism. It is common enough for a "hard-hitting" political speech to contain numerous references to tendencies the speaker's constituents are known to be against, but it is decidely uncommon in America for a high official to display the whole characteristic pattern of totalitarian ideas and images. Why should a man who stereotypes and distantiates people unlike himself in ethnic background and social class also wish to punish people who deviate from narrow norms of sexual behavior? And why should a man who does these things also wish to suppress intellectuals? The answer lies in the story of the development of authoritarianism—in an individual or in a culture. Social scientists have an obligation to tell this story, to point to manifestations and the implications of totalitarianism in high places as well as in low.

The implications of public utterances like those of the vice president are not hard to discover. "I think," a 19-year-old infantryman told Helen Emmerich of the *San Francisco Examiner*, "someone ought to kill those long-haired, queer bastards back in the world. Anyone who demonstrates against the war ought to be lined up and killed, just like any gook here." We know from personal experience that this is not an uncommon sentiment.

At the same time, it must be admitted that "the government has fallen into the hands of men;" in other words, that decisions on national policy are made by men who are all too human and that their behavior is often heavily influenced by unrecognized group-psychological processes. We know this from Arthur Schlesinger, Jr.'s and Theodore Sorensen's accounts of the meetings to decide on the Bay of Pigs invasion, and from James Thompson's and Townsend Hoopes' writings about decisions to escalate the Vietnam war. Social scientists can make an important contribution by carrying out such analyses and disseminating their knowledge.

If some of us are disposed to blame our elected officials for wrong policies in Vietnam, these officials are quick enough to pass the responsibility back to the general public, pointing to opinion polls and silent majorities that favor these policies. These officials have a good point. We as a people do bear much of the responsibility for Mylai. The guilt is in large part collective. It can certainly be argued that the massacre would not have happened had our soldiers not been brought up in a culture in which racism and a Manichaean approach to international relations are deeply rooted. It is quite possible that a larger number, perhaps a critically larger number, of the soldiers would have refused to take part in the massacre had they not been raised on a psychic diet of television violence, which almost every day of their lives impressed its lesson of the cheapness of life. Few of us, social scientists or not, have done much that was personally inconvenient to discover or to fight against either the root sources or the proximal causes of Mylai. Yet the case is certainly different with those citizens who have opposed the war than it is with those who have favored it; and those who have reluctantly given assent are in a different psychological situation from those who have participated vicariously in "body counts" and the "victories." There are in other words different degrees of actual responsibility and of potentiality for feelings of guilt.

Some light is shed on these matters by a survey of reaction to Mylai carried out by one of us with the assistance of students and staff members of the Wright Institute. Almost all of those interviewed coped with the news of the massacre by minimizing its emotional import, either by outright denial that a massacre occurred, or by self-reassurance that such massacres are after all routine, or by justification of the massacre, or by pointing to mitigating circumstances. "Hawks" used the more extreme of these defensive mental maneuvers more often than "doves," but even the latter tried, most often with ominous success, to remain emotionally unruffled. And, in striking parallel to Morris Janowitz's study of German reactions to Nazi war crimes, no one extended the scope of responsibility to himself or to the American people in general. In the America that chose Richard Nixon as leader, as in Hitler's Germany, the silent majority are determined to engross themselves in their private lives; they resist knowing the unpleasant facts about Vietnam; they find it both comforting and effortless to put their trust in their leaders.

Is there any point in focusing on responsibility and guilt in the face of massive resistance to dwelling on these matters? We believe that there is. We must make sure that as many people as possible know the truth and are guided by it. Unless a substantial number of people who can speak and write with authority strive to keep the evil of Mylai and of the larger policy of which it is an expression before the public, it is hard to see what will prevent our military from persisting in genocide in Vietnam and in future Vietnams.

But dealing with this guilt-laden subject will not be easy, for guilt that is on the edge of consciousness can lead to further destructiveness more easily than to contrition. Charles Manson, the alleged leader of the group accused of the Sharon Tate murders, seeing that his followers were shaken after their night's work, reportedly insisted that they commit more murders the next night. This psychological stratagem was used regularly in the Nazis' training of the SS. Efforts to induce consciousness of guilt in people who lack the inner strength to bear it can backfire, evoking behavior that relieves queasiness by demonstrating that what is feared can be done, even more and worse, without catastrophic consequences to oneself.

Public breast-beating, whether self-flagellation or condemnation of everyone except oneself, is probably futile at best and a dangerous indulgence at worst. Constructive handling of feelings about Mylai will require attention to what we can do to prevent future Mylais, to end the Vietnam war and to block the next Vietnam.

Social scientists in particular need not be part of a silent majority as, with rare exceptions, we so far have been. Psychologists can make themselves heard in investigating what makes some killing psychologically "close" and shocking, while the same death by bomb or shell is a matter of indifference. Sociologists have not yet reported on the structural aspects of the military reward system that insures that almost all war crimes remain unreported. Economists can calculate and publicize the enormous indirect costs of the war, such as disability pensions and survivor benefits that will continue into the twenty-first century. Historians could try to make the public aware of the nearly fatal effects of the Indochinese and Algerian wars on French democracy. Survey researchers, psychiatrists and clinical psychologists could assay the extent of long-lasting alienation and anomie among returned Vietnam veterans. The social sciences could join together in examining the pervasive distortion in information as it passes up and down the chain of military and civilian command, and how this distortion is used to justify and rationalize mass murder.

The psychology, sociology, economics and history of colonial wars particularly deserve more attention. One of the most insidious arguments for continuation of the Vietnam war is the proposition that termination in less than victory would produce a massive political backlash. We would do well to study and to make much better known the French experience after the Algerian war and the British experience following their withdrawals from India and from Suez. For that matter, it would be well to study some of our own retreats from political-military intervention abroad. President Nixon professedly fears being the first American president to "lose a war," but retreat is not "losing" and this historical fact must be made a psychological reality if we are to extricate ourselves from the Vietnam morass. Backing out of rather important military interventions—for example, the Bay of Pigs, the expeditionary force sent to Russia in 1919, etc.—has not sapped the will, ruined the economy or spoiled the society of the United States in the past; and these bugaboos, which are within the legitimate subject matter of the social sciences, need to be expunged from our minds. That will take work.

Funding such work will be difficult, but if social scientists think the work is important enough, they can find the means of sponsorship and support. There are times when to know and to remain silent is to be an accomplice. One of the lessons of Mylai is that silence in the face of such human disaster can no longer be an acceptable form of professional response.

March 1970

FURTHER READING

My Lai 4 (New York: Random House, 1970) by Seymour M. Hersh.

"Lessons on Mylai" by Edward M. Opton, Jr. in *Toward Social Change: A Handbook for Those Who Will* (New York: Harper & Row, 1971) edited by Robert Buckhout et al.

ALTERNATIVES IN GREAT POWER INTERACTION

The Brezhnev-Johnson
Two-World Doctrine

EDWARD WEISBAND and THOMAS M. FRANCK

In August 1968, the Soviet Union and its Warsaw Pact allies invaded the Socialist Republic of Czechoslovakia. Thirty years after this brave people had been betrayed by Britain and France and attacked by Hitler, the streets of Prague, one of Europe's classically beautiful cities, were once again lined with tanks and occupying military forces, which again included, to make the irony more poignant, troops from East Germany.

The invasion came unexpectedly. Observers in the West, exhilarated by Alexander Dubcek's attempt to impose a human face on socialism, watched closely as he tried to placate the Soviet Politburo at meetings in Cierna and at Bratislava. They were relieved when it seemed that he had succeeded in forging a modus vivendi with the Russians. But the excitement within and outside of Czechoslovakia generated by this for once genuine experiment in socialist democracy was short-lived. The Warsaw Pact invasion of August 20-21 crushed the visions and hopes of virtually all the Czechs including even pro-Soviet elements and in so doing unified them.

For a week after the invasion, this traditionally divided nation displayed a degree of discipline, will, courage and solidarity which eventually dismayed the soldiers of the occupying armies. Russian commanders had to replace a number of soldiers in the advanced units who had broken under the pressure brought to bear by the Czechs. Some soldiers were reported by the Prague underground to have been seen crying in a fit of almost total psychological disintegration. One was known to have committed suicide.

The forces that spearheaded the invasion had been briefed that the invasion was necessary to prevent Nazi revanchists aided by imperialistic capitalists from taking over Czechoslovakia. The Russians went so far as to publicize the discovery of a cache of weapons in a sewer which they imputed to be evidence of the machinations of the CIA. The occupying troops came prepared, therefore, to root out the U.S.-inspired, German re-vanchist conspiracy against Czechoslovakia. After they arrived, however, the Czechs made it abundantly clear that they perceived the Warsaw Pact powers as oppres-sors. The original rationale for the invasion thus broke down and with it many soldiers who took to senseless shooting during the night. As *Lidova Demokracie,* one of the many underground newspapers spontaneously published during the first week of the occupation, reported on August 26, 1968, "The night belongs to the occupiers, to their helpless rage; the day belongs to the people of Prague."

During that entire week following the invasion, the

Czechs deliberately set about preventing any action that might be misconstrued as the work of revanchists. At the behest of the underground, liquor, for example, was not readily sold in order to prevent anyone from undertaking a foolhardy provocation against the Warsaw Pact forces. Czech youth removed the swastikas that they had put up in protest against the Soviet Union, lest the occupying armies came to regard this as evidence of Nazi activity. Free Radio Prague, the voice of the underground, was called upon on several occasions to deny rumors that Dubcek had been killed. "It is probably a provocation aimed at inciting people to react violently against the occupiers," the Radio observed.

The reasoning behind this self-control was straightforward: the Soviets must be given no basis for legitimating the occupation. Throughout the resistance, the Czechs tried to prevent the Warsaw Pact powers from deriving any justification for their invasion on the basis of what the Czechs were doing. The Czech underground reasoned that any direct confrontation with the Soviet Union and its Warsaw Pact allies would be futile and would, on the contrary, tend to lend greater credence to Soviet contentions that reactionary elements were at work in Prague. So the word went out to resist, but to resist passively.

And it almost worked. The Soviets invaded apparently believing that a collaborationist regime would quickly emerge from the ranks of the Central Committee of the Czechoslovakian Communist Party (CCP), one that would claim that it was the legitimate government, reject the Dubcek reforms, and assert that it called the Warsaw Pact powers to save Czechoslovakia. Although the Strougal-Indra-Bilak faction of hard-core pro-Soviet hardliners inside the Czechoslovakian government cheered the invasion, they were insufficient to provide the proper semblance of legitimacy. Thus it is true to say that the vast majority of the Central Committee of the CCP remained faithful to the people at this moment of history.

The resistance was nonetheless doomed. The story of what broke its back is well known. Czech power could last only as long as Czech unity. In the end, the people were demoralized, not by Soviet tanks, but by Dubcek's and President Svoboda's capitulation to Soviet demands. The Soviets broke Dubcek by force. Svoboda they broke by holding Dubcek ransom in Moscow. It was not the same Dubcek who returned to Prague; his compromise, even in the name of avoiding the worst, led to the disintegration of the resistance and the passing of the Prague Spring.

But Czech discipline helped to win a moral victory which, although it may seem meaningless to them in the context of their daily lives today, could not be destroyed by Soviet tanks. The Soviets could not make credible their excuse that they were invading Czechoslovakia to prevent revanchist elements from taking over in Prague. They therefore had to develop new concepts to justify the action of the Warsaw Pact powers in the eyes of the world. In this situation they enunciated the so-called Brezhnev "doctrine of limited sovereignty" which, like all verbal strategy, seeks to locate state conduct in the context of principles which will advance national interests. Significantly, our government, although perhaps unwittingly, played a key role in devising the Brezhnev principles. We promulgated them and applied them in relation to states within "our" regional bloc, Latin America, and thereby perhaps signaled the Soviets that we were prepared to accept their reciprocal application of such principles against the states within "their" region—Eastern Europe.

The Brezhnev doctrine, which continues to govern the policies of the Warsaw Pact governments, to some degree represents a trade-off or division of the world by the Soviet Union and the United States into spheres of influence or "regional ghettos." Not that our policy-makers in Washington planned it that way: little or no evidence has been adduced to show that the U.S. government ever willfully intended to trade control over Latin America for recognition of absolute Soviet dominance over Eastern Europe. Nor can it be said that any actions we have taken in relation to Latin America are the same as Russia's brutal suppression of Czechoslovakia. It is not the purpose of this chapter to obfuscate the difference between our relations to Latin America and those of the Soviet Union toward Eastern Europe. What we do wish to assert is that virtually every concept of the Brezhnev doctrine can be traced to an earlier arrogation of identical rights by the United States vis-à-vis Latin America. The Brezhnev doctrine faithfully echoes official U.S. pronouncements made during the covert "CIA-engineered" overthrow of the government of Guatemala in 1954, during the Cuban missile crisis of 1962 and during the U.S. invasion of the Dominican Republic of 1965. When the Soviets resorted to the doctrine of limited sovereignty to explain their ending of the Prague Spring, *they* were able to claim, credibly, that the principles upon which they were acting were those we ourselves had devised to justify our conduct in the Americas. This deprived Americans of the right to point the finger at Russia, thereby, we believe, lowering the political and moral costs to the Soviet Union of the Czechoslovak invasion. If one finds ugly or distasteful the rule under which the Dubcek regime was eliminated by Soviet aggressive might, it is important to realize that the search for new norms in the world must begin with a clear understanding that we, as much as the Russians, bear responsibility for conceptualizing the Brezhnev norms.

This is not to suggest that the adoption on the part of the Soviet Union of the Brezhnev doctrine caused them to invade Czechoslovakia. Quite clearly, the Soviet Politburo made its strategic determination which indicated that the benefits from their point of view justified the costs. We do wish to assert, however, that had the United States not placed itself hostage to a similar set of principles in relation to its ghetto in the years prior to 1968, the costs as perceived by the Soviet leadership may have been higher. Indeed, given the fact that the Soviet Politburo was as divided in its decision to invade Czechoslovakia as it was, such costs may have indeed been prohibitive. As it was, the Soviet Union was merely acting in a way supportive of the system which our verbal strategy to some extent had helped to create. Having said this, moreover, we do not wish to be misconstrued as saying that what the United States did in the Dominican Republic is the operative cause of the Soviet suppression of Czechoslovakia. Coincidence is not causality, nor does congruence necessarily reflect meaningful correlation. The political factors which have constructed the dual ghetto system are far more complex than the adoption of certain enunciated concepts. But we do claim, however, that the United States employed an inflated rhetoric to justify its actions in relation to Latin America which the Soviets adopted when they decided to invade Czechoslovakia; that our verbal strategy helped to create an international system where such invasions on the part of superpowers were the rule rather than the exception; that the Soviets quite possibly realized this when they opted for invasion.

Finally, it is important to note that our concept of verbal strategy differs from other approaches to verbal behavior in that it proposes the planned, deliberate development and use of principles, concepts and enunciated norms as a conscious part of the conduct of foreign policy. This does not imply the retrospective use of fanciful apologia for acts already decided upon, nor does it suggest propaganda. Rather, verbal strategy, like other aspects of foreign policy decision-making, introduces into the weighing of policy options an awareness that actions taken must also be explained and that the explanation may be, in the long run, more costly or more beneficial to the national interest than the act itself. No action should ever be undertaken without assessing the long-run strategic and systemic costs and benefits of what is said to explain and justify the action. Verbal strategy, in other words, requires the same careful planning as any other aspect of strategy for the achievement of national goals. Before an option is chosen, before a verbal strategy is decided upon, its short-, medium- and long-term effects should be estimated. Such prediction, in turn, involves an effort to predetermine the effect of one's proposed verbal strategy on all the other players in the game and particularly on one's principal opponent.

It is useful, therefore, to outline the norms or principles contained in the Brezhnev doctrine and to compare these against the assertions of our own policymakers towards Latin America. This is not a pleasant task. The underlying purpose, however, is to stress the significance of verbal strategy in defining the actions of superpowers, that is, the importance of listening to ourselves as if we were the enemy speaking.

On September 25, 1968, *Pravda* published an article entitled "Sovereignty and International Duties of Socialist Countries." This article, representing the first public declaration of the Brezhnev doctrine asserts the following six legal principles or norms of state conduct:

☐ A nation member of a regional or ideological community cannot ever be withdrawn or withdraw itself from that community's jurisdiction;

☐ The community may impose norms of behavior in the realm of domestic policy and foreign policy on its members. These norms set out the basic standards of conduct which must be followed by all the members in order that the community and its prevailing sociopolitical system can survive and the security of its members can be protected against its opponents. These norms constitute an obligatory duty of membership in the community;

☐ Whether a member of the community is living up to these normative obligations in any given instance is determined by the other members of the community, and not by the unilateral self-determination of any single member;

☐ If the other members determine that one member is in dereliction of its duties, they may use military force to alter the policies and government of the delinquent. Such use of force is not aggression but rather the opposite: collective self-defense, an action in which the community organization is defending itself, its sacrosanct collective integrity, against the encroachment of an alien ideology;

☐ In particular, any socioeconomic or political doctrine

or system which varies from the one exclusively established in the community is by definition alien, and its espousal, even by the citizens and government of a member of the community, in effect constitutes foreign subversion of, and aggression against, the community in response to which collective force may be used in self-defense;

□ The territory of a member-state of the community may be invaded by the armies of the other states acting collectively under the treaty of the community in response to a summons by any persons the community designates as loyalist "leaders" of the invaded state, even though these are not recognized as the legal government of that state even by the other members of the community.

The Brezhnev doctrine maintains the right of a regional grouping to proscribe certain ideologies as being alien and to require on the part of each of its members rigid acceptance of regional norms. To do otherwise is to risk forceful intervention by the regional family in the name of collective defense. Capitalism, for example, is an alien ideology, the mere partial acceptance of which in any country in Eastern Europe constitutes aggression against the entire Warsaw Pact. According to *Pravda,* Czechoslovakia "is responsible not only to its own people, but also to all the socialist countries." As a "socialist state" Czechoslovakia's sovereignty cannot be exercised in a way "opposed to the interests of the world of socialism" because a socialist country's sovereignty is subject to the norms of the socialist community. Therefore, no socialist state should expect to rely on such international legal concepts as self-determination, coexistence or the right not to be coerced by other states. "When a danger arises to socialism itself in the particular country," when "anti-socialist and revisionist elements . . . under the guise of 'democratization' . . . befog the minds of the masses, stealthily hatching a counter-revolutionary coup," when a socialist state permits "encroachment on the foundations of socialism, on the basic principles of Marxism-Leninism," then the socialist community must act jointly to protect the sovereignty of that member of the community. It is for the socialist community and not just for the government of Czechoslovakia, to determine when Czechoslovak freedom, which is to say its socialist orthodoxy, is endangered; it is for the community to decide when to react with force. To protect

the principles of proletarian internationalism, the Soviet Union and the other socialist countries have undertaken joint actions for the defense of the achievements of socialism in fraternal Czechoslo-vakia . . . against the encroachments of domestic and foreign enemies . . . and toward insuring the conditions for the free development of a sovereign socialist country.

Such an action on the part of the socialist community is not illegal, *Pravda* argues, because the ordinary yardstick of international law does not apply within the community. When Czechoslovakia was found by the other members of the socialist community to be in danger of drifting into alien heresy, then the community had the right to use force to save Czechoslovak socialism and the community's solidarity. The rescuing Warsaw Pact troops arrived, Soviet apologists argued, in the nick of time to preserve freedom and democracy:

The anti-socialist forces in Czechoslovakia, which worked systematically for months to undermine the prestige of the Communist Party and to deprive it of its leading role, created a situation which could have led to the restoration of capitalism in Czechoslovakia and a reorientation of her foreign policy.

It was not that all the Czech leaders were a part of this conspiracy. Rather, the problem was that some did not recognize the power and the subtlety of the forces of counterrevolution which were threatening to displace them and to transform de-Stalinization into de-socialization. Such action, furthermore, by the community is purely an internal family matter and not open to international scrutiny. When certain members of the United Nations sought to take up the matter in the Security Council, they were firmly rebuffed by Soviet Representative Malik:

> The events taking place in Czechoslovakia are a matter for the Czechoslovak people and the States of the socialist community, linked together as they are by common responsibilities, and are a matter for them alone.... None of them has asked for a meeting of the Security Council, not only because they regard it as unnecessary in the present circumstances but also because they consider the matter as lying outside the purview of the Security Council.

In the Soviet view, regional determinations and prerogatives take precedence over those of the international community including the United Nations. These points represent the essence of the Brezhnev doctrine.

The news of the Warsaw Pact nations' invasion of Czechoslovakia, as Secretary of State Rusk said, "sent a shock wave of indignation and apprehension around the world." The United States reacted with proper indignation at this blatant violation of human dignity and international law. "The cynicism of the Kremlin move, made in violation of the most elementary canons of international law," the *New York Times* declared on the morning of the invasion, "is underlined by the bare-faced hypocrisy of the *Tass* claim that the invasion was made at the request of Czechoslovak Government and Communist Party leaders." President Johnson spoke for all humanity when he said, "The tragic news from Czechoslovakia shocks the conscience of the world." Richard Nixon, then campaigning for the presidency, described the Soviet action as "an outrage against the conscience of the world." In the United Nations, the U.S. delegate to the U.N. Special Committee on Principles of International Law, Herbert Reis, strongly rebutted the concept that a socialist "community" has special rights to act with force against a delinquent unable or unwilling to redress a situation regarded by the other members as a dereliction of the duties and norms of membership. He reminded the committee that

the charter governs the relations between all member states, including Eastern European states. These countries are entitled to charter rights and the observance of charter duties in their relations among themselves. . . . From a legal point of view, there is no basis for asserting that the relationships of the Eastern European states among themselves are the concern of that group of states alone.

What U.N. Representative Reis, Secretary of State Rusk, President Johnson, candidate Richard Nixon, even the editorial board of the *New York Times* were not prepared to see or admit was that these principles had originated in Washington.

It was the United States which first insisted on the right of a geographical or ideological grouping to demand orthodox conformity to the regional norms as determined by us; it was spokesmen for the U.S.

government that first claimed the right to exclude the United Nations from participating actively in intra-regional disputes.

What has been described by the *New York Times* as "The CIA-engineered revolution against the Communist-oriented President of Guatemala, Jacobo Arbenz Guzman," began in mid-June 1954. A particular feature of this "revolution"—aside from the clandestine role of the United States—was the manner in which the regional system of the Americas was utilized to legitimate aggression against the Arbenz regime and to run interference against the United Nations.

Shortly before the commencement of the actual operation against Guatemala from bases in adjacent Nicaragua and Honduras—operations which included bombing of Guatemalan cities by American planes with American pilots—the stage was set by the Tenth Inter-American Conference which met at Caracas, Venezuela, from March 1 to 28, 1955. At this meeting of American foreign ministers, according to the State Department

> One of the principal objectives of the United States delegation... headed by Secretary Dulles, was to achieve maximum agreement among the American Republics upon a clear-cut and unmistakable policy determination against the intervention of international communism in the hemisphere, recognizing the continuing threat which it poses to their peace and security and declaring their intention to take effective measures, individually and collectively, to combat it.

Here we find for the first time the idea that communism, as an alien ideology, constitutes aggression against the entire Inter-American system whenever and wherever it appears in the Western Hemisphere, and that the American states have a duty to take collective and individual measures to defend the system against it. The double-think runs like this: communism is aggression: its very presence within a Latin American government constitutes an act of intervention by a foreign power— the Soviet Union against the entire hemisphere. It follows that an attack on Guatemala is self-defense if it saves the Guatemalan people from their leftist regime. Thus a new principle asserted itself: a regional organization may designate a particular socio-political ideology as alien to the region. At the urging of the United States the Inter-American Conference also declared that "international communism, by its antidemocratic nature and its interventionist tendency, is incompatible with the concept of American freedom"; that "the activities of the international communist movement" constitutes "intervention in American affairs"; and that these communist activities are invariably pursued "in the interests of an alien despotism."

To remove any lingering doubt, the U.S. Senate on June 25, 1954, at the actual time of the so-called Guatemalan revolution, passed Concurrent Resolution 91. This found

> strong evidence of intervention by the international Communist movement in the State of Guatemala, whereby government institutions have been infiltrated by Communist agents, weapons of war have been secretly shipped into that country, and the pattern of Communist conquest has become manifest.

The term *conquest* in this context is particularly significant, as no overt change in Guatemalan government had occurred since 1944, and no foreign bases or troops had been located there. What matters, however, is not whether the allegations made in Congressional Resolution 91 were true or those contained in the Warsaw Letter were false. The nub of the matter is, surely, whether any regional system should have the right to require nations in the region to conform to its norms on pain of having its national deviation, first, judged, by other states in the family, then, treated as an act of aggression against the system and, finally, eradicated by collective self-defense of the region. Congress, and the Caracas Conference, came close, for the first time, to answering the question affirmatively.

The Guatemalan revolution caused us to propound another important new principle. In those days of June 1954, there arose the first occasion to test in practice the uneasy balance between the primacy of regional and world organization. As soon as hostilities had begun, Guatemala, despite an earlier, tentative approach to the Organization of American States, appealed to the United Nations Security Council for observers to investigate the source of the aggression. The United States representative, Henry Cabot Lodge, together with other OAS states' representatives on the Security Council, took a firm—and successful—line in preventing this. They steadfastly insisted that the Guatemalan complaint was "precisely the kind of problem which, in the first instance, should be dealt with on an urgent basis by an appropriate agency of the Organization of American States." Ambassador Lodge argued that "the United Nations should be supplementary to and not a substitute for or impairment of the tried and trusted regional relationships." Darkly, he added that

if the United Nations Security Council does not respect the right of the Organization of American

States to achieve a pacific settlement of the dispute between Guatemala and its neighbors, the result will be a catastrophe of such dimensions as will gravely impair the future effectiveness both of the United Nations itself and of regional organizations such as the Organization of American States.

Guatemala, at this time, was clamoring for U.N. action as the invasion by Colonel Castillo Armas' U.S.-supported and Nicaraguan-based army proceeded. The United States along with the other American states, however, succeeded in keeping the dispute bottled up in the Inter-American Peace Committee of the OAS until the Arbenz Guzman government had collapsed.

At first, the United States attempted to deal with Fidel Castro and his brand of communism as it had with Arbenz Guzman. The lesson Havana learned from the Bay of Pigs was that its powerful neighbor would probably, in various increasingly direct ways, continue to seek to infringe upon its sovereignty. When Cuba attempted to take its fears to the Security Council, the United States steadfastly replied that

recourse of the Cuban Government to the Security Council. . . is not in harmony with its treaty obligations under the Inter-American Treaty of Reciprocal Assistance signed at Rio de Janeiro on 2 September 1947 and the Charter of the Organization of American States signed at Bogotá on 30 April 1948.

Yet in the same speech Ambassador Lodge noted that the OAS was itself a complainant against Castro. The principles of the Monroe Doctrine, Lodge noted:

are now embodied in treaty obligations among the American States, notably in the Charter of the Organization of American States and in the Rio de Janeiro Treaty, which provide means for common action to prevent the establishment of a regime dominated by international communism in the Western Hemisphere.

Thus Cuba stood condemned by the regional organization, but was precluded by the regional system from taking its dispute to the U.N. The United States was thus demanding that the wayward canary be judged by the community of cats.

Throughout the period, between the time Castro first came to power and the Cuban missile crisis, the United States labored intensely to keep its dispute with Cuba within the OAS and out of the Security Council. In pursuing this objective, the State Department worked to reinforce the principle of hemispheric solidarity. It persuaded the OAS Foreign Ministers' meeting at San José to proclaim in August 1960, "that all members of the regional organization are under obligation to submit to the discipline of the Inter-American system, voluntarily and freely agreed upon." At the Punta del Este meeting of the Organ of Consultation, convoked at U.S. initiative, in January 1962, the content of this discipline was spelled out

[The] adherence by any member of the Organization of American States to Marxism-Leninism is incompatible with the Inter-American system and the alignment of such a government with the communist bloc breaks the unity and solidarity of the hemisphere.

Specifically, it was decided that "the present Government of Cuba, which has officially identified itself as a Marxist-Leninist government, is incompatible with the principles and objectives of the Inter-American system." Then, having reiterated the right of the American family to set norms of conduct for its members, and after reiterating the Guatemala norm outlawing alien Marxism-Leninism from the hemisphere, the family proceeded, at the ninth meeting of the Organ of Consultation in July 1962, to apply sanctions against Cuba in accordance with Articles 6 and 8 of the Rio treaty.

The culmination of the use of coercive sanctions against the deviant Havana regime was prompted by the Soviet deployment of nuclear missiles on Cuban soil. President Kennedy's speech of October 22 requires, therefore, close attention. The United States justified the Cuban quarantine and imposed its demands for the removal of Soviet missiles by reference to the following principles which parallel those later found in the Brezhnev doctrine.

1. Cuba, as a nation belonging to the American bloc, cannot escape the jurisdiction of that bloc: President Kennedy, for example, declared that Cuba is "in an area well known to have a special and historical relationship to the United States and the nations of the Western Hemisphere."

2. The bloc may impose its norms on Cuba: According to President Kennedy, "the nations of this hemisphere decided long ago against the military presence of outside powers" in this area. Moreover, the importation of

large, long-range, and clearly offensive weapons of sudden mass destruction—constitutes an explicit threat to the peace and security of all the Americas, in flagrant and deliberate defiance of the Rio Pact of 1947, the traditions of this Nation and hemisphere, the joint resolution of the 87th Congress, the Charter of the United Nations, and my own public warnings to the Soviets on September 4 and 13.

At the time, it should be noted, none of these was binding on Cuba, except the U.N. Charter. The statement clearly assumes a limitation on Cuban sovereignty predicated upon its geography and history as part of the American family.

3. It is the United States or its bloc which determines whether the norms set by it have been complied with by Cuba: In his address of October 22, President Kennedy judged Cuba to have violated a rule laid down for it by the U.S. Congress in joint resolution. This resolution determined, in part, that:

> Whereas the international Communist movement has increasingly extended into Cuba its political, economic, and military sphere of influence. . . the United States is determined a) to prevent by whatever means may be necessary, including the use of arms, the Marxist-Leninist regime in Cuba from extending, by force or the threat of force, its aggressive or subversive activities to any part of this hemisphere; b) to prevent in Cuba the creation or use of an externally supported military capability endangering the security of the United States.

A similar finding of deviation from the established norms was contained in the OAS Council's resolution of October 23. This stated that

> Incontrovertible evidence has appeared that the Government of Cuba, despite repeated warnings, has secretly endangered the peace of the continent by permitting the Sino-Soviet powers to have intermediate and middle-range missiles on its territory capable of carrying nuclear warheads.

According to the Council, "These steps are far in excess of any conceivable defense requirements of Cuba." The regional grouping thus asserted its right to decide on the sufficiency of the defense requirements of states within the region.

4. If the members of the bloc determine that Cuba is in dereliction of its duty to abide by the norms established by the bloc, then force may be used to secure the necessary compliance. The use of force, in such circumstances, is not aggression but collective self-defense: In addition to proclaiming his quarantine, and calling "an immediate meeting of the Organ of Consultation under the Organization of American States, to consider this threat to hemispheric security, the president told the Cuban people that "your leaders are no longer Cuban leaders inspired by Cuban ideals. They are puppets and agents of an international conspiracy which has turned Cuba against your friends and neighbors in the Americas." In other words, if a regime deviates from regional conformity, it thereby forfeits the rights to which a sovereign government is otherwise entitled. In view of Cuba's violations of the norms set for her by the United States and by the Inter-American bloc, it was thus appropriate for the Council of the OAS to recommend to its members to

> take all measures, individually and collectively, including the use of armed force, which they may deem necessary to ensure that the government of Cuba cannot continue to receive from the Sino-Soviet powers military material and related supplies.

These measures included a sea blockade, which in U.S. officials' terminology "involved the use of naval force to interfere with shipping on the high seas." The blockade effectively restrained the exercise by two sovereign states, Cuba and the Soviet Union, of their right to choose the means by which to cooperate in military matters. It was, however, defended by the United States as an act both of "anticipatory" self-defense and as collective regional action short of actual enforcement. According to Abram Chayes, then the State Department's chief legal adviser, "The Soviet missiles in Cuba were a threat to the security of the United States and the Western Hemisphere. As such they endangered the peace of the world." Chayes went further, citing a new version of the U.N. Charter in support of the U.S. initiative. Writing in *Foreign Affairs* he said, "The Charter obligation to refrain from the use of force is not absolute. Article 51, of course, affirms that nothing in the Charter impairs 'the inherent right of individual or collective self-defense.' " By inserting a period and ending the reference to Article 51 before the last and inconvenient phrase which actually limits the right of self-defense to a case of armed attack (which in this instance had not in fact occurred), the charges helped to construct the rhetorical basis for a new principle of international conduct, or the return of an old one, which permits each state to use force against another whenever it deems its interests threatened. The United States may have been justified in attempting to maintain its security by preventing deployment of Soviet missiles on Cuba, but the verbal strategy it used to explain its reasons for doing so was specious and inflated.

5. The expansion of an alien communist ideology into the American family will be tolerated only within strict limits which the family itself sets and which it may impose with force on a deviating member of the family. Ambassador Adlai Stevenson, himself, in his

opening statement before the Security Council on October 23, drew this principle to the attention of the world community:

For 150 years the nations of the Americas have painfully labored to construct a hemisphere of independent and cooperating nations, free from foreign threats. An international system far older than this [U.N.] one—the Inter-American system—has been erected on this principle. The principle of the territorial integrity of the Western Hemisphere has been woven into the history, the life, and the thought of all the people of the Americas. In striking at that principle the Soviet Union is striking at the strongest and most enduring strain in the policy of this hemisphere. It is disrupting the the convictions and aspirations of a century and a half. It is intruding on the firm policies of 20 nations. To allow this challenge to go unanswered would be to undermine a basic and historic pillar of the security of this hemisphere.

These five points exactly anticipate those of the Brezhnev Doctrine. The sixth point, namely, that a bloc may not only use coercive force to compel the deviate to adhere to bloc norms but may specifically extend coercion to include the use of armed force to invade the deviant's territory and reconstitute its government was carefully avoided by President Kennedy. But the same restraint was not shown by President Johnson during the crisis over the Dominican Republic in 1965.

The nature of the Dominican crisis of 1965 is still disputed. Many observers including the governments of some of the most important and democratic American states such as Chile, Mexico, Peru, Uruguay, Colombia and Venezuela as well as many observers inside the

United States did not accept our perception of the nature and extent of communist danger in the revolution which ousted Santo Domingo's right-wing military dictatorship on April 24, 1965 and tried to restore the social democratic regime of former President Juan Bosch. A serious case can indeed be made that the United States did act to impose a rightist regime as a reaction against the threat of a takeover by a non-Communist leftist one. The fact is, in any event, that between the end of April and the middle of May 1965, the United States landed 21,500 army, marine and air force personnel in the Dominican Republic. The force eventually peaked at about 25,000 and the last part of it was only withdrawn on September 21, 1966, almost 17 months later.

The verbal strategy of the United States in support of the troop landings was a masterpiece of muddled and ineffective planning. This was in part due to short-sightedness and in part to divisions within the government. The first justification advanced by President Johnson was that the troops were engaging in a humanitarian rescue of U.S. citizens caught in a tragic civil war. On April 30, President Johnson, in a television broadcast, asked the nation to understand that the troops had been sent "when, and only when, we were officially notified by police and military officials of the Dominican Republic that they were no longer in a position to guarantee the safety of American and foreign nationals." He emphasized the argument that the intervention had been requested by the Dominican Republic itself. However, this time the phrase "and to preserve law and order" was added, as well as the suggestion, still vague, that "there are signs that people trained outside the Dominican Republic are seeking to gain control." This was, however, a double-edged principle, since most foreign-trained personnel in the Dominican Republic were military officers trained in the United States.

By May 1, the pattern of Washington's verbal behavior had begun to shift. The president declared to the OAS:

Our goal in the Dominican Republic . . . is that the people of that country must be permitted freely to choose the path of political democracy, social justice, and economic progress. . . . We intend to carry on the struggle against tyranny no matter in what ideology it cloaks itself. This is our mutual responsibility . . . and the common values which bind us together.

The "humanitarian" basis of the intervention had not yielded to another unilateral finding of "fact": the communist conspiracy against the Dominican Republic and against the hemisphere.

The next day the specifically anti-communist objective of the invasion was openly declared. On May 2, the president, beginning simply enough, unveiled a momentous concept of compulsory hemispheric solidarity: "I was sitting in my little office reviewing the world situation with Secretary Rusk, Secretary McNamara and Mr. McGeorge Bundy," he began. "Shortly after 3 o'clock I received a cable from our ambassador, and he said that things were in danger; he had been informed that the chief of police and governmental authorities could no longer protect us." "Us" in this instance appeared to mean U.S. residents in the Dominican Republic. In fact, however, none had been in any way harmed up to this point. Mr. Johnson did not linger on this aspect. Instead, he went on to assert the unilateral right of the United States to intervene militarily in any sovereign state of the hemisphere if, in the opinion of the United States, that state were in danger of falling to the communists. He drew no distinction between communist accessions achieved by external invasion, internal coup or democratic election; nor did he distinguish between communist influence upon, infiltration into, or control of a revolutionary movement.

Why did the armed intervention begin with one justification and then shift in midstream to quite another? By May 2, more than half the U.S. civilians in Santo Domingo had already been evacuated. Obviously, the evacuation of U.S. civilians could not be used once again to justify a new expansion of the U.S. forces from a few thousand to over 20,000. Then, too, the days between April 28 and May 2 had seen the unraveling of another part of the original "humanitarian" justification for the U.S. invasion. It had soon become apparent that the invitation by Dominican authorities had, in fact, come not from neutral officials responsible for law and order but from Colonel Benoit, the head of the rightist junta faction. Moreover, the junta's reasons for calling in the United States were obviously not humanitarian but partisan. Although Colonel Benoit on the one hand maintained that he had made the request solely because he did not have enough troops to provide the protection urgently wanted by the diplomatic missions, yet he boasted, on the other, that he had not taken the city of Santo Domingo solely to prevent rebel casualties, although "he had enough forces to do so." These claims are contradictory and unconvincing. A more credible estimate of the junta's military position before the U.S. landings was given by Leonard C. Meeker, the legal adviser in the Department of State, who candidly reported that during "the course of April 28 the antirebel forces lost their momentum after earlier progress." Thus, by May 2, there was a widespread belief that U.S. troops had been called in only after the junta had faltered in its efforts to capture Santo Domingo and put down the revolution.

The original reasons for the intervention, therefore, no longer sufficed and were widely regarded as having been ill-advised. President Johnson took this into account in his broadcast that day. "Our goal, in keeping with the great principles of the Inter-American system, is to help prevent another Communist state in this hemisphere." He finally revealed the facts which he accepted as the basis for his choice of action necessary to preserve the national interest:

> The revolutionary movement took a tragic turn. Communist leaders, many of them trained in Cuba, seeing a chance to increase disorder, to gain a foothold, joined the revolution. They took increasing control. And what began as a popular democratic revolution, committed to democracy and social justice, very shortly moved and was taken over and really seized and placed into the hands of a band of Communist conspirators.

In the haste and urgency of the moment, the president accidentally repeated this entire foregoing paragraph a second time some moments later in his speech. He spoke of the "international conspiracy from which United States servicemen have rescued the [Dominican] people." He then went on to enunciate the Johnson doctrine: "American nations cannot, must not, and will not permit the establishment of another Communist government in the Western Hemisphere." To justify this, he cited the precedents of OAS actions, including sanctions and the quarantine in the case of Cuba and indicated that he was aware that his action on behalf of this principle constituted the first overt, unilateral U.S. military intervention in a sovereign state since the establishment of the United Nations.

There were among Mr. Johnson's advisers several who would have preferred the emphasis of the president's words to have been not, as Mr. Stevenson paraphrased them, on a total prohibition against any hemispheric state going communist by fair means or foul, but on a theory of collective self-defense against international aggression. But who could be said to have attacked the Dominican Republic? Helpfully, the State Department's legal adviser was able to produce an aggressor by means of another new doctrine:

> Participation in the Inter-American system, to be meaningful, must take into account the modern day reality that an attempt by a conspiratorial group inspired from the outside to seize control by force can be an assault upon the independence and integrity of a state.

An essentially similar term: "inspired by an outside power" is used again later in the legal adviser's memorandum and in subsequent pronouncements. Its significance lies in devising a conceptual strategy by which Dominicans can be deemed to be foreign aggressors even in their own country if they support efforts to establish a government which is "inspired" by a foreign regime or by an alien ideology. By virtue of this new definition of aggression, it becomes unnecessary to show an actual overt or covert armed attack by one state upon another before sending in U.S. troops for collective self-defense. It is enough that elements seeking a change in government are inspired from abroad: by training, money, teaching and propaganda, or perhaps just by example.

Once a Dominican becomes inspired by Cuba, Russia or China, the argument suggests, he ceases to be a true Dominican and is transformed into a vicarious instrument of Cuban, Russian or Chinese expansion. The political, revolutionary struggle in which he engages likewise ceases to be an internal one and becomes vicariously international, a case of aggression against which the superpower and the regional organization may respond in self-defense under Article 53 of the U.N. Charter and Article 3 of the Rio Pact. All of these concepts were made to order for the Soviets and the Warsaw Pact in the summer of 1968.

The import of the Johnson doctrine is virtually identical to that of the Brezhnev doctrine and the significance of this goes directly to the heart of national strategy. The Johnson doctrine and the Brezhnev doctrine are both enunciated principles, When a superpower sets out to explain its conduct to another superpower, and to the world in general, it engages in verbal strategy: that is, it seeks to locate its conduct in the context of principles which will advance the national interest. Effective verbal strategy demands not only that the principles being enunciated help to achieve the immediate object of current actions but also that they do not later redound against the longer-term interest of the enunciator. To this end, certain points should be kept in mind. One is that conduct, explained by principles inconsistent with those applied previously in similar circumstances, tends to transform the system. This means that the other superpower will, in the future, expect to have recourse to the same principles. A second point is that verbal strategy constitutes an element—by no means all, but an important part—of the complex of signals by which we—to employ Thomas

Schelling's definition of deterrence—influence the other side's expectations of our behavior in such a way as to influence their choice of behavior. Not only what we do, but what we say we are doing, creates a psychological expectation by the other side that they will not be prevented from acting in accordance with the same principles. Our opponents know that we believe that they believe that they will be acting within the permissible ambit of the principles we ourselves devised. Deterrence cannot be credible if we ourselves proclaim the right to do the very thing we wish another superpower to believe we will use force to prevent them from doing.

October 1971

FURTHER READING

Word Politics: Verbal Strategy Among the Superpowers (New York: Oxford University Press, 1971) by Thomas M. Franck and Edward Weisband.

International Politics Today (New York: Dodd, Mead, 1971) esp. Chap. 3, "Public Opinion and Foreign Policy" by Donald James Puchala.

Arms and Influence (New Haven: Yale University Press, 1966) by Thomas C. Schelling.

The Big Two: Soviet-American Perceptions of Foreign Policy (New York: Pegasus Books, 1971) by Anatol Rapoport.

The Psychological Dimension of Foreign Policy (Columbus, Ohio: Charles E. Merrill, 1968) by Joseph de Rivera.

International Behavior: A Social-Psychological Analysis (New York: Holt, Rinehart and Winston, 1965) by Herbert C. Kelman.

Crises in Foreign Policy: A Simulation Analysis (New York: Bobbs-Merrill, 1969) by Charles F. Hermann.

New Ways to Reduce
Distrust between the
U.S. and Russia

MILTON J. ROSENBERG

"Nations are not people, and therefore the troubles between them cannot be understood through psychology." So runs a complaint that psychologists often hear from political scientists these days.

This point of view strikes me as both justified and unjustified, depending upon the kind of psychological approach being considered. Worthy of condescension is the sort of shallow psychologizing that suggests that national frustration leads directly to national aggression, or that attempts to explain particular wars as due to the madness of some specific historical figure or the basic personality structure of a whole people.

Another approach to the psychology of international relations, however, has been quietly maturing over the last decade. This approach assumes that the interests of various nations are frequently in real conflict—but that it is also common for international rivalries of the war-risking kind to be based largely upon attitudes that have no clear factual support. A guiding purpose in this new approach is to achieve a better understanding of the psychological forces that tend to drive both types of conflict toward limited, and then unlimited, war.

One important development is the attempt to focus some of the major theories of attitude change upon the relations between national elites. This may point ways out of dangerous international antagonisms that are rooted mainly in attitudes. And even where the clash of national interests is apparently "intractable, ' the alteration of background attitudes may still point ways out of the dilemma.

In this article, I hope to show how two of the major theories of attitude change might be applied in lowering some of the barriers to realistic settlement of international issues.

For simplicity I shall deal mainly with the interaction between the American and Soviet policy elites. But what is suggested here could be readily applied to aspects of the U.S.-Chinese or the Soviet-Chinese relationships—or, for that matter, to those of Israel and Egypt or any other set of national elites locked into mutual disdain and suspicion but not yet caught in long-term regression to active war, as we now are in Vietnam.

The *instrumental-learning* model of attitude dynamics was developed by Carl I. Hovland and Irving L. Janis and their associates, first in field experiments conducted for the Army during World War II and then at Yale. At its core is the idea that we learn to like or dislike (or to trust or distrust) someone or something by *reinforcement*—that is, because in the past the expression of our like or dislike has brought us rewards or reduced our needs.

The largest amount of experimental study has been

devoted to two types of rewards. One is tied directly to what a person can gain if he changes some specific attitude—for instance, a person could reduce his anxiety over his health if he adopted an uncompromisingly negative attitude toward smoking. The second type of reward is due to increased social acceptance gained by moving one's attitudes toward the attitudinal standards set by others. Usually this happens not through mere cynical compliance, but through a gradual and "internalized" reorientation.

Changing the attitude of another person, according to this model, requires a series of steps:
—attract the attention of the person or groups whose attitudes you want to change;
—establish your credibility and trustworthiness;
—provide well-planned and informative communications that cast doubt upon the reasons and rewards that bolster the present attitude, and make change seem desirable by highlighting the rewards associated with the new, advocated attitude; and
—get the person or group to "rehearse" the new attitude for a while—to make its promised rewards seem more real and immediate.

Experimental work conducted by the Yale group and others has identified a number of factors that determine the success with which the various stages are negotiated. Among them are the basic credibility of the source of the persuasive communication; the way in which the communication is structured; the use of anxiety arousal; "role-playing" as a way of getting the person to consider the arguments and incentives that support the new attitude; the importance to the person of groups that support his attitude or its opposite; and personality factors making for general persuasibility or rigidity.

Clearly, this model is relevant to changing the

attitude pattern of distrust that continues to hamper movement toward true American-Soviet conciliation. The policy elites involved are composed of men playing roles that reduce flexibility. What limits these men most is that they feel *required* to distrust the opposing power and the assurances offered by its elite. Yet each side recognizes that the other's attitude of distrust must be converted toward trust if anything better than an easily-upset détente is to be achieved. Specifically, each side faces the problem of getting the other to believe its assurances that it will refrain from a surprise nuclear attack; that it will abide by arms-control and disarmament agreements (even when these cannot be effectively policed); that it will scrupulously adhere to sphere-of-influence agreements; and that it will accept necessary limitations of sovereignty as new and powerful international institutions are developed.

How are such attitudes of trust to be cultivated while policy elites still pursue and protect national interests? How can the Soviet-American "credibility gap" be closed?

The Yale experiments on credibility indicated that what seems to count most are the communicator's apparent status and expertise. But these have little bearing upon relations between policy-elite representatives, who are usually perceived by their opposite numbers as possessing both of these qualities in more than sufficient degree.

At this level there is, however, a more direct route toward cultivating attitudes of trust. Though difficult to pursue, it must be taken, even while each nation strives to preserve and advance its own national interests. That route, to speak bluntly, is to stop posturing, faking and lying.

Is it possible—even conceivable—that nations, in their

relations with one another, can abandon the deceit that, since Machiavelli, has seemed essential to statecraft? Many specialists would immediately answer, in the tones of revealed doctrine, "As it was in the beginning, is now, and ever shall be, world without end. Amen." But at the risk of sounding naive, I believe that we need to take a fresh look.

I suggest that the present international system is so inadequate and dangerous that the American and Soviet leaders have very compelling reasons to go beyond the limits of conventional *Realpolitik* and impose some moral order on their relationships. The exploration of this radical possibility could best begin with a direct assault upon the attitudinal problem of international distrust. There are probably many ways in which the behavioral sciences might help to mount such an assault. One would be the use of inter-nation gaming and simulation techniques—to provide "dry run" tests of an international system based upon a principle of general-ized trust. Such studies might clarify just how feasible, how resistant to breakdown, a system of this sort would be, and how it might best be instituted.

But we need not wait. Immediate initiatives in honesty and self-revelation are now available for the seizing. Even though a great deal remains secret, even though the international system remains more closed than open, much could still be revealed to an antagonist under conditions that would allow him the opportunity for verification. There are possibilities in the direct revelation of data about arms technology, economic plans, the policy-formulation process itself. Such candor might well invite reciprocation. It might, in fact, set in motion expanding cycles of reciprocity that could eventually encompass most of the matters now sur-rounded by suspicion.

Another way of attempting to reduce attitudes of distrust would be, simply, to seek occasions that will require promises to be given—particularly promises that seem to incur some disadvantage for the promiser—and then to make sure that they are conscientiously fulfilled. This serves as almost incontrovertible evidence of reliability and credibility.

Additional useful suggestions can be drawn from the work of the Hovland group when we consider their emphasis (well backed by many experimental studies) upon appeals to the motives and incentives of individuals. How does this translate to the situation of one elite communicating with another? It highlights the importance of conducting diplomatic interaction so as to make clear to the other side the gains that are available if it will undertake an accommodating shift on some issue under negotiation.

This recommendation applies not so much to the general goal of reducing attitudes of distrust as to the conciliation of more specific issues. What if the United States offered the Soviet Union something it wanted in return for an arms quarantine of the Middle East? Or what if the Soviet Union offered us some equally meaningful reward for a U.S. guarantee that West Germany would not be allowed access to nuclear arms? In either instance the consequence might be conciliatory yielding. This would be due to changes of attitudes on the particular issues. But an exchange of such yieldings, particularly if accompanied by the recurring experience of promises kept, could alter the more basic attitudes of distrust that still persist between the American and Soviet policy-making groups.

Why, then, has this approach to conciliation rarely been used? One reason: Ingrained attitudes of mutual distrust inhibit easy exploration and flexible exchanges of conciliatory shifts. Another: The incentives occasionally offered to change attitudes are usually negative, not positive—threats and harassment, not attractive rewards. Leaders on either side may sometimes be forced to bow to such pressures, but their distrust and hostility will hardly diminish. Just the opposite: The elite group forced to yield, especially if humiliated, will await its opportunities for retribution.

The United States and Russia will continue to try to control each other's attitudes and actions by negative means as long as their leaders view their relationship as an extended zero-sum game—one side can win only if the other loses. Some issues, of course, are zero-sum; but many can be so structured that mutual gain *is* possible. Peace itself, after all, is a mutual gain.

Still, it is clear that possibilities for mutual gain cannot be found in each and every conflict. It would be better, therefore, to systematically rely on cross-trading. In other words, the advantage in one interest conflict is given to one side, while the advantage in another conflict is given to the other side. For example, the Soviet Union's refusal to allow unlimited inspection of its atomic facilities, and the United States' commitment to some form of nuclear force within NATO, are both seemingly unbudgeable stances. Might full, unscheduled inspections in the Soviet Union be traded for the permanent cancellation of plans for a NATO nuclear force?

The opportunities are vast. Both sides could continually review their priorities. How strongly do they desire particular concessions? What are they willing to offer in trade? Permanent tradeoff negotiations could lead to large and thoroughgoing patterns of settlement.

After some initial success in trade-off negotiations,

both groups would have experienced gains: the reduction of tensions, and domestic improvements made possible by shifting economic resources away from the defense sector. These gains would probably foster additional significant change in the attitudes of competitiveness and distrust that presently impede progress in American-Soviet conciliation. And this, in turn, would be likely to produce, on both sides, the strengthened conviction that trade-off negotiations are generally profitable even though they require abandonment of some earlier policy goals.

It would also be very useful if the United States and the Soviet Union were to immediately expand the search for shared problems that do *not* raise the apparent or fundamental issues of the lingering Cold War—problems in such comparatively manageable areas as technological development, scientific techniques, urban design, educational methods, crime control and administrative organization. An institutionalized system that would foster greater East-West cooperation in the solution of such cross-national, domestic problems would probably be of clear benefit to both nations, as well as to the members of their respective blocs. And this, too, would further invalidate basic attitudes of competitiveness and distrust and foster further progress in resolving issues that have persisted in the framework of Cold War competition.

At least one other recommendation can be drawn from the instrumental-learning model of attitude change. Studies at Yale and elsewhere have shown that role-playing is a direct and effective method of changing attitudes. The subject becomes a kind of devil's advocate: He is required to argue for a viewpoint quite different from his own. In laboratory experiments, this often leads to attitude change—though exactly why and how this happens remains controversial.

In discussions between opposing groups of policy-makers, one would not expect or desire such facile shifts of attitude. But there is good reason to expect that role-playing techniques could help policy-makers of opposed groups to reexamine and, where necessary, revise the attitudes of suspicion and distrust they approach one another with. Further formal research on this process, and real-life experiments with it, would add considerably to the development of a technology of conciliation.

A word of warning is required. When a formerly hostile and untrusting opponent is beginning to change his attitudes, when he is letting his guard down, the temptation to take advantage of his new and tentative trust will often be great. Though short-run strategic and political gains may beckon in such a situation, they must be completely rejected—for nothing will so easily destroy the credibility of conciliatory communications and actions than a lapse into even a single unscheduled seizure of advantage.

The *consistency* theories represent a second major approach to attitude change, and they can add a good deal to our understanding of how to reduce distrust between policy elites. Though they differ in important ways, all these theories see an attitude as a combination of elements bound together in a kind of internal balance, so that any sizable disruption will bring into play a self-regulating dynamic that restores the original harmony. The basic assumptions, then, are that human beings need attitudinal consistency and are intolerant of inconsistency—and that when this consistency is disrupted, they often restore it through the process of attitude change.

So goes the general consistency-theory analysis. But to show its relevance to the problem of inter-elite distrust, we must get down to the particulars of one of the major theories of this type. The one that I will use is my own, though it reflects aspects of a related theory developed in cooperation with Robert Abelson. The fact that I use it here does not mean that it is superior to the other consistency models of attitude change, but simply that it is convenient for probing deeper into the problem of cross-elite attitude change.

Basic to this model is the definition of an attitude as a kind of psychological stance in which elements of *affect* and *cognition* are intimately related. The affective core of the attitude is simply the person's habitual feeling of like or dislike toward some "object," be that a person, an issue, a proposal, an institution, or an event. The cognitive component is simply his total set of beliefs about that liked or disliked object, particularly beliefs about how it is related to other things he is interested in and has feelings about.

To exemplify just what we mean by affective-cognitive consistency, and by the kind of inconsistency that fosters a change of attitude, we need to work through a concrete illustration. Let us take a hypothetical U.S. senator standing on the periphery of the American decision-making circle just before the ratification of the atmospheric nuclear test-ban treaty. He approves of the treaty and plans to vote for it. This reflects his affective component—how he *feels* about the treaty.

In public debate he gives some of his reasons—the cognitive component: "The ban will slow the nuclear race. It will protect us from radioactive poisoning of the air. It will show the world that we mean it when we say we want peace." Privately, he adds other considerations: "It will probably freeze the nuclear race where it is now, while we still have a big advantage. Also, it should eventually open up some Eastern European markets we can use." Still another of his private reasons: "Judging by the latest polls, my stand should go over well with the liberal church and women's groups back home. Anyway, it should get the White House off my back and maybe get me better support from the National Committee in my next campaign."

If we check all of these reasons (technically, each is a cognition about the relationship between the attitude object and some other emotionally significant object), we find an interesting fact: The attitude object (the test-ban treaty) toward which the senator has a positive feeling is, to him, positively related to such welcome developments as "opening up some Eastern European markets" and negatively related to such unwelcome possibilities as "radioactive poisoning of the air." This demonstrates a general principle: A positively evaluated attitude object will typically be seen as bringing about desired goals or preventing undesirable ones; a negatively evaluated object will be seen as blocking the way to desired goals, or fostering undesirable ones. Such affective-cognitive consistency has often been shown to be characteristic of stable attitudes. Furthermore, research has shown that the stronger and more extreme the basic positive or negative feeling toward the attitude object, the greater will be the person's certainty about the supporting beliefs.

How then, according to this model, can attitudes be changed? One must begin by trying to break up the internal harmony of beliefs and feelings—by inducing, or increasing, inconsistency. Most often, this is attempted by presenting arguments, data, and "facts" from sources that are seen as authoritative because of their prestige or expertise. The purpose is either to undermine beliefs that support the affective core of the attitude ("Experts say we can't be sure of our test-detection system, so how can we know the Russians won't keep testing and get far ahead of us?") or to introduce new assertions that cast a different light—and thus induce contrasting feelings—on the subject ("If we stop testing, we simply cannot develop a good low yield, antimissile missile").

Introduce enough inconsistency and the subject will no longer be able to tolerate it. How much internal inconsistency a person can stand varies from attitude to attitude, situation to situation, and person to person. But everyone must reach a point where the piling up of inconsistency forces him to try to do something about it.

When a person's internal inconsistency becomes unbearable, one of three things will usually happen:

1. He will simply retreat from the conflict. He will try to find some way to disregard the whole area of inconsistency.

2. He will reject and expel the new cognitions that are upsetting the old balance and restore the initial attitude. (Incidentally, we may assume that this is what our hypothetical senator did, since it is just what many real senators did. The arguments *against* the nuclear test-ban treaty were simply not so telling and credible, or so important in the values they referred to, as were the arguments in favor of the treaty. In this case, the easiest route to reducing internal inconsistency was, ultimately, to reject the arguments that had generated it.)

3. He will yield to the new inconsistency-arousing cognitions, and—by changing his feelings about the attitude object—restore consistency.

This last is, of course, what is usually meant by attitude change.

Consistency theory also predicts, and has experimentally demonstrated, that the reverse form of attitude change is possible: *Feelings* can be altered first, and cognitions will follow. But, in real life, affect change resulting from prior cognition change is far more common.

What determines whether internal inconsistency brings about an overall change of attitude? First, the nature of the attitude itself. An attitude will probably be more easily changed by inconsistency if:

1. The number of beliefs that support the attitude is small.
2. The attitude object is believed to serve comparatively unimportant goals.
3. The person already holds a few beliefs that are inconsistent with his overall attitude.
4. The original attitude is isolated from most of the other attitudes of the individual—is itself, therefore, in a sense an inconsistency. (An example with a real senator: Everett M. Dirksen's support of an earlier civil-rights bill was on the periphery of his essentially conservative concerns; his stance on civil rights later underwent several sea changes.)

A second factor determining whether inconsistency leads to attitude change is how important the attitude is to a person's needs and essential motivations. The less the holding of the attitude serves to meet his real needs, the more easily—if threatened by inconsistency—it can be changed. Similarly, his attitudes are more easily altered when he does not need them for the roles he plays or for maintaining good standing in the groups he identifies with.

From the foregoing, it is apparent why changing the attitudes of national leaders has been so difficult during the Cold War—even though both sides wanted to find some way out. The core attitudes of distrust, hostility and competition have been so thoroughly anchored and buttressed by supporting beliefs, so strongly influenced by what leaders think their positions and "roles" require of them, that there has been very little room for flexibility.

This does not mean that evidence of good will or pacific intentions has been totally useless. But what usually happens is that these gestures are reinterpreted in ways that reduce their power to generate inconsistency and thus their power to affect attitudes. For example, an American offer of wheat sales would typically be interpreted by the Russians as a tactic to help the U.S. economy. And American leaders are likely to interpret Soviet offers to share information about industrial nuclear technology as a ploy to save the costs of research—rather than really to further general cooperation. Many leaders traditionally interpret gestures for peace as a mask for hostile intent—and bellicose gestures as proof of it.

Perhaps, therefore, the greatest positive good that came from the few very dangerous confrontations between the United States and the Soviet Union—particularly the Cuban missile crisis—has been that they gave the leaders of both nations some appreciation of how deeply each wanted to avoid stumbling into nuclear war. Since then, a number of steps toward avoiding danger have been taken, and they have probably thrown some inconsistency into the attitudes of mutual distrust. As a result, there is probably a fair opportunity today for each side to act in ways that could ultimately bring about changed attitudes. How can this best be done? The consistency approach offers some leads.

One clear recommendation is that, before the competing policy groups undertake to revise each other's attitudes, they study what these attitudes really are, and what beliefs are built into them. Too often policy-makers seem confused about the perceptions and purposes that lie behind the policy positions taken by the competing power. "Riddles wrapped in mysteries inside enigmas" lie more often in the eye of the observer than the observed. Surely, within the great mass of white papers, diplomatic conversations, propaganda releases and policy rationalizations that flow from Washington or Moscow there should be enough material for an educated reconstruction of how opposing leaders really think and feel about an issue, and how they structure policy around it. Close study of this sort would help isolate the issues on which the other side would be comparatively receptive to actions and messages that could generate internal inconsistency.

Obviously these issues, at the present time, would be on the outer edge of major policy and have little immediate effect on important conflicts. But the real purpose of such early efforts is to lower the opposing side's defense against information and action that might create inconsistency in more central attitudes. If either side could convince the other that it really *does* favor cultural exchange in order to reduce tension, rather than to make propaganda—or that it really *wants* disengagement in Central Europe to avoid military confrontations, rather than to gain some devious advantage—then the day will be much closer when the very center of the web of distrust and competition can be directly assaulted.

But can such direct assault succeed when the core issues still seem virtually irreconcilable? How is this to be done? This is where the consistency approach is especially pertinent. It suggests strongly that *there are no truly intractable, unchangeable attitudes.* Instead, there are less resistant and more resistant ones. Where resistance is high, this is because the affective portion of the attitude is supported by a large number of detailed beliefs that are consistent with it—and also because the attitude itself is consistent with the role demands and ideologies that leaders must live up to. For such an attitude to be changed it must be bombarded with a continuing, unrelenting stream of inconsistency-generating communications and events—and the more peripheral attitudes to which it is tied must also be exposed to pressures for change.

To reverse the attitudes of distrust with which the Soviet and American elites approach and misinterpret each other, either or each of them must undertake an unflagging display of trustworthiness—and give strong, unequivocal evidence that its paramount desire is conciliation. In this light Charles Osgood's GRIT strategy is very relevant. Osgood recommends a long series of unilateral, tension-reducing initiatives on the part of the United States, even if no sign of reciprocation appears from the Soviets for some time. He also maintains that concrete actions speak much louder—and less ambiguously—than words.

For too long both the United States and the Soviet Union have been lagging in this regard. On the American side, occasional actions in the Kennedy years and in the last period of the Eisenhower era may have worked, whether by intention or not, to generate some inconsistencies in Soviet core attitudes of distrust. But these actions were never designed as part of a strong, well-focused plan for reducing tension. Today the situation is worse. What probably stands out most to the Soviets is our past escalation of the Vietnam war and our continuing rejection of those opportunities for realistic settlement that are apparently available.

Still other recommendations can be drawn from the consistency approach, particularly from the variants developed by other authors. Here is one example out of a number of possibilities: Both Fritz Heider and Theodore Newcomb have studied the kind of consistency that is found *between* rather than *within* the attitudes of separate people. And both have reported considerable supporting evidence for this proposition: People who are tied together by friendship or more formal role relationships tend toward mutual consistency on important attitude issues. Nevertheless, they will sometimes encounter inconsistency between their separate attitudes. When this happens, the formally or emotionally subordinate person will usually alter his attitude to bring it into consistency with that of the other person.

This proposition is not surprising, but put this way it does have considerable practical value. What it suggests is that attempts to produce attitude change through arousing inconsistency will work best if we first learn as much as possible about members of the "target group" and their relationships with one another. Who are the key men, why, and what are they like?

The most influential, in governmental as in business elites, are not always the most visible. When we know who the crucially placed people in the opposing elite are—and, particularly, when their importance is based upon their analytic or strategic skills—we have found the people toward whom our initial attempts at inconsistency arousal ought to be especially directed. If *their* attitudes begin to shift, the effect may spread across the elite group more rapidly than could otherwise happen.

In all that I have said up to now I have been urging greater adventurousness in the attempt to reduce inter-elite distrust. But, of course, real-life constraints and responsibilities often inhibit the taste for adventure and innovation. The policy-elite groups of the contesting powers are still limited by their attitudes of distrust toward one another, and by concerns over the domestic political consequences of a too rapid or dramatic movement toward international conciliation. Also they are sometimes hampered by the "prudential" (the word is borrowed from certain strategic analysts) definition of their roles—that is, they sometimes take it as their obligation to imagine the worst they can about the opposing power's motives and intentions and then to act on the assumption that what they have imagined is accurate.

Thus most of the suggestions made here would probably not be acceptable to typical members of the policy elites of the contesting powers. However, desperation over the impasse imposed by the Cold War, and fear of escalation, have moved some leaders to reexamine their own attitudes about the plans and intentions of their opposite numbers. This development had, in fact, progressed quite far—until it began to languish and lose relevance in the wake of the Vietnam war.

If the Vietnam war should end with a setback for those American policy-makers still committed to the John Foster Dulles "roll-back of Communism" and "brinksmanship" doctrines, we may see an energetic renewal of the search for meaningful conciliation.

Awareness of the possibilities discussed here could make that search much more productive. And in the meantime it can foster preparation for new peace initiatives and help to keep alive the prospect of ultimate concilation.

April 1968

FURTHER READING:

Communications and Persuasion (New Haven, Conn.: Yale University Press, 1953) by Carl I. Hovland, Irving L. Janis and Harold H. Kelley.

An Alternative to War or Surrender (Urbana, Ill.: University of Illinois Press, 1963) by Charles Osgood.

Attitude Organization and Change (New Haven, Conn.: Yale University Press, 1960) by Milton J. Rosenberg, Carl I. Hovland et al.

International Behavior: A Social-Psychological Analysis (New York: Holt, Rinehart & Winston, 1965) edited by Herbert C. Kelman. See "Images in Relation to the Policy Process—American Public Opinion on Cold-War Issues" by Milton J. Rosenberg.

ALTERNATIVE ROLES FOR POLICY SCIENTISTS

The Pentagon Papers
and
Social Science

IRVING LOUIS HOROWITZ

Today, no major political event, particularly one so
directly linked to the forging of American foreign policy
as the publication of the Pentagon Papers by the *New
York Times* and the *Washington Post* can be fully
described without accounting for the role of the social
scientist. In this case, the economists clearly performed
a major role. From the straightforward hawkish pre-
scriptions offered in 1961 by Walt W. Rostow to the
dovishly motivated release of secret documents on the
conduct of the war in 1971 by Daniel Ellsberg, the
contributions of social scientists were central. As a
consequence, it is fitting, nay imperative, that the
import of these monumental events be made plain for
those of us involved in the production and dissemina-
tion of social science information and insight.

The publication of the Pentagon Papers is of central
importance to the social science community in at least

two respects: social scientists participated in the development of a posture and position toward the Vietnam involvement; and at a more abstract level, the publication of these papers provides lessons about political participation and policy-making for the social sciences.

We live in an age in which the social sciences perform a special and unique role in the lives of men and in the fates of government, whatever be the status of social science theory. And because the questions of laymen are no longer "is social science scientific," but "what kinds of recommendations are offered in the name of social science," it is important that social scientists inquire as to any special meaning of the Pentagon Papers and documents, over and above the general and broad-ranging discussions that take place in the mass media. Thus, my effort here is not to be construed as a general discussion of issues, but rather a specific discussion of results.

I. Findings

The Pentagon's project director for a *History of United States Decision-Making Progress on Vietnam Policy* (now simply known as *The Pentagon Papers*), economist Leslie H. Gelb now of Brookings, remarked: "Writing history, especially where it blends into current events, especially where the current event is Vietnam, is a treacherous exercise." Former Secretary of Defense Robert S. McNamara authorized this treacherous exercise of a treacherous conflict in 1967. In initiation and execution this was to be "encyclopedic and objective." The actual compilation runs to 2.5 million words and 47 volumes of narrative and documents. And from what has thus far been made public, it is evident that this project was prepared with the same bloodless, bureaucratic approach that characterizes so much federally inspired social science and history. The Pentagon Papers attempt no original hypothesis, provide no insights into the behavior of the "other side," make scant effort to select important from trivial factors in the escalation process; they present no real continuity with past American foreign policy and in general eschew any sort of systematic survey research or interviewing of the participants and proponents. Yet, with all these short-comings, these materials offer a fascinating and unique account of how peace-keeping agencies became transformed into policy-making agencies. That this record was prepared by 36 political scientists, economists, systems analysts, inside dopesters and outside social science research agencies provides an additional fascination: how the government has learned to entrust its official records to mandarin types, who in exchange for the cloak of anonymity are willing to prepare an official record of events. An alarming oddity is that, in part at least, the chronicle was prepared by analysts who were formerly participants.

For those who have neither the time nor the patience to examine every document thus far released, it might be worthwhile to simply summarize what they contain. In so doing, it becomes clear that the Vietnam War was neither a Democratic nor a Republican war, but a war conducted by the political elite, often without regard to basic technical advice and considerations, and for reasons that had far less to do with curbing communism than with the failure of the other arms of government in their responsibility to curb executive egotism. The publication of these papers has chronicled this country's overseas involvement with a precision never before available to the American public. Indeed, we now know more about decision-making in Vietnam than about the processes by which we became involved in the Korean War. For instance, we have learned that:

1. The United States ignored eight direct appeals for aid from Ho Chi Minh in the first half-year following World War II. Underlying the American refusal to deal with the Vietnamese leader was the growth of the cold war and the opposition to assisting a communist leadership.

2. The Truman administration by 1949 had already accepted the "domino principle," after the National Security Council was told early in 1950 that the neighboring countries of Thailand and Burma could be expected to fall under communist control if Vietnam were controlled by a communist dominated regime.

3. The Eisenhower administration, particularly under the leadership of Secretary of State John Foster Dulles, refused to accept the Geneva accords ending the French-Indochina war on the grounds that it permitted this country "only a limited influence" in the affairs of the fledgling South Vietnam. Indeed, the Joint Chiefs of Staff opted in favor of displacing France as the key influence rather than assisting the termination of hostilities.

4. The final years of the Eisenhower administration were characterized by a decision to commit a relatively small number of United States military personnel to maintain the Diem regime in Saigon and to prevent a détente between Hanoi and Saigon.

5. The Kennedy administration transformed the limited risk gamble into an unlimited commitment. Although the troop levels were indeed still quite limited, the Kennedy administration moved special forces units into Vietnam, Laos and Cambodia—thus broadening the conflict to the area as a whole.

6. The Kennedy administration knew about and approved of plans for the military coup d'état that overthrew President Diem. The United States gave its support to an army group committed to military dictatorship and no compromise with the Hanoi regime.

7. The Johnson administration extended the unlimited commitment to the military regime of Saigon. Under this administration between 1965 and 1968, troop levels surpassed 500,000 and United States participation was to include the management of the conflict and the training of the ARVN.

8. After the Tet offensive began in January 1968, Johnson, under strong prodding from the military Chiefs of Staff, and from his field commanders, moved toward full scale mobilization, including the call-up of reserves. By the termination of the Johnson administration, the United States had been placed on a full-scale war footing.

Among the most important facts revealed by the Papers is that the United States first opposed a settlement based on the Geneva accords, signed by all belligerents; that the United States had escalated the conflict far in advance of the Gulf of Tonkin incident and had used congressional approval for legitimating commitments already undertaken rather than as a response to new communist provocations; and finally that in the face of internal opposition from the same Department of Defense that at first had sanctioned the war, the executive decided to disregard its own policy advisers and plunge ahead in a war already lost.

II. Decisions

Impressive in this enumeration of policy decisions is the clinical way decisions were made. The substitution of war-game thinking for any real political thinking, the total submission of the Department of State to the Department of Defense in the making of foreign policy, and the utter collapse of any faith in compromise, consensus or cooperation between nations, and the ludicrous pursuit of victory (or at least non-defeat) in Vietnam, all are so forcefully illustrated in these Pentagon Papers, that the vigor with which their release was opposed by the Attorney General's office and the executive branch of government generally, can well be appreciated.

Ten years ago in writing *The War Game* I had occasion to say in a chapter concerning "American Politics and Military Risks" that "a major difficulty with the thinking of the new civilian militarists is that they study war while ignoring politics." The recent disclosure of the Pentagon Papers bears out that contention with a vengeance; a kind of hot house scientology emerges, in which the ends of foreign policy are neatly separated from the instruments of immediate destruction. That a certain shock and cynicism have emerged as a result of the revelations in these papers is more attributable to the loss of a war than to the novelty of the revelations. The cast of characters that have dragged us through the mire of a bloody conflict in Southeast Asia, from Walt W. Rostow to Henry A. Kissinger, remain to haunt us and taunt us. They move in and out of administrations with an ease that belies political party differences and underscores the existence of not merely a set of "experts," but rather a well defined ruling class dedicated to manufacturing and manipulating political formulas.

The great volume of materials thus far revealed is characterized by few obvious themes: but one of the more evident is the utter separation of the purposes of devastation from comprehension of the effects of such devastation. A kind of Howard Johnson sanitized vision of conflict emerges that reveals a gulf between the policy-makers and battlefield soldiers that is even wider and longer than the distance between Saigon and Washington. If the concept of war gaming is shocking in retrospect, this is probably due more to its utter and contemptible failure to provide battlefield victories than to any real development in social and behavioral science beyond the shibboleths of decision theory and game theory.

III. "Scientists"

A number of researchers as well as analysts of the Pentagon Papers were themselves social scientists. There were political scientists of considerable distinction, such as Morton Halperin and Melvin Gurtov; economists of great renown, such as Walt W. Rostow and Daniel Ellsberg; and systems analysts, such as Alain Enthoven. And then there was an assorted group of people, often trained in law, such as Roger Fisher and Carl Kaysen, weaving in and out of the Papers, providing both point and counterpoint. There are the thoroughly hawkish views of Walt Rostow; and the cautionary perspective of Alain Enthoven; and the more liberal recommendations of people like Roger Fisher. But it is clear that social scientists descend in importance as they move from hawk to dove. Walt Rostow is a central figure, and people like Carl Kaysen and Roger Fisher are at most peripheral consultants—who in fact, seem to have been more often conservatized and impressed by the pressurized Washington atmosphere than to have had an impact on the liberalization or softening of the Vietnam posture.

The social scientific contingency in the Pentagon, whom I christened the "new civilian militarists" a decade ago, were by no means uniform in their reactions to the quagmire in Vietnam. Political scientists like Morton H. Halperin and economists like Alain C. Enthoven did provide cautionary responses, if not outright criticisms of the repeated and incessant requests for troop build-ups. The Tet offensive, which made incontrovertible the vulnerability of the American posture, called forth demands for higher troop levels on the part of Generals William C. Westmoreland and Maxwell Taylor. Enthoven, in particular, opposed this emphatically and courageously:

> Our strategy of attrition has not worked. Adding 206,000 more U.S. men to a force of 525,000, gaining only 27 additional maneuver battalions and 270 tactical fighters at an added cost to the U.S. of $10 billion per year raises the question of who is making it costly for whom. . . . We know that despite a massive influx of 500,000 U.S. troops, 1.2 million tons of bombs a year, 200,000 enemy killed in action in three years, 20,000 U.S. killed in action in three years, 200,000 U.S. wounded in action, etc., our control of the countryside and the defense of the urban areas is now essentially at pre-August 1965 levels. We have achieved stalemate at a high commitment. A new strategy must be sought.

Interestingly, in the same month, March 1968, when Enthoven prepared this critical and obviously sane report, he wrote a curious paper on "Thomism and the Concept of Just and Unjust Warfare," which, in retrospect, seemed to be Enthoven's way of letting people like myself know that he was a dissenting voice despite his earlier commitment to war game ideology and whiz-kid strategy.

As a result of these memoranda, Assistant Defense Secretary Paul Warnke argued against increased bombing and for a bombing pause. He and Assistant Secretary of Defense for Public Affairs, Phil G. Goulding, were then simply directed to write a draft that "would deal only with the troop issue;" hence forcing them to abandon the internal fight against an "expansion of the air war." And as it finally went to the White House, the report was bleached of any criticism. The mandarin role of the social scientists was reaffirmed: President Johnson's commitments went unchallenged. The final memo advocated deployment of 22,000 more troops, reserved judgment on the deployments of the remaining 185,000 troops and approved a 262,000 troop reserve build-up; it urged no new peace initiatives and simply declared that a division of opinion existed on the bombing policy, making it appear that the division in opinion was only tactical in nature. As the Pentagon Papers declared:

> Faced with a fork in the road of our Vietnam policy, the working group failed to seize the opportunity to change directions. Indeed, they seemed to recommend that we continue rather haltingly down the same road, meanwhile, consulting the map more frequently and in greater detail to insure that we were still on the right road.

One strange aspect of this war game strategy is how little the moves and motives of the so-called "other side" were ever taken into account. There is no real appreciation of the distinction between North Vietnam and the National Liberation Front of South Vietnam. There is not the slightest account taken of the actual decisions made by General Giap or Chairman Ho. The

Tet offensive seems to have taken our grand strategists by as much surprise as the political elites whom they were planning for. While they were beginning to recognize the actual balance of military forces, Wilfred Burchett had already declared, in 1967 to be exact, that the consequences of the war were no longer in doubt— United States involvement could not forestall a victory of the communist factions North and South. Thus, not only do the Pentagon Papers reveal the usual ignorance of the customs, languages and habits of the people being so brutally treated, but also the unanticipated arrogance of assuming throughout that logistics would conquer all. Even the doves like George W. Ball never doubted for a moment that an influx of a certain number of United States troops would in fact swing the tide of battle the way that General Westmoreland said it would. The argument was rather over tactics: is such a heavy investment worth the end results. In fact, not one inner circle "wise man" raised the issue that the size of the troop commitment might be basically irrelevant to the negative (from an American viewpoint) outcome of the Southeast Asian operations. One no longer expects good history or decent ethnography from those who advise the rulers, but when this is compounded with a heavy dose of impoverished war gaming and strategic thinking in the void, then the question of "science for whom" might well be converted into the question of "what science and by whom."

All of this points up a tragic flaw in policy-making by social science experts. Their failure to generate or to reflect a larger constituency outside of themselves made them continually vulnerable to assaults from the military and from the more conservative sectors of the Pentagon. This vulnerability was so great that throughout the Pentagon Papers, one senses that the hawk position is always and uniformly outspoken and direct, while the dove position is always and uniformly ubiquitous and indirect. The basis of democratic politics has always been the mass participation of an informed electorate. Yet it was precisely this informed public, where a consensus against the war had been building, that was cut off from the policy-planners and recommenders. Consequently they were left in pristine isolation to pit their logic against the crackpot realism of their military adversaries within the bowels of government.

IV. Disclosures

Certain serious problems arose precisely because of the secrecy tag: for example, former Vice President Hubert Humphrey and Secretary of State Dean Rusk have both denied having any knowledge whatsoever of these papers. Dean Rusk went so far as to say that the research methodology was handled poorly: "I'm rather curious about why the analysts who put this study together did not interview us, particularly when they were attributing attitudes and motives to us." (*New York Times,* Saturday, July 3, 1971.) Perhaps more telling is Dean Rusk's suggestion that the Pentagon Papers have the characteristics of an anonymous letter. Along with Dean Rusk, I too believe that the names of the roughly 40 scholars connected with the production of these papers should be published. To do otherwise would not only prevent the people involved from checking the veracity of the stories attributed to them, but more important, would keep the social science community from gaining a clearer insight into the multiple roles of scholars, researchers, professors and government analysts and policy-makers. The nature of science requires that the human authorities behind these multi-volumes be identified, as in the precedent established by the identification of the authors of the various bombing surveys done after World War II and the Korean War.

One serendipitous consequence of the Pentagon Papers has been to provide a more meaningful perspective toward the proposed "Code of Ethics" being advanced by so many social science professional associations. They all deal with the sanctity of the "subject's rights." All sorts of words guarding privacy are used: "rights of privacy and dignity," "protection of subjects from personal harm," "preservation of confidentiality of research data." The American Sociological Association proposals for example are typical:

> Confidential information provided by a research subject must be treated as such by the sociologist. Even though research information is not a privileged communication under the law, the sociologist must, as far as possible, protect subjects and informants. Any promises made to such persons must be honored. . . . If an informant or other subject should wish, however, he can formally release the promise of confidentiality.

While the purpose of this code of ethics is sincerely geared to the protection of individuals under study, if taken literally, a man like Daniel Ellsberg would be subject to penalty, if not outright expulsion, on the grounds that he was never allowed by the individuals concerned to make his information public. What so many professional societies forget is that the right to full disclosure is also a principle, just as significant as the right of the private subject to confidentiality, and far more germane to the tasks of a social scientific learned society. The truly difficult ethical question comes not with the idea of maintaining confidentiality, but with determining what would be confidential, and when such confidentiality should be violated in terms of a higher principle. All social science codes of ethics presume an ethical standpoint which limits scientific endeavor, but when it is expedient to ignore or forget this ethical code, as in the case of the Pentagon Papers, the profession embarrassingly chooses to exhibit such a memory lapse. The publication of the Pentagon Papers should once again point the way to the highest obligation of social science organizations: to the truth, plain and simple, rather than the preservation of confidentiality, high and mighty. And unless this lesson is fully drawn, a dichotomous arrangement will be made between making public the documents of public servants whose policies they disapprove of and keeping private the documentation on deviants whom supposedly the social scientists are concerned with protecting. This is not an ethical approach but an opportunistic approach. It rests on political and professional expediency. The need therefore is to reassert the requisites of science for full disclosure, and the ethics of full disclosure as the only possible ethics for any group of professional scientists. If the release of the Pentagon Papers had done nothing else, it has reaffirmed the highest principle of all science: full disclosure, full review of the data, full responsibility for what is done, by those who do the research.

V. Secrets

Another area that deeply concerns the social scientist and that is highlighted in the Pentagon Papers is the government's established norms of secrecy. While most officials in government have a series of work norms with which to guide their behavior, few forms of anticipatory socialization have applied to social scientists who advise government agencies. The professionalization of social scientists has normally been directed toward publicity rather than secrecy. This fosters sharp differences in opinion and attitudes between the polity and the academy, since the reward system for career advancement is so clearly polarized.

The question of secrecy is intimately connected with matters of policy, because the standing assumption of policy-makers (particularly in the field of foreign affairs) is not to reveal themselves entirely. No government in the game of international politics feels that its policies can be candidly revealed for full public review; therefore, operational research done in connection with policy considerations is customarily bound by the canons of government privacy. But while scientists have a fetish for publicizing their information as a mechanism for professional advancement no less than as a definition of their essential role in the society, the political branches of society have as their fetish the protection of private documents and privileged information. Therefore, the polity places a premium not only on acquiring vital information, but on maintaining silence about such information precisely to the degree that the data might be of high decisional value. This leads to differing premiums between analysts and policy-makers and to tensions between them.

Social scientists complain that the norm of secrecy oftentimes involves yielding their own essential work premises. A critical factor reinforcing an unwilling acceptance of the norm of secrecy by social scientists is the allocation of most government research funds for military or semi-military purposes. Senate testimony has shown that 70 percent of federal funds targeted for the social sciences involve such restrictions.

The real wonder turns out to be not the existence of the secrecy norm but the relative availability of large chunks of information. Indeed, the classification of materials is so inept that documents (such as the Pax America research) designated as confidential or secret by one agency may often be made available as a public service by another agency. There are also occasions when documents placed in a classified category by sponsoring government agencies can be gotten without charge from the private research institute doing the work.

But the main point is that the norm of secrecy makes it extremely difficult to separate science from patriotism and hence makes it that much more difficult to question the research design itself. Social scientists often express the nagging doubt that accepting the first stage—the right of the government to maintain secrecy —often carries with it acquiescence in a later stage—the necessity for silence on the part of social researchers who may disagree with the political uses of their efforts.

The demand for government secrecy has a telling impact on the methodology of the social sciences. Presumably social scientists are employed because they, as a group, represent objectivity and honesty. Social scientists like to envision themselves as a wall of truth off which policy-makers may bounce their premises. They also like to think that they provide information which cannot be derived from sheer public opinion. Thus, to some degree social scientists consider that they are hired or utilized by government agencies because they will say things that may be unpopular but nonetheless significant. However, since secrecy exists, the premises upon which most social scientists seek to work are strained by the very agencies which contract out their need to know.

The terms of research and conditions of work tend to demand an initial compromise with social science methodology. The social scientist is placed in a cognitive bind. He is conditioned not to reveal maximum information lest he become victimized by the federal agencies that employ his services. Yet he is employed precisely because of his presumed thoroughness, impartiality and candor. The social scientist who survives in government service becomes circumspect or learns to play the game. His value to social science becomes seriously jeopardized. On the other hand, once he raises these considerations, his usefulness to the policy-making sector is likewise jeopardized.

Social scientists believe that openness is more than meeting formal requirements of scientific canons; it is also a matter of making information universally available. The norm of secrecy leads to selective presentation of data. The social scientist is impeded by the policy-maker because of contrasting notions about the significance of data and the general need for replication elsewhere and by others. The policy-maker who demands differential access to findings considers this a normal return for the initial expenditure of risk capital. Since this utilitarian concept of data is alien to the scientific standpoint, the schism between the social scientist and the policy-maker becomes pronounced precisely at the level of openness of information and accessibility to the work achieved. The social scientist's general attitude is that sponsorship of research does not entitle any one sector to benefit unduly from the findings—that sponsorship by federal agencies ought not place greater limitations on the use of work done than sponsorship by either private agencies or universities.

VI. Loyalties

A major area that deeply concerns social scientists is that of dual allegiance. The Pentagon Papers have such specific requirements and goal-oriented tasks that they intrude upon the autonomy of the social scientist by forcing upon him choices between dual allegiances. The researcher is compelled to choose between participating fully in the world of the federal bureaucracy or remaining in more familiar academic confines. He does not want the former to create isolation in the latter. Thus, he often criticizes the federal bureaucracy's unwillingness to recognize his basic needs: 1) the need to teach and retain full academic identity; 2) the need to publicize information; and above all 3) the need to place scientific responsibility above the call of patriotic obligation—when they may happen to clash. In short, he does not want to be plagued by dual or competing allegiances.

The norm of secrecy exacerbates this problem. Although many of the social scientists who become involved with federal research are intrigued by the opportunity to address important issues, they are confronted by some bureaucracies which oftentimes do not share their passion for resolving social problems. For example, federal obligations commit the bureaucracy to assign high priority to items having military potential and effectiveness and low priorities to many supposedly idealistic and far-fetched themes in which social scientists are interested.

Those social scientists, either as employees or as

consultants connected with the government, are hamstrung by federal agencies which are in turn limited by political circumstances beyond their control. A federal bureaucracy must manage cumbersome, overgrown committees and data gathering agencies. Federal agencies often protect a status quo merely for the sake of rational functioning. They must conceive of academicians in their midst as a standard bureaucratic type entitled to rise to certain federal ranks. Federal agencies limit innovating concepts to what is immediately useful, not out of choice and certainly not out of resentment of the social sciences but from what is deemed as impersonal necessity. This has the effect of reducing the social scientist's role in the government to that of ally or advocate rather than innovator or designer. Social scientists begin to feel that their enthusiasm for rapid change is unrealistic, considering how little can be done by the government bureaucracy. And they come to resent involvement in theoryless application to immediacy foisted on them by the "new utopians," surrendering in the process the value of confronting men with the wide range of choices of what might be done. The schism, then, between autonomy and involvement is as thorough as that between secrecy and publicity, for it cuts to the quick well-intentioned pretensions at human engineering.

The problem of competing allegiances is not made simpler by the fact that many high ranking federal bureaucrats have strong nationalistic and conservative political ideologies. This contrasts markedly with the social scientist, who comes to Washington not only with a belief in the primacy of science over patriotism but also with a definition of patriotism that is more open-ended and consciously liberal than that of most appointed officials. Hence, he often perceives the conflict to extend beyond research design and social applicability into one of the incompatible ideologies held respectively by the social scientist and entrenched Washington bureaucrats. He comes to resent the proprietary attitude of the bureaucrat toward "his" government processes. The social scientist is likely to consider his social science biases a necessary buffer against the federal bureaucracy.

VII. Elitists

The publication of the Pentagon Papers sheds new light on political pluralist and power concentrationist hypotheses. When push finally did turn to shove, President Nixon and the government officials behaved as members of a ruling class and not as leaders of their political party. President Nixon might easily have chosen to let the Democratic party take the burn and bear the brunt of the assaults for the betrayal of a public trust. Indeed the Nixon administration might have chosen to join the chorus of those arguing that the Democratic party is indeed the war party, as revealed in these documents; whereas the Republican party emerges as the party of restraint—if not exactly principle. Here was a stunning opportunity for Mr. Nixon to make political capital at a no risk basis: by simply drawing attention to the fact that the war was constantly escalated by President Truman, who refused to bargain in good faith with Ho Chi Minh despite repeated requests, by President Kennedy, who moved far beyond anything President Eisenhower had in mind for the area, by making the fatal commitment not just to land troops but to adopt a domino theory of winning the war, by President Johnson, whose role can well be considered as nefarious: coming before the American people as a peace candidate when he had already made the fatal series of commitments to continuing escalation and warfare. That the president chose not to do so illustrates the sense of class solidarity that the political elites in this country manifest; a sense of collective betrayal of the priesthood, rather than a sense of obligation to score political points and gain political trophies. And that too should be a lesson in terms of the actual power within the political structure of a small ruling elite. Surely this must be considered a fascinating episode in its own right: the reasons are complex, but surely among them must rank the belief that Mr. Nixon behaved as a member of the ruling elite, an elite that had transcendent obligations far beyond the call of party, and that was the call of class.

One fact made clear by the Pentagon Papers is the extent to which presidentialism has become the ideology and the style in American political life. The infrequency of any reference to the judicial situation with respect to the war in Southeast Asia and the virtual absence of any reference to congressional sentiments are startling confirmations of an utter change in the American political style. If any proof was needed of the emerging imbalance between the executive and other branches of government, these papers should put such doubt to rest. The theory of checks and balances works only when there are, in fact, groups such as senators or stubborn judges who believe in the responsibility of the judiciary and legislative branches to do just that, namely, establish check and balance. In the absence of such vigor, the war in Southeast Asia became very much a series of executive actions. And this itself should give pause to the advocates of consensus theory in political science.

The failure of the Vietnam episode has resulted in a reconsideration of presidentialism as the specific contemporary variant of power elite theory. The renewed vigor of Congress, the willingness, albeit cautionary willingness, of the Supreme Court to rule on fundamental points of constitutional law, are indicative of the resurgence of pluralism. In this sense, the darkest hour of liberalism as a political style has witnessed a liberal regrouping around the theme of mass politics. Even the domestic notions of community organization and states rights are indicative of the limits of presidentialism—so that Mr. Nixon, at one and the same time, is reluctantly presiding over the swan song of presidentialism in foreign affairs, while celebrating its demise in domestic affairs. The collapse of the Vietnam War and the trends toward neo-isolationism are in fact simply the reappearance of political pluralism in a context where to go further in the concentration of political power in the presidency would in all likelihood mean the upsurge of fascism, American style. If the concept of a power elite was reconfirmed in the Pentagon Papers, so too, strangely, was the concept of political pluralism in the public response to them. The countervailing influence of the Supreme Court was clearly manifested in the ringing affirmation of the First Amendment, in the denial of the concept of prior restraint and prior punitive actions, and in the very rapidity of the decision itself. This action by the judiciary, coupled with a show of muscle on the part of the Senate and House concerning the conduct of the war, military appropriations, boondoggles and special privileges for a select handful of aircraft industries in their own way served to underscore the continued importance of the open society and the pluralistic basis of power. Even executives, such as Hubert H. Humphrey, have declared in favor of full disclosure and reiterated the principles guiding the publication of the Pentagon Papers.

Power elites operate behind a cloak of anonymity. When that cloak is lifted, an obvious impairment in the operational efficiency of elites occurs. What has happened with the release of the Pentagon Papers is precisely this collapse of anonymity, no less than secrecy. As a result, the formal apparatus of government can assert its prerogatives. This does not mean that the executive branch of government will be unable to recover from this blow at its prestige, or that it will no longer attempt to play its trump card: decision-making by executive fiat. It does mean, however, that the optimal conditions under which power elites operate have been seriously hampered. The degree of this impairment and the length of time it will obtain, depend exclusively on the politics of awareness and participation, no less than the continuing pressures for lowering the secrecy levels in high level international decision making.

Probably the most compelling set of reasons given for President Nixon's bitter opposition to the release of the Pentagon Papers is that provided by Melvin Gurtov, one of the authors of the secret Pentagon study and an outstanding political scientist specializing in Asian affairs. He speaks of three deceits in current American Vietnamese policy: "The first and most basic deceit is the Administration's contention that we're winding down and getting out of the war." In fact, Vietnamization is a "domestic political ploy that really involves the substitution of air power for ground power." The second deceit is that "we're truly interested in seeing the prisoners of war released." Gurtov notes that "as far as this administration is concerned the prisoners of war are a political device, a device for rationalizing escalation, by saying these are acts that are necessary to show our concern for the prisoners." The third deceit "is that under the Nixon Doctrine the United States is not interested in making new commitments in Asia." In fact, the administration used the Cambodia coup "as an opportunity for creating for itself a new commitment in Southeast Asia, namely the survival of a non-Communist regime in Pnompenh." This outspoken position indicates that the defense of the power elite of the past by President Nixon might just as well be construed as a self-defense of the power elite in the present.

VIII. Conspiracies

The Pentagon Papers provide much new light on theories of power elite and power diffusion and also provide an equal measure of information on conspiracy theory. And while it is still true that conspiracy *theory* is bad theory, it is false to assert that no conspiracies exist or are not perpetrated by the government. It might indeed be the case that all governments, insofar as they are formal organizations, have secrets; and we call these secrets, conspiracies. From this point of view, the interesting question is how so few leaks resulted from an effort of such magnitude and involving so many people as setting policy in the Vietnam War. Rather than be surprised that these papers reached the public domain four to six years after the fact, one should wonder how the government was able to maintain silence on matters of such far-ranging and far-reaching consequence.

Cyrus Eaton, American industrialist and confidant of many communist leaders, indicates that the Vietnamese almost instantaneously were made aware of United States policy decisions. But I seriously doubt that they actually had copies of these materials. Rather, like the American public itself, they were informed about the decisions but not the cogitations and agitations that went into the final decision. Perhaps this is the way all governments operate; nonetheless, it is fascinating—at least this once—to be privy to the process and not simply the outcome, and to see the foibles of powerful men and not just the fables manufactured for these men after the fact.

These papers tend to underwrite the common-sensical point of view that governments are not to be trusted, and to undermine the more sophisticated interpretation that governments are dedicated to the task of maintaining democracy at home and peace abroad. As bitter as it may seem, common sense cynicism has more to recommend it than the sophisticated, well elaborated viewpoints which take literally the formal structure of government and so readily tend to dismiss the informal response to power and pressure from men at the top. The constant wavering of Lyndon B. Johnson, his bellicose defiance of all evidence and information that the bombings were not having the intended effect, followed by shock that his lieutenants like Robert McNamara changed their position at midstream (which almost constituted a betrayal in the eyes of the president) were in turn followed by a more relaxed posture and a final decision not to seek the presidency. All of this forms a human drama that makes the political process at once fascinating and frightful; fascinating because we can see the psychology of politics in action, and frightful because the presumed rationality is by no means uniformly present.

The publication of the Pentagon Papers, while a considerable victory for the rights of a free press and of special significance to all scientists who still uphold the principle of full disclosure as the norm of all political as well as scientific endeavor, is not yet a total victory for a democratic society—that can only happen when the concept of secrecy is itself probed and penetrated, and when the concept of undeclared warfare is finally and fully repudiated by the public and its representatives. The behavior of the government in its effort to suppress publication of the Pentagon Papers cannot simply be viewed as idiosyncratic, but rather as part of the structure of the American political processes in which the expert displaces the politician, and the politicians themselves become so beholden to the class of experts for information, that they dare not turn for guidance to the people they serve. For years, critics of the Vietnam War have been silenced and intimidated by the policy-makers' insistence that when all the facts were known the hawk position would be vindicated and the dove position would be violated. Many of the facts are now revealed—and the bankruptcy of the advocates of continued escalation is plain for all to see. Hopefully, this will strengthen the prospects for peace, and firm up those who, as an automatic reflex, assume the correctness of the government's position on all things military. It is to be hoped that the principle of democracy, of every person counting as one, once more becomes the source of fundamental decision-making and political discourse.

September 1971

FURTHER READING

The Use and Abuse of Social Science (New Brunswick, N.J.: Transaction Books, 1971) edited by Irving Louis Horowitz examines the increasing involvement of social scientists in the formulation and execution of policy making.

The Rise and Fall of Project Camelot (Cambridge, Mass.: MIT Press, 1967) edited by Irving Louis Horowitz presents the viewpoints of social scientists, political scientists and statesmen who were involved in controversial research on sensitive political situations in developing countries.

Beyond Vietnam

MILTON J. ROSENBERG and SIDNEY VERBA

In our book, *Vietnam and the Silent Majority* we tried
to analyze the data on public opinion objectively and
with some concern for the inner complexity of those
data and the phenomena they reflect. That analysis gives
no comfort to those who believe that there is a "silent
majority" of the American public standing firmly
behind the President and willing to stick with him
through any kind of military venture.

On the other hand, our analysis does press some hard
facts upon those who hope to find within the American
public an easily mobilized force for peace, and who
believe that the general unhappiness with the war in
Vietnam implies that the American people are adopting

This chapter originally appeared in *Vietnam and the Silent
Majority: The Dove's Guide* by Milton J. Rosenberg, Sidney
Verba and Philip E. Converse. Copyright © 1970 by Harper &
Row, Publishers, Inc.

a general orientation toward basic revision in overall foreign policy. Rather, our data suggest that there are clear potentialities for moving the American public in the direction of greater support for peace but the task will be difficult and there are many obstacles to overcome. Hopefully, these obstacles can be more easily overcome if one achieves a fairly sophisticated understanding of public opinion and of the ways in which it can be changed—and our main attempt has been to advance that kind of understanding.

In our effort to do this, we stayed rather closely with the issue of Vietnam. We chose to do this out of a belief that this is the first priority issue for American policy and that progress elsewhere depends upon its early resolution. At the same time, we remain aware of—and, in fact, are deeply concerned over—some other, more far-reaching questions that are vividly highlighted by our nation's Vietnam policy and by the long-lasting domestic political crisis that it has precipitated. These questions will not fade away even if we achieve a full extrication from Southeast Asia in the next year.

The many questions that concern us can be reduced to two basic ones, and they can be put rather simply. The first is this: From the point of view of assessing the purpose and style of our involvements in the world, what can, and ought, this nation learn from the Vietnam saga? The second question is: Will foreign policy design and revision (which have at least temporarily engaged the interests of millions of Americans) once again become a private preserve of the Washington governmental elite? Or, to be more candid in signaling our concern and our value preferences, we could ask: What can be done to keep foreign policy issues in the public realm—and to improve the quality, while maintaining the quantity of public attentiveness toward basic policy issues, choices and philosophies?

The first question simply cannot be ignored. If we (meaning the "peace community") are interested in changing the attitudes of many of our fellow citizens, it is necessary that we be very clearheaded about the real content of our own attitudes. Equally, we must spell out the details of our own critical evaluation of present policy and of the kinds of extensive policy change we hope for.

To agree simply that we want our nation out of Southeast Asia soon and completely and on a nonreversible basis is not enough. If our thought and convictions venture only that far, we will not be able to effectively argue our position with the more thoughtful and more truly policy-oriented persons who support present policies. For they will, quite properly, want to know how the Vietnam undertaking can be abandoned without abandoning a whole, and far more extensive, policy pattern which, as they see it, is also a *necessary* policy pattern.

There is another reason why we must get beyond Vietnam in our own probing and thinking. Unless we do, we will have no guarantee that we will not soon be facing other, still more depleting and dangerous Vietnams elsewhere. Within some sectors of the policy community in Washington (and in its academic outposts), and in conversation with military professionals, one often hears something like the following as the lessons of Vietnam are being drawn: There *will* be more Vietnams. The Chinese and even the Soviets will continue to foment, or attempt to capitalize upon, discontent in the emerging nations. From this will come insurgencies which test our staying abilities and attempt to diminish our influence and our geopolitical security. The present Vietnam war if it is to be closed out can only be terminated if we can leave behind a block of anti-Communist regimes that can hold up—though, for them to have that capability, continued American logistic and economic support will be required, as well as a commitment on our part to send emergency forces back in when and where they are required. Meanwhile we have learned a great deal about "insurgency" and how to counter it. We shall meet it again but we shall be better prepared—not only with new, sharpened military techniques and technology but also with a new sense of the domestic political problems that our policies create. And what we have learned on *that* side of the picture should also be valuable for handling things better the next time they must be handled.

The foregoing is a caricature version—but only by virtue of its simplified and direct statement—of one line of "sophisticated" realism that is now abroad. Immediately one must hasten to add that this sort of view is completely rejected and actively opposed by many persons in positions of policy influence. Such persons are to be found in Congress—particularly in the Senate— in some sectors of the State Department, even in some corners of the Department of Defense. And if some university specialists have helped to develop this modern brand of *Realpolitik*, others of their colleagues have been critically analyzing it for some time and are devoting their full careers to elaborating alternative models of international reality and of national purpose.

But the choice, as we see it, hangs in the balance—and it can only be tipped toward a resolution that makes the world safe for the United States and the United States safe for the world if all those who feel deep concern over the Vietnam tragedy commit themselves to the hard work of thinking through its true origins and its symptomatic meanings. For the present great debate must continue beyond Vietnam, and basic alternatives to our present policy style (or is it a rigidified drift?) must be clarified and advocated.

These last passages have been hortatory by intent. We have as yet said little about our own views on what has been *basically* wrong with this nation's foreign policy and how it should be conducted. But, having urged our readers to concern themselves with such matters if they hope to keep us out of new Vietnams after we are extricated from the old one, it may not be inappropriate to spend a few paragraphs in *asserting* (proof and argument are beyond our present task definition) what sort of critical analysis of present policy orientation we think to be immediately required.

In rather thin outline, then, the analytic perspective toward which we tend comes down to these basic points:

1. A definition of national interest in terms of geopolitical standards of physical security simply does not accord with present reality. But it does lead us into interventions that regularly risk the transformation of "conventional" war into immolative, nuclear war.

2. The conventional detachment of foreign policy from domestic policy renders many of our policy makers dangerously insensitive to the problems and priorities of our domestic life. And the readiness to maintain American dominance or "security" by recourse to military adventures (adventures which commit American power to impossible goals and thus mire us in long-range involvements that must

be maintained for the sake of our "credibility") produces consequences for our domestic society that are unacceptably costly and injurious.

3. The maintenance of this whole pattern is based upon a "hard reality" that simply happens to be untrue. We speak of the common belief that the rise of new, low-power states organized along socialist lines is a threat to our own security or to our economic prospects. Even more patently absurd, in the face of the obvious polycentrism of Communist movements around the world, is the notion that some superpower (once it was the Soviet Union, but now our strategists seem more focused upon China) can control such emerging nations in a way that threatens our national survival or sociopolitical viability.

4. The present international system—if allowed to function with minimum disruption by the old geopolitics and the old uses of threat and war—is evolving toward a new kind of stability. Mastery of the problems of development and of industrialization can, in time, create a de-ideologized world order. In such an order, great states will remain great in their land mass, in their economic advancement, and in their pretensions of special access to the best and most just modes of sociopolitical organization. But, in fact, the healthy trend toward the evolution of international institutions (a trend required by the modernization process that is sweeping the world) will make great states less significant and less prominent. In consequence, it will become possible for them (it is close to being possible now if only their national traditions and power models did not fuzz the perceptions of their

policy makers) to live more quietly in the world—
to turn to their own most compelling inner
problems and devitalize their current obsessive
involvement in the game of nations.

5. Finally, in this brief sketch of one of a number of
possible critical approaches to present foreign
policy, we come to the aspiration that is pressed
upon us by the Vietnam war, as well as by recent
horrifying developments in arms policy. That
aspiration is simply that policy makers and their
publics will come to recognize that continuing to
play the game of nations in the Clausewitzian style
("War is the continuation of policy by other
means") necessarily fosters a militarization of
foreign policy. A war-oriented system of great
states—given what modern war or the readiness for
it requires in terms of expenditure and
technology—moves the military toward dominance
over the policy-making function. The consequence
is ultimately as ruinous for the political institutions
of a society and for its domestic economic life as it
is for international relations as such. Thus any
movement toward a more rational and safer international order must begin with significant cutbacks
not only in military spending but in the militarization of the national system and its policy-setting
institutions. Realistically, this cannot be done or
begun by one great state alone. In current and
coming attempts by the United States and the
Soviet Union to find a way of freezing and,
hopefully, of rolling back current levels of nuclear
assault capability, there lies a great opportunity. It
is the opportunity to begin extricating those states
from the profoundly dangerous and inhumane

dilemmas into which they, and their immediate allies, have plunged themselves, and into which they have drawn the peoples of many emerging nations. But this opportunity cannot be grasped—arms-limitation negotiations cannot succeed and take on continuing momentum—in an international climate such as now obtains. We mean a climate in which the great states frighten one another (and thus force one another back to an international politics of distrust and geopolitical jockeying) by their separate incursions into the affairs of smaller nations. No more Vietnams—and no more Czechoslovakias—must be the first new rule of responsibility in any modern and rational approach to foreign policy. And, probably, such a rule must in itself be negotiated and made the cardinal item of agreement between the great powers.

We are aware that in these comments we have rushed in where careful scholars fear to tread—or fear to tread so lightly. But we have done so more as a way of raising the kinds of questions and concerns that we think Americans committed to the struggle for real peace must draw into their active attentiveness.

In saying this, we are entering the lists in another great debate—one far older than the current national struggle over Vietnam policy. For at least two centuries, men in government and students of governmental process have been contesting the question of whether policy (and particularly foreign policy) is best conducted when the general public has withdrawn (or never developed) an interest in such matters, or whether it is best conducted when the general public cares about such matters, follows them with interest and investment, and acts to influence the policy decisions of their leaders.

The issue breaks down into many familiar questions—familiar at least to specialists but, in reality, vitally important to actively concerned citizens of the sort to whom this book is addressed. Among these questions are the following: Can judicious policy choices be made, and executed with the adeptness they require, if the public is always looking on, judging and sometimes complaining and protesting? Or, on the other hand, can a separated elite of policy makers avoid the rigidities of their narrowly specialized conceptions of international relations unless their choices are under public scrutiny—are submitted to public debate?

As far as we are concerned, we lean to the view that foreign policies designed and put in motion beyond public scrutiny are, at least in this latter day, far more likely to fail in their purpose and to do unintended damage to the national life. In this we opt for the ideals that are often highlighted by the political philosophy of democracy. Indeed, we take the Vietnam disaster as a prime case in point of just how much international and national disaster can be wrought through policy planning that occurs (as originally it did) far beyond the public's claim to the rights of scrutiny and consultation.

Yet, having said this much, we must back away—or at least shift from idealization toward realism. And the standard of realism requires immediately that two things be acknowledged. The first is that the general American public, like the general publics in most of the mass democracies, is usually rather indifferent to the details of our international problems and opportunities. And that indifference is correlated with a rather low level of information and a rather easy (if variable) yielding to governmental justifications for current policies and international gambles and capers. From such a general public (even if its indifference and comparative ignorance are partly the fault of government itself; that is, of government's tendency to propagandize a quick and sloganistic justification for its foreign undertakings) one cannot expect much in the way of useful participation in the processes of policy review and evaluation.

But this brings us to the second factual consideration that realism forces upon us. If the general public is largely indifferent, underinformed, and lacking in attentiveness on foreign policy matters, that is compensated by the existence of "attentive" publics. Some are attentive only in one rather narrow issue sector (e.g., the current excitement and division among Americans of Greek descent over our government's policies toward the regime of the colonels). But some have been drawn toward general and more long-lasting interest in broad sectors of foreign policy.

The key problems of current foreign policy seem to be organized around our relations with the established Communist states, with the emerging nations, and with our own military strategists and visionaries. Two broad sectors of the general public have developed high interest and some sophistication on these matters in recent years. They differ in their overall views and in the ways in which they relate their values to foreign policy issues. The one group essentially endorses the "hard line" against Communist incursions on our national power and security; it favors high levels of military readiness and, of course, it has comprised the highly *vocal* minority in support of the Vietnam war. The other group began to shape up around the desire for an end to nuclear testing, came to see "containment policy" as a source of American misadventures in the world, quite early grew restive and rejecting toward the

Vietnam involvement, and today is deeply concerned over the dangers of militarization of our society.

These two vocal minorities differ in their social and demographic characteristics. Both have had influence upon the general public, and the latter group can, at the moment, be said to be exerting more persuasive force, recruiting more Americans to limited endorsement of its Vietnam position (but only that position) than the former group. This is not necessarily due to its greater diligence or the greater depth of its acquired expertise. Rather, it is as much due to the fact that events have played into its hands—that the Vietnam war has exacted far too high a cost for far too little visible gain. In other words, events and unavoidably vivid disappointments have generated an inner-attitudinal inconsistency in the Vietnam attitudes of the general public, and the members of the attentive peace public have been reaping the reward. They might, however, reap still more.

The purpose that animates us here is to warn them that these rewards may be rather ephemeral unless they examine their situation—their opportunities and obstacles—thoroughly. The effort that the attentive peace public is now launched upon may well succeed. They may in coming months be able to move the American majority into outright opposition to any solution to the Vietnam problem except full, early, irreversible withdrawal. And, clearly, it is desirable that this effort be undertaken and that it succeed.

But the hope often heard these days that the general American public will then be committed to a totally different view of how we should in the future conduct ourselves in the world—that it will, through Vietnam, come at last to a post-Cold War concern for international conciliation and demilitarization—is, we think, a wishful fantasy. Inattentiveness, sluggishness, preoccupation with the manageable and more immediate concerns of private life and, at most, of *domestic* politics will, we fear, again preempt the attention of typical Americans.

And perhaps this is all we should hope for as regards the broad, total public. Perhaps it is all that our political institutions can, in fact, sustain; for the conservative Burkean political philosophers may have a compelling practical point when they suggest that leadership too slavishly tied to placation of mass publics cannot function but can only temporize. The profoundly unsatisfying aspect of this view is that it suggests that our governing elite should be left free to take us where it will in foreign affairs without any countervailing agency that will test, challenge and, where necessary, oppose its often profoundly mistaken readings of international reality, its increasingly primitivized dependence upon postures of dominance and implacable toughness in its relations with other more truly pragmatic nations.

But the long interregnum in which foreign policy was supposed to be bipartisan (that is, unquestioned, undebated—a matter of unshaken consensus elaborated in rather closed, elite circles) seems to have passed. Countervailing agencies—sources of basic opposition to, and informed criticism of, our foreign policy style and long-range plans—have now sprung up within government, particularly on the part of a vocal minority in the Senate. This has been made possible by the gradual buildup (much aided by the growing national disenchantment with the Vietnam war) of a sizable and vocal peace constituency—that very new attentive public of which we have spoken.

That public must remain *attentive* whether or not it becomes a statistical majority of the American people. Only if the attentive peace public persists as an activist body, striving to bring occasionally concerned, but less attentive, others into active rejection of such grossly visible defaults as the Vietnam war, can its representatives within government continue their absolutely essential struggle.

Even so, that struggle waged within government may not be enough to produce true and basic revision of our foreign policy. It is certainly necessary but probably not sufficient. What is additionally required is that the attentive peace public comprise *itself* as a countervailing agency. This, as we see it, means a number of things. It must remain focused on the task of reaching the policy makers, delivering electoral threat and putting new men, equipped with new perspectives, in office. But, living with the knowledge that it probably, for the foreseeable future, cannot become a mass movement, the attentive peace public must also understand that its power lies not only in its size but in its presence—in its very attentiveness.

There are other ways of reaching men in office and charged with policy responsibilities—ways which precede and also go beyond electoral politics, though electoral politics must always be used. The foremost of these is, simply, to maintain intelligent and vigilant scrutiny and to mobilize all of one's communicative powers for effective advocacy. Men at the very top of the policy-setting apparatus these days are increasingly confused and thus, perhaps, far more open to influence than peace workers suspect.

At any rate, until such time as the general American public is redeemed from the confusion and disorientation into which it has been pushed by the combination

of overwhelming events and the mendacity or in-
competence of many of its leaders, someone must stand
guard and speak strongly for humane and rational
change in our whole foreign policy orientation. This, as
we see it, is the long-range task of the attentive peace
public. To meet the requirements of that task, it must
be aware of the danger that it may dissolve, as an
activist constituency, after the Vietnam war is finally
over—and it must by conscious readiness prepare to
overcome that danger. Also, it must realize that to be
influential, to play the role of a significant countervailing force, it must press upon itself, upon its sizable
informal membership, the necessity for deepening its
own sophistication, extending the scope of its detailed
and relevant knowledge about the *many* issues that
together constitute the great problem of rectifying our
overall foreign policy.

We do not presume to offer specific advice on how
these requirements should be met. Awareness of the
challenge and of the obstacles is what we urge—that,
plus the staying power and stamina that are obviously
required in coming years. Happily, that staying power
can be reinforced by particular successes; and the
opportunity now available to the peace constituency of
turning the country around on the Vietnam issue can
provide just such a success. It can also *begin* the long
process of restoring the American people as a whole to
some sense of their own competence and their own
rights in the realm of international affairs.

We are aware that in voicing this last point we verge
upon paradox or indeed perhaps even upon inconsistency! We have indicated our troubled doubt about how far
the general public can presently be moved toward true
civic responsibility in international affairs. We have also

ambivalently resonated the classic concern over how government can function responsibly in the face of *mass* attentiveness. Yet we do truly believe in the redemptive power of intelligence and humane concern—and we believe that the broad and total American public is potentially rich in these resources. The struggle to deepen American understanding about the Vietnam war and to convince the majority, silent or otherwise, that it must vocally demand a change in that policy may signal a great beginning—the beginning of a rediscovery by the American people that their ideals are relevant to the stance their nation takes in the world.

We are willing to live with paradox if it carries us toward hopefulness. And, at this moment, we find some hopefulness in the potential for persuading the American people to shift toward peace on the Vietnam issue; and we find even greater hopefulness in the emergence of a multitude, perhaps millions, of dedicated persuaders.

FURTHER READING

"Vietnam, the Urban Crisis and the 1968 Election: A Preliminary Analysis" (Paper delivered at the American Sociological Association Meetings. San Francisco: September 1969) by Richard A. Brody, Benjamin Page, Sidney Verba and Jerome Laulicht.

"Continuity and Change in American Politics: Parties and Issues in the 1968 Election" (*American Political Science Review* Vol. LXIII, December 1969) by Philip E. Converse, Warren E. Miller, Jerrold G. Rusk and Arthur C. Wolfe.

" 'Silent Majorities' and the Vietnam War" (*Scientific American,* June 1970) by Philip E. Converse and Howard Schuman.

"A Structural Theory of Attitude Dynamics" (*Public Opinion Quarterly* 24, 1960) by Milton J. Rosenberg.

"Images in Relation to the Policy Process: American Public

Opinion on Cold War Issues" by Milton J. Rosenberg in *International Behavior: A Social Psychological Analysis* (New York: Holt, Rinehart & Winston, 1965) edited by H. C. Kelman.

"Attitude Change and Foreign Policy in the Cold War Era" by Milton J. Rosenberg in *Domestic Sources of Foreign Policy* (New York. Free Press, 1967) edited by J.N. Rosenau.

Attitude, Organization and Change (New Haven: Yale University Press, 1960) by Milton J. Rosenberg, C. I. Hovland, W. J. McGuire, R. P. Abelson and J. W. Brehm.

"Public Opinion and the War in Vietnam" (*American Political Science Review,* June 1967) by Sidney Verba, Richard A. Brody, Edwin E. Parker, Norman H. Nie, Nelson W. Polsby, Paul Ekman and Gordon S. Black.

"Participation, Preferences and the War in Vietnam" (*Public Opinion Quarterly,* Fall 1970) by Sidney Verba and Richard A. Brody.

About the Authors

Frank Church ("Gunboat Diplomacy and Colonialist Economics"), United States senator from Idaho, is a member of the Senate Foreign Relations Committee and co-author of the Cooper-Church amendment of 1970. His articles have appeared in the *New York Times, Harpers'* and many other publications.

Richard A. Falk ("Mylai: War Crimes and Individual Responsibility") is Milbank Professor of International Law at Princeton University. He is author of *This Endangered Planet, Legal Order in a Violent Order*, editor of *The Vietnam War and International Law* and co-editor with Saul H. Mendlovitz of *The Strategy of World Order*.

Thomas M. Franck ("The Brezhnev-Johnson Two-World Doctrine") is director of the Center for International Studies at New York University. His most recent publications include *Word Politics: Strategy Among the Superpowers* (with Edward Weisband) and *The Structure of Impartiality*. Franck also served as a consultant to AID in 1970-71.

Lucien M. Hanks ("Corruption and Commerce in Southeast Asia"), a psychologist by training and an anthropologist by experience, has worked many years with the lowland and upland peoples of Thailand. He is a senior research associate at Cornell University.

Irving Louis Horowitz ("The Pentagon Papers and Social Science") is chairman of the department of sociology of Livingston College at Rutgers University and editor-in-chief of **Society** (formerly *trans*action) magazine. Among his books are *The Rise and Fall of Project Camelot: Studies in the Relationship between Social Science and Practical Politics* and *The War Game*.

Marvin Kalkstein ("ABM and the Arms Race") is a faculty member of the Experimental College at the State University of New York at Stony Brook. His recent work includes "Time for a Fresh Look at U.S. Nuclear Weapons Test Policy" (a paper delivered before the hearings of the Senate Foreign Relations Committee on Underground Weapons Testing, September 29, 1969) and an article in *Science and the Future of Man*, a forthcoming volume edited by Bentley Glass.

Robert Jay Lifton ("Vietnam: Betrayal and Self-Betrayal") is professor of psychiatry at the Yale University medical school. He is author of *Boundaries: Psychological Man in Revolution* and editor, with Richard Falk and Gabriel Kolko, of *Crimes of War*.

Seymour Melman ("Pentagon Bourgeoisie") is professor of industrial engineering at Columbia University. He has written and edited many books and articles, among them *The War Economy of the United States, Pentagon Capitalism: The Political Economy of War,* and *Conversion of Industry from a Military to Civilian Economy.*

Hyman Minsky ("Passage to Pakistan") is professor of economics at Washington University, St. Louis. He has also served as a consultant to the Federal Deposit Insurance Corporation and the board of governors of the Federal Reserve System.

Leslie Nulty ("Pakistan: The Busy Bee Route to Development") is a graduate student at the University of Cambridge and is working on agricultural economics with the European Research Unit, Ltd., Oxford.

Timothy Nulty ("Pakistan: The Busy Bee Route to Development") is a tutor in- economics and statistics at Ruskin College, Oxford. He spent 18 months in Pakistan with the Harvard Development Advisory Service.

Edward M. Opton, Jr. ("Lessons of Mylai") is senior research psychologist and associate dean of the Graduate Division at tne Wright Institute. A contributor to numerous professional journals, Opton has also worked as a radio correspondent in Southeast Asia.

John R. Raser ("The Failure of Fail-Safe") is associate professor of political studies at the University of Otago, Dunedin, New Zealand.

Milton J. Rosenberg ("New Ways to Reduce Distrust Between the U.S. and Russia" and "Beyond Vietnam") is professor of social psychology at the University of Chicago. Senior author of *Attitude Organization and Change* and co-author of *Theories of Cognitive Consistency*, he has contributed numerous articles on the social psychology of international relations.

Bruce M. Russett ("The Price of War") is professor of political science and director of the World Data Analysis Program at Yale University. He is the author of numerous books on comparative and international politics, including *What Price Vigilance? The Burdens of National Defense, No Clear and Present Danger: A Skeptical View of the United States Entry into World War II*, and editor, with Alfred Stepan, of *The Military Force and American Society*.

Nevitt Sanford ("Lessons of Mylai") is scientific director of the Wright Institute.

Sidney Verba ("Beyond Vietnam") is professor of political science at the University of Chicago where he is also a director of the National Opinion Research Center. A specialist in the comparative study of political attitudes, Verba is co-author of *The Civic Culture* and author of *The International System* and of *Comparative Survey Analysis*.

Edward Weisband ("The Brezhnev-Johnson Two-World Doctrine") is assistant professor of politics at New York University and associate director of the Center for International Studies there. He is co-author of the forthcoming *Turkish Foreign Policy 1943-45: A Case Study of Small State Diplomacy and Great Power Politics*.